# Epistemic Forces in International Law

ELGAR INTERNATIONAL LAW

**Editorial Board:** Jean d'Aspremont, *University of Manchester, UK and University of Amsterdam, the Netherlands*; Fausto Pocar, *University of Milan, Italy and ICTY, The Hague, the Netherlands*; Christian Tams, *University of Glasgow, UK*; Nigel D. White, *University of Nottingham, UK*; Jacob Katz Cogan, *University of Cincinnati, USA*; and Hilary Charlesworth, *Australian National University*

This important series will present high quality monographs that analyse current thinking and research across the field of international law, rigorously examining key concepts as well as provoking debate and questions for further research. Some volumes will draw on insights from disciplines other than law, such as economics and politics, in an attempt to arrive at a genuinely inter-disciplinary perspective. Seeking to attract original thinking and new, challenging research, proposals are encouraged that primarily engage with new and previously under-developed themes in the field, or alternatively offer an innovative analysis of areas of uncertainty in the existing law.

# Epistemic Forces in International Law

Foundational Doctrines and Techniques of International Legal Argumentation

Jean d'Aspremont

*Professor, University of Manchester, UK and University of Amsterdam, the Netherlands*

Edward Elgar
PUBLISHING

Cheltenham, UK • Northampton, MA, USA

© Jean d'Aspremont 2015

All rights reserved. No part of this publication may be reproduced, stored in a retrieval system or transmitted in any form or by any means, electronic, mechanical or photocopying, recording, or otherwise without the prior permission of the publisher.

Published by
Edward Elgar Publishing Limited
The Lypiatts
15 Lansdown Road
Cheltenham
Glos GL50 2JA
UK

Edward Elgar Publishing, Inc.
William Pratt House
9 Dewey Court
Northampton
Massachusetts 01060
USA

Paperback edition 2016

A catalogue record for this book
is available from the British Library

Library of Congress Control Number: 2014954955

This book is available electronically in the **Elgar**online
Law subject collection
DOI 10.4337/ 9781781955284

ISBN 978 1 78195 527 7 (cased)
ISBN 978 1 78195 528 4 (eBook)
ISBN 978 1 78195 529 1 (paperback)

Typeset by Columns Design XML Ltd, Reading
Printed in Great Britain by Clays Ltd, St Ives plc

# Contents

| | |
|---|---|
| *Preface* | vi |
| *Prologue: consistency and conceptual variations* | vii |
| Introduction: the socialization of international lawyers | 1 |

## PART I   THE FOUNDATIONAL DOCTRINES

| | |
|---|---|
| 1. Subjects | 33 |
| 2. Sources | 61 |
| 3. Law-making | 111 |
| 4. Institutions | 139 |
| 5. Effectivity | 167 |

## PART II   THE ARGUMENTATIVE TECHNIQUES

| | |
|---|---|
| 6. Methodology | 177 |
| 7. Interpretation | 199 |
| 8. Academic writing | 225 |
| 9. Dissemination | 237 |
| 10. Expert blogging | 246 |
| *Index* | 253 |

# Preface

The preface of a book usually sheds light on some of the institutional, inter-personal and substantive dynamics against the backdrop of which the manuscript has been written and by which the latter has been inspired. As far as this book is concerned, however, no such account is possible. Indeed, many of the following chapters, even though they have been subjected to substantial updates, additions and extensive rewriting, originate in articles and essays that have appeared elsewhere. All the chapters of this book have thus been written at different times and for different audiences. Each of them comes with its own history and would deserve to be situated separately. For the same reason, too many colleagues and friends have taken part in the discussions that informed the writing of these chapters for this preface to be able to list them all. The same disaggregated history explains why the style, the tone, the footnoting, and the orientation of each of the chapters varies greatly.

Notwithstanding this heterogeneity, it remains that all the following studies and essays are grounded in an identical thread, namely the idea that international law is an argumentative practice constituted of key doctrines which are themselves deployed through argumentative techniques specific to professional international lawyers. Gathering all these studies in one single volume is not only meant to give the latter a new thrust but also to provide a new dimension to both doctrinal and theoretical debates in international legal scholarship.

Although it would be impossible, for the above-mentioned reasons, to thank all those friends and colleagues whose insights, advice and intelligence have fed into the following lines, a few specific expressions of gratitude must be formulated. My gratitude goes to Iain Scobbie, André Nollkaemper, Ingo Venzke, Sahib Singh, and Valerio Priuli for their substantive insights during the finalization of this book as well as Ben Booth and Jennifer Stanley at Edward Elgar for their patience and continuous guidance.

Amsterdam, September 2014

# Prologue: consistency and conceptual variations

International lawyers, and especially legal academics, like to think of international law as an all-integrated notion. They let themselves (and their action) be guided by one single concept of international law that is supposedly exclusive in the way it describes, explains and makes demands on the world. One's understanding of international law ought to apply consistently across the board, informing anything one does in relation to (or in the name of) international law. This faithfulness to a single concept of international law *per capita* is usually strictly enforced among international lawyers. Failing to demonstrate fidelity to one single concept of international law often comes with severe social, professional and institutional opprobrium, most of the time under the holy offence of inconsistency.

There certainly are virtues in conceptual consistency but far less in the forced dogmatic consolidation of concepts. International law can be given many different facets – that is, it can be constructed in many different ways – without one having any ascendency over the other. What is more, I am convinced that variations in one's concept of international law, albeit the occasional cause of incommensurable views on the world explained or called for by international law, enrich rather than diminish the value of one's work. In the opinion of this author, the descriptive, explanatory or normative incommensurability produced by the variations in one's concept of international law necessarily creates contradictions. After all, contradictions only arise between qualities or facets that are commensurable.[1] Provided that one sufficiently discloses one's conceptual choices for the argumentative move at stake, there is not necessarily any inconsistency in *simultaneously* thinking of international law as a set

---

[1] For a discussion on the question of rational argumentation between incommensurable positions see G.-L. Lueken, *Inkommensurabilität als Problem rationalen Argumentierens*, Stuttgart/Bad Cannstatt 1992. This was brought to my attention by V. Priuli.

of rules and institutions,[2] a set of authoritative processes,[3] a combination of rules and processes,[4] a set of legal relations,[5] a discourse,[6] a tool to create authoritative claims,[7] a political project,[8] etc. It may be time to bring an end to the impoverishing social expectation that each international lawyer constantly and invariably abides by the same one-dimensional concept of international law and commend those who have built for themselves a large portfolio of cognitive standpoints on which they can draw to create different images of international law and its practice. This certainly does not mean valuing those argumentative tactics that purposely promote semantic instability.[9] Conceptual self-awareness dictates that variations in one's concept of international law always ought to be acknowledged and delineated. That international law can equally be looked at from very diverging but equally valid perspectives should make it socially acceptable to let one's concept of international law fluctuate to

---

[2] In a previous work, I have pondered the theoretical difficulties associated with a dynamic rule-based approach to international law and especially the problem of infinite regress or of normative arbitrariness behind the empirical foundations of a rule-based system. See J. d'Aspremont, *Formalism and the Sources of International Law* (Oxford University Press, 2010) (reprinted as paperback in 2013).

[3] It is the well-known legacy of the New Haven School of International Law to think of international law as a process.

[4] It is Hart's merit to have offered a concept of law that combines the idea of law as a product and law as practice. On this aspect of Hart's theory, see W. van der Burg, "Two Models of Law and Morality", 3 *Associations* (1999) pp. 61–82, at 68.

[5] Ph. Allott, "The True Function of Law in the International Community" 5 *Global Legal Studies Journal* 1998 391, at 400.

[6] M. Koskeniemmi, "Law, Teleology and International Relations: An Essay in Counterdisciplinarity", 26, *International Relations*, 3, at 3; see also M. Koskenniemi, "Methodology of International Law", *Max Planck Encyclopedia of Public International Law*, para. 1. For some critical remarks on the move to discourse, see Onuf, "Do Rules Say What They Do? From Ordinary Language to International Law", 26 *Harvard International Law Journal* 385 (1985), at 393.

[7] See J. d'Aspremont, *Customary International Law as a Dance Floor: Part I* at http://www.ejiltalk.org/customary-international-law-as-a-dance-floor-part-i/ and J. d'Aspremont, *Customary International Law as a Dance Floor: Part II*, at http://www.ejiltalk.org/customary-international-law-as-a-dance-floor-part-ii/; J. d'Aspremont, "Wording in International Law", 25 Leiden *Journal of International Law* (2012), pp. 575–602.

[8] M. Koskenniemi, "The Fate of Public International Law: Between Technique and Politics", *The Modern Law Review*, 1997, 1–30, at 1.

[9] For a criticism of those argumentative tactics, see below chapter 8.

produce contrasts in the way international law describes, explains and makes demands on the world[10] and should not be socially reprehensible, but rather, valued.

---

[10] I nonetheless agree with MacIntyre that perspectivism *sensu stricto* is an oxymoron as variations in perspectives always unfold within a certain tradition. See A. MacIntyre, *Whose Justice? Which Rationality?*, Duckworth, 1988, at 352–3.

# Introduction: the socialization of international lawyers

## I. THE PREMISES: A COMMUNITARIAN APPROACH TO FOUNDATIONAL DOCTRINES AND ARGUMENTATIVE TECHNIQUES

Although this may be a feeling sometimes more pronounced and accepted in other social sciences,[1] the main purpose of any introduction is the disclosure, with as much self-awareness as possible, of the conceptual premises of the subsequent argument. Needless to say that complete awareness of one's conceptual premises is unattainable, if not a contradiction in terms. Indeed, self-reflectivity remains carried out according to structures that are inherited from tradition and for which full awareness is not always conceivable.[2] Yet, it seems at least possible to shed light on one's (self-understanding of the) conceptual premises informing the study that follows. This is the object of the present introduction.

In the following chapters, international law is construed as an argumentative practice that articulates itself around a set of *foundational doctrines*, themselves deployed through a variety of *argumentative techniques*. According to this understanding, these doctrines and techniques are not considered to have *a priori* validity and are not postulated in the abstract. Rather they are thought of as being both constitutive and constituted by the community of international lawyers that is organized around international law. This means that, for the chapters that follow, acquiring the mastery of the foundational doctrines and argumentative techniques of international law is what socializes international lawyers as

---

[1] In international relations literature, there is much more systematic depiction of one's concepts than in international law literature. This certainly does not mean there is more conceptual transparency. For some critical observations on the way in which international lawyers write and construct their arguments, see chapter 8.
[2] A. MacIntyre, *Whose Justice? Which Rationality?*, Duckworth, 1988, 352–3, at 367.

much as those social international lawyers shape those foundational doctrine and argumentative techniques.

These elementary premises are all but controversial.[3] Claiming that international law is an argumentative practice, albeit not always substantiated,[4] is commonplace in contemporary international legal scholarship.[5] Likewise, a large number of international lawyers, increasingly informed by insights of other social sciences,[6] have come to accept the idea that foundational doctrines and argumentative techniques operate in a dialectical relation with their social environment, for doctrines and argumentative techniques, on the one hand, and international lawyers (and the community they constitute), on the other, are now held to be simultaneously constitutive of one another.[7]

Although the mutually nourishing and constituting relation between foundational doctrines and argumentative techniques of international law and the community of international lawyers is a rather simple idea, it leaves international lawyers with the possibility to look at a myriad of

---

[3] As is argued by I. Venzke, international law as practice appears to be a compromise between the idea that law is the expression of the will of the speakers and the idea that law is the image of structural forces. I. Venzke, "Multidisciplinary Reflections on the Relationship between Professionals and The(ir) International Law" *ESIL* 2013/ 5th Research Forum: International Law as a Profession, Conference Paper No. 4/2013, pp. 1–2.

[4] On this finding, see I. Venzke, "What Makes for a Valid Legal Argument? (Editorial)", 27 *Leiden Journal of International Law* (2014) (pp. 844–46). (He argues that while scholars and practitioners concur about the idea that international law constitutes an argumentative practice, they disagree on what they understand to be the nature of arguing.)

[5] M. Koskeniemmi, "Law, Teleology and International Relations: An Essay in Counterdisciplinarity", 26, *International Relations*, 3, at 3; see also M. Koskenniemi, "Methodology of International Law", *Max Planck Encyclopedia of Public International Law*, para. 1.

[6] On the pitfalls of the current craving for interdisciplinarity, see however, J. Klabbers, "The Relative Autonomy of International Law and the Forgotten Politics of Interdisciplinarity" 1 *Journal of International Law and International Relations* 35; see also M. Koskenniemi, "Constitutionalism as Mindset: Reflections on Kantian Themes about International Law and Globalization", 8 *Theoretical Inquiries in Law* (2006) 9, at 14; M. Koskenniemi, "The Mystery of Legal Obligation", 3 *International Theory* (2011), 319–25, at 319. For some additional observations, see below chapter 6.

[7] For an application of the idea that structures produce agents while also being the product of agents, see T.J. Berard, "Rethinking Practices and Structures" (2005) 35 *Philosophy of the Social Sciences* 196–230; A. Giddens, *Central Problems in Social Theory. Action, Structure and Contradiction in Social Analysis* (Macmillan, 1979), 69.

different facets of international law and international legal practice. In other words, if approached according to the abovementioned dialectical model, international law still lends itself to many different types of inquiries. One can grapple with the dialectics themselves and zero in on how output and input structuring dynamics coexist and interact in the formation of foundational doctrines and argumentative dynamics and how they impact on the international society. This approach would be mostly of a sociological character, necessitating the resort to tools and methods of other social sciences. This is not the approach favored in this study that consciously focuses mostly on one single aspect of these dialectical dynamics. This book makes a decided communitarian turn and zeroes in on the way the community of international lawyers conditions the doctrines and argumentative techniques of international lawyers. This communitarian approach – which is not without constructivist overtones[8] – informs the majority of the chapters that follow. Said differently, the bulk of this book is devoted to the way in which (and the reasons informing how) the community of international lawyers designs the foundational doctrines of international law and uses argumentative techniques. Thus, this book is primarily an exploration of how the community of international lawyers impacts the way in which those doctrines and techniques are cast and deployed in contemporary legal scholarship and practice.

This is not to say that this book turns a blind eye to the other facet of the mutually-nourishing relation between foundational doctrines and argumentative techniques on the one hand and the community of scholars on the other. It seems difficult to study one facet without showing minimal awareness for the other. This is why, while the rest of the book explores the communitarian dynamics at works in the design of doctrine and the deployment of argumentative techniques, this introduction concentrates on the way in which foundational doctrines and argumentative techniques socialize international lawyers and determine both their identity and that of the community they constitute.

---

[8] See e.g. N. Rajkovic, "Rules, Lawyering, and the Politics of Legality: Critical Sociology and International Law's Rule", 27 *Leiden Journal of International Law* (2014), 331–52.

## II. THE OBJECT OF THE INQUIRY: INTERNAL AND FUNCTIONAL SITUATIONALISM

Approaching international law from a communitarian perspective is hardly unheard of, especially since the second half of the twentieth century.[9] Since French sociology made its first foray into international legal studies, international lawyers have grown aware that arguing, studying, and invoking international law constitute highly structured activities in the sense that the juridical field is permeated by social structures which directly impinge on the production of the legal discourse.[10] The idea that applying international law is embedded within a social context pervaded by "highly rationalized struggles" between jurists, each competing to construct an "official representation of the social world"[11] is no longer controversial. International lawyers have also learnt from French sociologists that power not only comes in forms of centralized constraints but is dispersed, ubiquitous and even at work in the production of reality. In that sense, they know too well that arguing about international law is an exercise of power aimed at objectifying particular modes of thought and normalizing formal and informal modes of social ordering.[12]

Notwithstanding being clearly informed by some of these sociological insights – some of which are spelled out in this Introduction, it must be repeated that this book is not a sociological exercise seeking to shed light

---

[9] I. Venzke argues that theories that give prime consideration to the concept of practice have for a while been mainly structuralist (and mainly Marxist). See I. Venzke, "Contemporary Theories and International Law Making", Amsterdam Centre for International Law No. 2013-23, at 18.

[10] This is one of the central ideas defended by Bourdieu in his studies of the legal field. See e.g. P. Bourdieu, "The Force of Law: Toward a Sociology of the Juridical Field" 38 *Hastings Law Journal* (1987) 805–53.

[11] Ibid., 805–53, at 805.

[12] On the step made between Bourdieu and Foucault and the distinct benefits of the insights provided by each of them for the study of international law, see the remarks of N. Rajkovic, "Rules, Lawyering, and the Politics of Legality: Critical Sociology and International Law's Rule", 27 *Leiden Journal of International Law* (2014), 331–52, at 341. N. Rajkovic, "Rules, Lawyering, and the Politics of Legality: Critical Sociology and International Law's Rule", 27 *Leiden Journal of International Law* (2014), 331–52, at 341, citing V. Tadros, "Between Governance and Discipline: The Law and Michel Foucault" (1998), 18 *Oxford Journal of Legal Studies*, 75, at 78; see also F. Ewald, "Norms, Discipline and the Law" (1990), 30 *Representations* 138, at 139–41; *A Foucauldian Approach to International Law. Descriptive Thoughts for Normative Issues*, by L.M. Hammer. Aldershot: Ashgate, 2007.

on the structural characteristics of the field and bring to the surface the exercise of power behind the production of knowledge. The ambition of this book lies elsewhere. It is not that the structures of the field are not worthy of investigation by international lawyers. Understanding those structures certainly helps explain why international legal thinking continues to oscillate between contradictory paradigms and eternally moves in circles, often in opposite terms.[13] Likewise, identifying those very structures that obfuscate the exercises of power constitutes a concern which international legal thinkers have rightly engaged with in recent years.[14] Yet, this book sets itself more modest ambitions and rather focuses on another aspect of the communitarian dimension of the argumentative practice of international law which has been, to the knowledge of this author, rarely explored in contemporary legal scholarship.

The chapters that follow approach foundational doctrines and argumentative techniques as distinct tools to impose *social arrangements* within and beyond the field. The social arrangements contemplated by foundational doctrines and argumentative techniques under examination here can often pertain to the organization of the "outside world" as much as that of the community of international lawyers itself. The social arrangement promoted by foundational doctrines and argumentative techniques can thus be of an internal or external nature. This book does not seek to unearth the social arrangements that the foundational doctrines and argumentative techniques under examination here seek to vindicate. This would reduce this book to another study of the "politics" of international law aimed at unveiling the external agenda of doctrines and argumentative techniques. Instead, the chapters that follow limit themselves to functionally situate the design of foundational doctrines and the deployment of argumentative techniques in relation to the community of international law itself, irrespective of the political agenda that is envisaged for the external world. The

---

[13] D. Kennedy, "When Renewal Repeats: Thinking Against the Box", 32 *New York University Journal of International Law and Politics* 335 (2000). For some nuances to the idea that the legal scholarship moves as a pendulum, N. Duxbury, *Patterns of American Jurisprudence*, OUP, 1997, at 2–4.

[14] Others like M. Koskenniemi have taken direct issue with those structures, like managerialism, in that they obscure the way power works. See M. Koskenniemi, "The Politics of International Law: 20 Years Later" 20 *European Journal of International Law* (2009) 7–19. This is why his culture of formalism seeks to reinstate international law as the only available surface over which managerial governance may be challenged. M. Koskenniemi, *The Gentle Civilizer of Nations: The Rise and Fall of International Law 1870–1960* (Cambridge University Press, 2002), at 500–508.

exercise, in contrast with numerous contemporary studies, is thus neither problem-solving nor complexity-reducing.[15] Its ambitions lie solely with shedding light on the *internal* social arrangements that are pursued by international lawyers when designing and deploying their foundational doctrines and argumentative techniques. It is inevitable, however, that in discussing internal social arrangements pursued by the community of international lawyers, the chapters below occasionally touched on the external social arrangements eyed by international lawyers. This, however, is never the primary focus of the inquiry.

The foregoing should suffice to show that this book, rather than a detour into the sociology of international law or the politics of international law, primarily constitutes an exercise of functional and internal *situationalism*.[16] Indeed, its aim is to internally contextualize the making and deployment of the foundational doctrines and argumentative techniques by exhuming the conditions that influence the limits and potential to which their architects and users are subjected.[17] Needless to say that exploring the situatedness of (the design or deployment of) foundational doctrines and argumentative techniques is nothing groundbreaking in contemporary scholarship. It is certainly the legacy of critical legal studies – although they were no pioneer in this respect – to have taught international lawyers exposed to it, and especially international legal scholars, not only to disclose their own agenda and conceptual premises, but also to try to situate the legal claims of others.[18] In today's international legal scholarship, the situatedness of legal claims and legal argument has even become a central object of inquiry.

It is well known that situatedness of an argument inextricably has multiple facets. One can situate a legal claim from a great variety of angles: anthropological, cultural, historical, traditional, political, socio-economical, socio-historical, etc. It seems fair to say that the mainstream

---

[15] On the necessity of legal scholarship to reduce complexity, see A. Peters, "Realizing Utopia as a Scholarly Endeavor", 24 *European Journal of International Law* (2013) 533–52.

[16] For an early elaboration of situationality, see K. Jaspers, *The Future of Mankind*, 1958 (transl) and *Man in the Modern Age*, 1932 (transl) (Berlin, 1932).

[17] O. Korhonen, *International Law Situated. An Analysis of the Lawyer's Stance Towards Culture, History and Community*, The Hague; London: Kluwer Law International (2000), 8.

[18] Situationalism was very central in legal realism. On the link between critical legal studies and legal realism, see N. Duxbury, *Patterns of American Jurisprudence*, OUP, 1997, at 6.

approach to situatedness in today's international legal scholarship is probably socio-historical and it seems no coincidence that one of the most seminal pieces of scholarship produced in the present century sought to situate international law within its socio-historical context.[19] As the foregoing has already indicated, this book departs from the main type of situationalism observed in the international legal literature and shies away from embarking on a discussion of the socio-historical situatedness of foundational doctrines and techniques considered below. Rather, this book construes the foundational doctrines and argumentative techniques of international law as purposive constructions and activities[20] and seeks to unearth the internal social arrangements that are pursued in the design and deployment of each of them.

It must be acknowledged that situationalism, albeit growing more common in international legal studies, is certainly not without problem. It is inevitably affected by self-referentiality,[21] and, in the context of socio-historical situationalism, an anachronism.[22] Indeed, the insights produced by situationalism are inevitably prejudiced by the pre-understandings of the one exploring the situatedness of any legal claim.[23] This is why it is acknowledged that situationalism is itself necessarily situated.[24] Those problems have, however, been deemed insurmountable,

---

[19] See generally M. Koskenniemi, *The Gentle Civilizer of Nations* (CUP, 2001). See the remarks on this aspect of M. Koskenniemi's project by J. Dunoff, "From Interdisciplinarity to Counterdisciplinarity: Is there Madness in Martti's Method?", 27 *Temple International and Comparative Law Journal* 309 (2013).

[20] This is certainly not ground-breaking. It is well-known that contemporary natural law thinkers construe law as a purposive enterprise. See L. Fuller, *The Morality of Law* (Yale University Press, 1964 second edition, 1969), p. 145. For an application to international law, see P. Capps, *Human Dignity and the Foundations of International Law*, Hart, 2009, 41–3.

[21] See the criticism of Fish's situatedness of interpretation and the de-reponsibilization of the self by P. Shlag. See P. Shlag, "Fish v. Zapp: The Case of the Relatively Autonomous Self", 76 *The Georgetown Law Journal* (1987) 36.

[22] On the problem of anachronism in socio-historical situationalism, see the comments and rebuttal by M. Koskenniemi, "Histories of International Law: Significance and Problems for a Critical View" 27 *Temple Journal of International and Comparative Law* (2013) 215.

[23] See O. Korhonen, (2000), *International Law Situated. An Analysis of the Lawyer's Stance Towards Culture, History and Community*, The Hague; London: Kluwer Law International, pp. 9–10.

[24] Stanley Fish, *Is there a text in this class?* Harvard University Press, 1980, 360; see also A. MacIntyre, *Whose Justice? Which Rationality?*, Duckworth, 1988, 367. In the context of legal argumentation, O. Korhonen recalls that critical

played down or turned on their head as a source of richness for scholarly inquiries.[25] It is not necessary to address them here. It seems more relevant to formulate a few additional caveats on the scope and purpose of the chapters that follow.

First, it should go without saying that determining one or several dimensions of the situatedness of a legal claim or legal argument does not make the claim or argument concerned more determinate as far as its substance is concerned.[26] In that sense, this book does not constitute an attempt to rein in the indeterminacy that inevitably shrouds the foundational doctrines of international law and that is unavoidably exacerbated by the deployments of the argumentative techniques of international lawyers.[27] Second, although they focus on the functional situatedness of the foundational doctrines of international law and the argumentative techniques deployed by international lawyers, the following chapters do not reduce doctrines and argumentative techniques to the choices of their architects or the social arrangements they contemplate. Likewise, this book should not be understood as an exercise of critical narrative analysis properly so called as this commonly requires an in-depth and systematic exploration of the various components of legal arguments.[28] The following chapters, as was explained above, limit themselves to the functional intellectual manoeuvres behind the design of foundational doctrines and the deployment of argumentative techniques. Third, as these chapters will make clear, the social arrangements contemplated by international lawyers when designing and deploying their foundational doctrines and argumentative techniques can very well be

---

method is not an ultimate universally valid method but also a form of submission to structure. See O. Korhonen, "New International Law: Silence, Defence or Deliverance?" 7 *European Journal of International Law* (1996), 1–28, 17.

[25] On the virtues of anachronism, see K. Koskenniemi, "Histories of International Law: Significance and Problems for a Critical View", 27 *Temple Journal of International and Comparative Law* (2013) 215, at 230–31.

[26] O. Korhonen, "New International Law: Silence, Defence or Deliverance?" 7 *European Journal of International Law* (1996), 1–28, at 5.

[27] It is an exaggeration to claim that this was the purpose of my previous work on the role of formalism and the sources of international law. I thus disagree with the reading of S. Singh, "Appendix 2: International Law as a Technical Discipline: Critical Perspectives on the Narrative Structure of a Theory" (May 26, 2013) in J. d'Aspremont, *Formalism and the Sources of International Law* (Oxford: OUP, 2013), pp. 236–61; University of Cambridge Faculty of Law Research Paper No. 22/2013

[28] See the critical remarks by S. Singh, "International Law as a Technical Discipline: Critical Perspectives on the Narrative Structure of a Theory", ibid.

unconscious. International lawyers may be mechanically reproducing narratives or methods through which they have been socialized without realizing the social arrangements envisaged by each of them. The (un)conscious character of the pursuit of social arrangements is, to some extent, irrelevant here, especially since the self-consciousness of international lawyers – albeit inevitably part of the social structures looked at – is not the primary object of the essays that follow.[29] Fourth, it should be made clear that approaching the practice of international law in communitarian terms does not mean that the community of international lawyers must itself be held a formal source of law.[30] Foundational doctrines and argumentative techniques are not approached from the perspective of the sources of international law. Neither is their validation by virtue of the mainstream doctrine of sources an object of inquiry. Of singular interest here is the pursuit of internal social arrangements by international lawyers when designing and deploying their foundational doctrines and argumentative techniques, irrespective of their implications for (and from the perspective of) the doctrine of sources of international law.

## III. THE SOCIALIZING OF INTERNATIONAL LAWYERS THROUGH THE ACQUISITION OF FOUNDATIONAL DOCTRINES AND TECHNIQUES

As was indicated in the previous section, this book adopts a communitarian approach to the relation between foundational doctrines and argumentative techniques and the community of international lawyers by examining the way in which the community of international lawyers impacts the design and the use of foundational doctrines and argumentative techniques. It particularly looks at the internal functional situatedness of the design and use of such foundational doctrines and argumentative techniques and seeks to exhume some of the social arrangements pursued by international lawyers on such occasions. So delineated, the object of inquiry of the chapters that follow obviously presupposes that there is

---

[29] For such an inquiry, see M. Koskenniemi, "Between Commitment and Cynicism: Outline for a Theory of International Law as Practice" in *The Politics of International Law*, Hart, 2011, at 271.
[30] On this debate, see gen. J. Kammerhofer, "Law-Making by Scholars" (November 30, 2012). C. Brölmann and Y. Radi (eds), *Research Handbook on the Theory and Practice of International Law-Making* (Cheltenham: Edward Elgar 2015) (forthcoming).

such a thing as a community of international lawyers to which consciousness and instrumental choices can be attributed. In other words, it presupposes that international lawyers naturally have coalesced into a community sharing some consciousness or disciplinary sensitivity and are capable of pursuing common social arrangements. And this is where this book, although it focuses primarily on the way communitarian dynamics informs the design and use of foundational doctrines and argumentative techniques, must turn its attention to the way in which those doctrines and techniques themselves shape the community of international lawyers.

The idea of a community of international lawyers is apprehended here through the notion of socialization. It is the process of socialization that makes individual agents coalesce into a collective association and become a member thereof. The notion of socialization is also what reveals the extent of the implications of the abovementioned dialectical understanding of the relation between foundational doctrines and argumentative techniques on the one hand and the community of international lawyers on the other. The socialization of international lawyers, as it is understood here, refers to international lawyers, despite diverging political commitment becoming possessed with certain doctrines as well techniques of reading and using the law.[31] In other words, becoming an international lawyer is to undergo a process of socialization whereby one is trained to the doctrines and argumentative techniques of international law, and more generally, to the "world view" of the discipline.[32] From the perspective of the process of socialization, the foundational doctrines and argumentative techniques can be considered a "grammar"[33] common to all international lawyers that determines what it is possible to say, to think and to hope with the language of international law. Said differently, through socialization, international lawyers are introduced to those rituals that function as symbolic validation mechanisms.[34] It is true that, from a more empirical perspective, it could be contended that a community of international lawyers could exist in the

---

[31] See the critical remarks of P. Bourdieu, "The Force of Law: Toward a Sociology of the Juridical Field" 38 *Hastings Law Journal* (1987) 805–53, at 827.

[32] O. Korhonen, "New International Law: Silence, Defence or Deliverance?" 7 *European Journal of International Law* (1996), 1–28, at 6.

[33] M. Koskenniemi, *From Apology to Utopia*, CUP, 2005, p. 589 ("a grammar is not a description of what native language-speakers say in fact – it is an account of what it is possible to say in that language").

[34] T. Franck, *The Power of Legitimacy among Nations*, NY, OUP, 1990, p. 92.

absence of international law.[35] Yet this book departs from such an empirical finding and embraces a notion of community whereby the foundational doctrines and argumentative techniques feed into the socialization process of international lawyers and allow the emergence of a consciousness that is itself constitutive of the community.

The point made here is thus that the acquisition of these foundational doctrines and argumentative techniques contributes to the socialization of international lawyers (and allows them to coalesce into a community) because it gives rise to a shared consciousness, understood here as a vocabulary of concepts and typical arguments[36] or some disciplinary sensitivity.[37] Here too there exists a myriad of different descriptive frameworks to apprehend the consciousness or sensitivity constitutive of the community. Some scholars have spoken of mindset or tradition.[38] Others have referred to the notions of cultural unity,[39] ethos,[40] legal culture,[41] normative universe (nomos),[42] or collective consciousness.[43]

---

[35] As J. Crawford put it when receiving the ASIL Hudson Medal (2012): "One does not need to believe in God to credit the existence of the clergy", 106 *ASIL Proceedings* 2012, p. 2). See also the critical remarks of J. d'Aspremont, *International Lawyers Live!* (May 23, 2013). Available at SSRN: http://ssrn.com/abstract=2271115.

[36] Duncan Kennedy, "Two Globalizations of Law and Legal Thought: 1850–1968", 36 *Suffolk University Law Review* (2003), 631, at 634.

[37] David Kennedy, "The Disciplines of International Law and Policy" 12 *Leiden Journal of International Law* 9–133 (1999), at 13 and 17.

[38] M. Koskenniemi seems to be using these words interchangeably. See M. Koskenniemi, "Constitutionalism as Mindset: Reflections on Kantian Themes about International Law and Globalization", 8 *Theoretical Inquiries in Law* (2006) 9, at 9.

[39] M. Prost, *The Concept of Unity in Public International Law* (Hart, 2012), pp. 153 and 159 (who refers to the "parameters for the product, the dispersion and the validation of juridical discourse" and argues that international law can be studied like any other cultural system).

[40] F. Megret, *International Law as Law* (September 6, 2010). *Cambridge Companion to International Law*, J. Crawford and M. Koskenniemi, eds, 2010, 64, at 66.

[41] See H.P. Glenn, *Legal Traditions of the World*, OUP, 2007 (putting the emphasis on the idea of continuity).

[42] R. Cover, The Supreme Court 1982 Term – "Foreword: Nomos and Narrative" 97 *Harvard Law Review* 4, at 4–5 (1983) (putting the emphasis on the whole normative corpus of a living community by virtue of which a community constitutes a community).

[43] E. Durkheim, *The Division of Labor in Society*, Glencoe, The Free Press, (1947), pp. 79–80 (who speaks of social psyche constituted by a group with common beliefs and sentiments).

Needless to say that the consciousness or disciplinary sensitivity constantly evolves over time, together with the foundational doctrines and argumentative techniques. It is a dynamic cognitive notion meant to capture a fluid factual phenomenon. By definition, it is inconceivable to apprehend (and delineate) what the consciousness of the discipline is at any moment in time. At best, one can represent, with broad strokes, what the mainstream understanding(s) of the foundational doctrines as well as what the mainstream use(s) of the argumentative techniques look like. The textbooks and the scholarship can constitute good indicators in this respect.[44] However, this book should certainly not be perceived as attempting, in any way, to provide a plain account of what is the consciousness or disciplinary sensitivity of the time.

Socialization occurs through visible (and conscious) and less-visible (and unconscious) channels. It would be of no avail to discuss them extensively here. It suffices to focus on two of the main mechanisms through which socialization is realized: education and scholarship.[45] It does not seem controversial to claim that training and education constitute the main instrument through which international lawyers are socialized, that is made proficient in the language of international law and acquire a consciousness shared with all those that have been trained the same way. Although there are significant geographical variations,[46] the

---

[44] For instance contemporary scholarship seems to indicate that, probably as a result of the rise and success of critical legal studies and deconstructivism in international legal thinking, the shared consciousness of international lawyers nowadays include self-doubt. For an elaboration on this theme, see generally M. Koskenniemi, "Between Commitment and Cynicism: Outline for a Theory of International Law as Practice" in *The Politics of International Law*, Hart, 2011, at 271.

[45] One could also think of the socialization that occurs by virtue of professional training in law firms, legal services of foreign affairs ministries or legal divisions of international organizations.

[46] Although this comes with a bit of oversimplification, it is commonly believed that, in the Anglo-Saxon tradition, the emphasis is first put on the acquisition of skills whereas, in civil law traditions and others, the focus is on the acquisition of knowledge. On this debate, see gen. M. Damaska, "A Continental Lawyer in an American Law School: Trials and Tribulations of Adjustment", 116 *University of Pennsylvania Law Review* (1968) 1363. See also H. Dagan, "Law as an Academic Discipline", Tel Aviv University Law School, Tel Aviv University Law Faculty Papers, Paper 171, (2013). Available at SSRN: http://ssrn.com/abstract=2228433. In recent years, some concern arises as a result of the move to interdisciplinarity, not only in legal scholarship, but also in legal education. See Weinrib, "Can Law Survive Legal Education" 60 *Vanderbilt Law Review* (2007) 401, at 403–4 and 410–11.

socialization of international lawyers through education and training is usually realized by virtue of a transmission of both knowledge (including foundational doctrines) and skills (including argumentative techniques).[47] In that specific mode of socialization, textbooks play a crucial formatting role.[48] Although education and training are two of the most powerful instruments of socialization, one should not underestimate the role played by scholarship in the process of acquisition of the doctrines and argumentative techniques of international law. Indeed, both the consumption of scholarship (as a reader) and the production of scholarship (as an author) contribute to the rise of a shared consciousness or disciplinary sensitivity. This does not seem controversial and hence does not call for any discussion here.

Whatever the channels of socialization may be, it seems unanimously recognized that they contribute to the reproduction of the very powerful structures of the field. This is a finding long made by sociologists[49] and it is now uncontested among international lawyers that the foundational doctrines as well as the argumentative techniques acquired through socialization processes open new argumentative spaces as much as they restrict them.[50] Those structures affect both the access to socialization as well as access to the community of socialized international lawyers. In that sense, it should be emphasized that, as a result of those powerful structures, socialization cannot be deemed synonymous to access to legal argumentation itself. Being socialized as an international lawyer does not necessarily provide access to authoritative and universal legal argumentation. Access to legal argumentation remains restricted. Not everyone is allowed to have their legal argumentation even considered. Being admitted as an authorized interpreter of international law – and thus deploying

---

[47] For G. Simpson, socialization through education and training is carried out in a "romantic" way, that is, by virtue of a series of compromises (or repressed theoretical contradictions). See Gerry Simpson, "On the Magic Mountain: Teaching Public International Law", 10 *European Journal of International Law* 1999, 70–92, 72.

[48] For some critical remarks, see the special symposium in the *European Journal of International Law* in "Symposium: A Colloquium on International Law Textbooks in England", 11 *European Journal of International Law* (2000) 615.

[49] See P. Bourdieu, "The Force of Law: Toward a Sociology of the Juridical Field" 38 *Hastings Law Journal* (1987) 805–53.

[50] J. Crawford and M. Koskenniemi, "Introduction", in J. Crawford and M. Koskenniemi (eds), *Cambridge Companion to International Law* (CUP, 2012), at 4; see also M. Koskenniemi, *From Apology to Utopia*, CUP, 2005, p. 589.

foundational doctrines and argumentative technique – is not a universal entitlement and is dependent on other – formal and non-formal – parameters. While access to socialization itself is restricted – especially when it materializes in the taking of an advanced university degree – access to legal argumentation will thereafter depend, among others, on one's affiliation or profession.[51] This is not to mention exclusion by power and practical constraints. These entry tariffs to legal argumentation vary according to the fragmentation of the community of the community of international lawyers.[52] The socialization discussed here should thus not be understood as seeking to open a "horizon" of a universal legal argumentation, as this has been yearned for by some international lawyers.[53]

It is probably not necessary to elaborate on those powerful enabling and restricting structures that bear upon the access to the socialization process and the access to the community of socialized international lawyers. One remark must however be made about the idiom in which

---

[51] To illustrate that point, it suffices to recall how suspicious we are when we open a book, an article or a working paper from someone whose name is unknown to us and who does not provide his or her professional affiliation. In such a case, and unless it comes with the recommendation of trustworthy peers or a very sexy title, there is a high chance that we do not even bother to read it. This is also why it always proves so important to mention one's affiliation on open access repositories and databases like SSRN.

[52] As a result, there exist various – sometimes overlapping – guilds, each of them with different entry tariffs for potential entrants. For some critical remarks, see A. Rasulov, "New Approaches to International Law: Images of a Genealogy", in J.M. Beneyto and D. Kennedy (eds), *New Approaches to International Law: the European and the American Experiences* (TMC Asser-Springer, 2012), pp. 151–91.

[53] This is the famous concept of "culture of formalism" floated by M. Koskenniemi. M. Koskenniemi, *The Gentle Civilizer of Nations: The Rise and Fall of International Law 1870–1960* (Cambridge University Press, 2002), at 500–508. For a discussion of that concept, see E. Jouannet, "Présentation critique", in M. Koskenniemi, *La Politique du Droit International* (Paris, Pedone, 2007), at 32–3. See also I. de la Rasilla del Moral, "Martti Koskenniemi and the Spirit of the Beehive in International Law", 10 *Global Jurist* (2010); J. von Bernstorff, "Sisyphus was an international lawyer. On M. Koskenniemi's 'From Apologia to Utopia' and the place of law in international politics", 7 *German Law Journal* (2006) 1015, at 1029–31; J.A. Beckett, "Rebel Without a Cause. M. Koskenniemi and the Critical Legal Project", 7 *German Law Review* (2006) 1045; see also the book review of M. Koskenniemi, "The Gentle Civilizer of Nations: The Rise and Fall of International Law 1870–1960" by N. Tsagourias, 16 *Leiden Journal of International Law* (2003) 397, pp. 398–9.

nowadays most of the abovementioned socialization occurs, be it through education and training or scholarship. Indeed, the dominant language in which international law is today taught and thought, not to say argued, has itself generated its own sets of enabling and restricting structures. With the rise of the English language as the lingua franca of international law[54] come a style of analysis and specific categories as well as a worldview, even for those for whom English is not a mother tongue.[55] This has not been without consequences on the distribution of power among international lawyers. Although they are today surrounded by an overwhelming majority of non-native speakers practicing international law in English, native speakers necessarily continue to enjoy some ascendency[56] and are more in a position to impose their categories, methods, cognitive frameworks, style, and to some extent, views of the discipline and views of the world.

There are of course many more structures that bear upon the socialization process of international lawyers and the access to the community of socialized international lawyers. Some of them will be touched upon in the following chapters.

## IV. THE COMMUNITY OF SOCIALIZED INTERNATIONAL LAWYERS: EPISTEMIC COMMUNITY, COMMUNITY OF PRACTICE, INTERPRETIVE COMMUNITY OR COMMUNICATIVE COMMUNITY?

As the previous section has shown, it is through socialization that the international lawyers coalesce into a community. It is by acquiring, among others, these doctrines and argumentative techniques, that they come to form a community – that community, in turn, impacting on how foundational doctrines and argumentative techniques operate. The community of international law that emerges through the socialization process briefly described above can of course be apprehended in a great

---

[54] For some similar observations, see A. Somek, "The Indelible Science of Law", University of Iowa Legal Studies Research Paper, Number 09-18, June 2010.
[55] Ibid., at 79.
[56] For a similar finding albeit in another context, see M. Koskenniemi, "Miserable Comforters: International Relations as New Nature Law", 15 *European Journal of International Relations* (2009) 395–422, at 395.

variety of ways. Until recently, international lawyers would only look at the community organized around international law through the angle of law-appliers,[57] *auctoritatis interpositio*,[58] or those undeveloped – but not unpopular – notions like the invisible college.[59] In recent years, however, other cognitive models have come to stand out, some of which have been inherited from other social sciences. It suffices to mention four of them briefly.[60]

First, from international relations theory, international lawyers have learned that their community could be understood as an *epistemic community*, that is in a non-systematically organized network of professionals with recognized expertise and authority that allow them to contribute to the making of policy-relevant knowledge in relation to their area of expertise.[61] According to this construction, international lawyers constitute an epistemic community, and thus not merely an interest group, or a social movement by virtue of a shared faith in certain –

---

[57] The notion of law-applier emerged in the context of a rule-based approach to international law. It finds roots in British analytical jurisprudence as well as German legal positivism. It quickly proved insufficient as it often remained equated with the idea of judicial authority. In recent years, the concept of law-applying authority has been subject to some dilution and pluralization in general theory of law and jurisprudence. See K. Culver and M. Giudice, *Legality's Borders – An Essay in General Jurisprudence*, OUP, 2010.

[58] The idea of *auctoritatis interpositio* is borrowed from C. Schmitt although it is used to refer to the Kantian idea – systematized by Kelsen – that by virtue of the indeterminacy of rules law is ultimately dependent upon human judgement. See C. Schmitt, *Politische Theologie: Vier Kapitel zur Lehre von der Souveränität* ((Berlin: Duncker und Humblot, 1979), at 41. See the discussion of that question by N. Rajkovic, "Rules, Lawyering, and the Politics of Legality: Critical Sociology and International Law's Rule", 27 *Leiden Journal of International Law* (2014), 331–52

[59] O. Schachter, "The Invisible College of International Lawyers" 72 *Nw. U. L. Rev.* 217 (1977–1978).

[60] The inquiry here is thus alien to an examination of the distinctiveness of the community of lawyers within the society as a whole. For a discussion of the various parameters that allow a differentiation between the community of lawyers and the rest of the society, see, F. Schauer, *The Force of Law* (Harvard University Press, forthcoming 2015), chapter 11. See more generally N. Luhmann, *The Differentiation of Society*, New York: Columbia University Press, 1984. See also Luhmann, *Das Recht der Gesellschaft*, Frankfurt a.M. 1995, 550 ss. (Engl.: *Law as a Social System*, Oxford, OUP, 2004).

[61] P. Haas, "Introduction: epistemic communities and international policy coordination", 46 *International Organizations* (1992) 1, at 2 and 3 (Peter Haas acknowledged that the notion has some Marxist origins but that he uses it in a different way).

allegedly scientific – methods as a way of generating truth.[62] The notion of epistemic community has proved rather appealing for many international lawyers to explain some of the dynamics at work in the creation of knowledge about international law.[63]

Second, from another strand of international relations, international lawyers have borrowed the more fluid and open idea of *community of practice*. According to such a construction, international lawyers constitute a community of practice as long as they "are informally as well as contextually bound by a shared interest in learning and applying a common practice"[64] while also sharing a common "repertoire of communal resources, such as routines, words, tools, ways of doing things, stories, symbols, and discourse".[65] This presupposes "social communication through which practitioners bargain about and fix meanings and develop their own distinctive identity and how to practice it".[66] The concept of community of practice is more fluid in that the members' shared sense of joint enterprise is constantly being renegotiated[67] and membership is not fixed as members constantly move in and move out.[68] Notwithstanding some inevitable incommensurable elements that distort any comparison between the two notions, it seems possible to say, with a good deal of oversimplification, that communities of practice constitute a more all-encapsulating notion than that of epistemic community, the latter being a special kind of community of practice. Like the notion of epistemic community, the notion of community of practice has found an echo in international legal scholarship, the doctrine of sources being

---

[62] Ibid. at 3 and at 18.

[63] M. Noortmann, "The International Law Association and Non-state Actors: Professional Network, Public Interest Group or Epistemic Community?", in J. d'Aspremont (ed.), *Participants in the International Legal System: Multiple Perspectives on Non-state Actors in International Law* (Routledge, 2015, 233–47); D.J. Galbreath and J. McEvoy, "How Epistemic Communities Drive International Regimes: the Case of Minority Rights in Europe" 35 *Journal of European Integration* (2013), 169–86; for an application of the notion by P. Haas himself, see P. Haas, "International Environmental Law: Epistemic Communities" in D. Bodansky, J. Brunée and E. Hey (eds), *The Oxford Handbook of International Environmental Law* (OUP, 2007), 791–806.

[64] E. Adler, *Communitarian International Relations: The Epistemic Foundations of International Relations* (Routledge, 2005), at 15.

[65] Ibid., at 15.

[66] Ibid., at 17.

[67] Ibid., at 14.

[68] Ibid., at 14.

considered one of the most elementary tools that allows social practice within the community.[69]

Third, international lawyers have found in literary and linguistic philosophy the notion of interpretive community. The concept does not need to be spelled out at length as it is further discussed later in this book.[70] It suffices to recall that the notion refers to the public and conventional point of view that orders and principles the argumentative practice of international law and constrain the production of meanings.[71] It presupposes a common understanding of what constitutes valid practice, such an understanding being occasionally translated into rules, like rules on interpretation or rules on sources of law.[72] According to that notion, international lawyers constitute an interpretive community as soon as they share a language which allows them to speak to one another and a system of principles that each of them has internalized and which comes to constrain the type of legal argumentation they recognize as valid.[73] Like the concept of community of practice, the notion of interpretive community is not fixed or finite.[74] Because of both its ordering and anti-indeterminacy virtues as well as its fluidity, it is not surprising that the concept of interpretive community has enjoyed a resounding success in international legal scholarship.[75]

---

[69] H. Cohen, "Finding International Law, Part II: Our Fragmenting Legal Community" 44 *NYU Journal of International Law and Politics* (2012) 1049.

[70] See below chapter 7 on interpretation.

[71] S. Fish, "Fish v. Fiss" 36 *Stanford Law Review* (1984) 1325–47, at 1331–2. S. Fish, *Is there a text in this class?* (Harvard University Press, 1980), pp. 13–14.

[72] For a challenge of the idea that rules on sources constitute rules properly so-called, see J. d'Aspremont, "The Idea of Rules in the Sources of International Law", 84 *British Yearbook of International Law* (2014) pp. 103–30.

[73] S. Fish, *Is there a text in this class?* Harvard University Press, 1980, at 5.

[74] S. Fish, "Fish v. Fiss" 36 *Stanford Law Review* (1984) 1325–47, 1329; see also S. Fish, *Is there a text in this class?* Harvard University Press, 1980, at 172. ("Of course, this stability is always temporary (unlike the longed for and timeless stability of the text). Interpretive communities grow larger and decline, and individuals move from one to another; thus, while the alignments are not permanent, they are always there, providing just enough stability for the interpretive battles to go on, and just enough shift and slippage to assure that they will never be settled.")

[75] A. Bianchi, "The International Regulation of the Use of Force: The Politics of Interpretive Method" 22 *Leiden Journal of International Law* 2009, 665; J. d'Aspremont, "Wording in International Law", 25 *Leiden Journal of International Law* (2012) 575–602; I. Johnstone, "Treaty Interpretation: The

Fourth, the community of international lawyers has also been apprehended by the idea of a shared platform of communication. According to this conceptualization, which has been deemed "communicative",[76] there is a community of international lawyers as soon as there is a striving for a shared vocabulary that allows communication and argumentation among scholars. Short of any communicative tool, international legal scholars cannot constitute a community of international law. This approach acknowledges that the shared vocabulary of the community is bound to be ever changing and fluctuate constantly.[77] Yet, it is this striving that creates the possibility of communication necessary for the

---

Authority of Interpretive Communities", 12 *Michigan Journal of International Law* 371 (1990–1991); E. Papastavridis, "Interpretation of Security Council Resolutions under Chapter VII in the Aftermath of the Iraqi Crisis", 56 *International and Comparative Law Quarterly* (2007) 83–118; A. Bianchi, "Textual interpretation and (international) law reading: the myth of (in)determinacy and the genealogy of meaning", in: P.H.F. Bekker/R. Dolzer/M. Weibel (Hrsg.), *Making Transnational Law Work in the Global Economy. Essays in Honour of D. Vagts*, Cambridge 2010, 34 ss., 51 ss.; D.F. Vagts, "Treaty Interpretation and the New American Ways of Law Reading", in: *EJIL*, Vol. 4, Nr. 1, 1993, 472 ss., 480 ss.; F. Zarbiev, "Le discours interprétatif en droit international: une approche critique et généalogique" (Geneva: Graduate Institute of International and Development Studies, PhD thesis, 2009), 98 ss.; V. Fikfak/Benedict Burnett, "Domestic Court's Reading of International Norms: A Semiotic Analysis", in: *International Journal for the Semiotics of Law*, Vol. 22, Nr. 4, 2009, 437 ss.; I. Johnstone, "Security Council Deliberations: The Power of the Better Argument", in: *EJIL*, Vol. 14, Nr. 3, 437 ss., 439.

[76] See J. d'Aspremont, "Wording in International Law" 25 Leiden *Journal of International Law* (2012) pp. 575–602. See also chapter 1 in J. d'Aspremont, *Formalism and the Sources of International Law* (OUP, 2011). It is no coincidence that T. Meyer has interpreted this work as seeking to preserve the possibility of communication and calling for a new theory of communication in international law. See T. Meyer, "Towards a Communicative Theory of International Law", *Melbourne Journal of International Law* (2013) 1.

[77] In the same sense, see A. Marmor, "Can the Law Imply More than It Says? – On Some Pragmatic Aspects of Strategic Speech", (December 3, 2009). USC Law Legal Studies Paper No. 09-43. Available at SSRN: http://ssrn.com/abstract=1517883, p. 14. There is "a certain degree of uncertainty about the relevant maxims of conversation or the level of adherence to them, that the parties are presumed to follow. It is precisely this lack of complete certainty about the maxims of conversation that enables the success of communication in spite of certain divergence of communicative expectations or intentions. The lack of certainty leaves certain content hanging in the air, as it were, leaving each party to the conversation with an option of understanding the full communicated content somewhat differently".

subsistence of the community of international law. Such a conceptualization has simultaneously come with a plea for a renewed idea of the sources of international law – deemed necessary to allow communication[78] – that nonetheless ought to radically depart from the static pedigree-determining blueprints found in the mainstream literature.[79] Such an understanding inevitably comes with its own self-created perils,[80] that is the hazard associated with a disaggregation of the language of the sources.[81]

All these cognitive models to apprehend the communitarian forces between the agents of international law have their own merits and weaknesses. It would be of no avail to try to evaluate each of them in the context of international law and determine which one offers the most useful construction of the community of professionals at work behind international law. It seems that each of them sheds light (and puts the emphasis) on a different – but equally relevant – aspect of the community of those socialized international lawyers. This is why the following chapters borrow from several of them, depending on the communitarian aspects of the foundational doctrines or argumentative techniques which

---

[78] See contra the work of D. Davidson, "A Nice Derangement of Epitaphs", in D. Davidson, *Truth, Language, and History* (New York: Oxford University Press, 1986) 89–108 (for him conventions are not necessary to allow communication). See the discussion in I. Venzke, in "Is Interpretation in International Law a Game?" (May 23, 2014), forthcoming in: A. Bianchi, D. Peat and M. Windsor (eds), *Interpretation in International Law* (OUP, 2014), Amsterdam Law School Research Paper No. 2014-34, Amsterdam Center for International Law No. 2014-21, Postnational Rulemaking Working Paper No. 2014-02 as well as see more generally, I. Venzke, *How Interpretation Makes International Law – On Semantic Change and Normative Twists* (OUP, 2012).

[79] J. d'Aspremont, *Formalism and the Sources of International Law* (OUP, 2011).

[80] S. Singh, "Appendix 2: International Law as a Technical Discipline: Critical Perspectives on the Narrative Structure of a Theory" (May 26, 2013) in J. d'Aspremont, *Formalism and the Sources of International Law* (Oxford: OUP, 2013), pp. 236–61; University of Cambridge Faculty of Law Research Paper No. 22/2013.

[81] This is a finding also made by H. Cohen, "Finding International Law, Part II: Our Fragmenting Legal Community", 44 NYU *Journal of International Law and Politics* (2012) 1049; see also J. d'Aspremont, "An Autonomous Regime of Identification of Customary International Humanitarian Law: Do Not Say What You Do or Do Not Do What You Say?" (March 8, 2013) in R. van Steenberghe (ed.), *Droit international humanitaire: un régime spécial de droit international?* 73 (Bruylant, 2013), available at SSRN: http://ssrn.com/abstract=2230345.

they seek to elucidate. For the sake of the exploration attempted in the following chapters, there is no need to espouse a single uniform universalized and neat concept of community to make sense of the communitarian dynamics against the backdrop of which foundational doctrines and techniques are shaped and deployed.

There is another – probably more fundamental – reason why it would be vain to seek to elect a single model of community at work behind the foundational doctrines and argumentative techniques of international law under discussion in the following chapters. There is indeed not one community but a great variety of communities of international lawyers, each of them of different nature and subject to different structures. There seems to be no one to contest that the professional community organized around international law is fragmented and made of several different sub-communities at the same time. Such a pluralistic configuration originates in – often unconscious – differentiations, estrangements and federating dynamics of very different kinds: methodological, conceptual, political, linguistic, professional, cultural, geographical, etc. For the sake of this current study, it is certainly not necessary to provide a cartographic overview of the various sub-communities of international lawyers. Nor is it necessary to ascertain all the levels at which the community of international lawyers is fragmented. The point that must be made here, however, is that the foundational doctrines and the argumentative techniques examined here can, at times, be the very dividing and fragmenting factor.[82] In that sense, the explorations that follow do not assume that the communitarian dynamics under examination are universal. They are generally those that can be observed in some of the dominant strands of the – mostly English speaking – international legal scholarship, that is among those international lawyers whose principal activity is of an academic nature.

---

[82] Different communities, past and present, have different concepts of law, different foundational doctrines and different argumentative techniques. Among others, see L.B. Murphy, "Better to See Law this Way" 83 *New York University Law Review* (2008) 1104–8; F. Schauer, "Postivism as Pariah" in R.P. George (ed.), *The Autonomy of Law: Essays on Legal Positivism* (Clarendon Press, 1996) 31–56 at 34; J. Waldron, "Normative (or Ethical) Positivism" in J.L. Coleman (ed.), *Hart's Postscript: Essays on the Postscript to The Concept of Law* (OUP, 2001) 411–33; J. Beckett, "Behind Relative Normativity: Rules and Process as Prerequisites of Law" 12 EJIL (2001) 627–50, at 648.

## V. SOCIAL VALIDATION IN THE COMMUNITY OF SOCIALIZED INTERNATIONAL LAWYERS

As most of the following chapters point out, validation of legal arguments in this community of socialized international lawyers is itself of a social nature. Albeit contested,[83] this does not seem to be particularly idiosyncratic. The concept of social validation has been extensively studied, in the theory of knowledge and literary philosophy[84] and does not need to be discussed here. For the argument made here, what matters is to highlight that, against the backdrop of the social validation of legal arguments, a valid legal argument is primarily one that is received as such by the other members of the community. Said differently, the valid argument is the one that is successful, rather than the one that is ontologically valid. This applies to academics, judges and practitioners.[85] This is not say that, because validation is social, acceptance is necessarily the unique criterion of validity. This does not mean that there cannot be procedural guarantees in the acceptance by the audience or in how the

---

[83] See e.g. I. Venzke, "What Makes for a Valid Legal Argument? (Editorial)", 27 *Leiden Journal of International Law* (2014) pp. 811–16. Some critical remarks have also been formulated by V. Priuli in his presentation on "How States Frame the Legality of Secession. An Argumentation Analysis of the ICJ Advisory Proceedings on Kosovo" at the Amsterdam Centre for International Law in July 2014.

[84] See T. Kuhn, *The Structure of Scientific Revolutions*, The University of Chicago Press, 50th anniversary edition, 2012. He famously argued that "paradigms gain their status because they are more successful than their competitors in solving a few problems that the group of practitioners has come to recognize as acute" (p. 24) and that there is no standard higher than the assent of the relevant community (p. 94). The same point is made by S. Fish, *Doing What Comes Naturally*, Duke University Press, 1989, 29–30 and 237. This has also been recognized by legal theorists. See e.g. C. Perelman, *Justice, Law and Argument* (D. Reidel Synthese Library, 1980), at 29.

[85] For an examination of the the techniques used by courts to convince governments, legislature and the public, see G. Davidov and M. Davidov, "How Judges Use Weapons of Influence: The Social Psychology of Courts", 46 *Israel Law Review* (2013), 7–24. See also: L.V. Prott, "Argumentation in International Law", in: *Argumentation, Vol. 5*, 1991, 299 ss. and "The Style of Judgment in the International Court of Justice", in: *Australian Yearbook of International Law, Vol. 5* (1970–1973), 1973, 75 ss. (applying the rhetorical theory of Perelman to the ICJ).

consensus is reached.[86] Social acceptance remains, however, in the view of the author of these lines, the primary validating parameter.

Social validation is complex. If an international lawyer is bound to convince her audience, it will be expected that she resorts to some of those foundational doctrines and argumentative techniques under discussion in the following chapters. However, it does not suffice to deploy the dominant foundational doctrines and argumentative techniques to secure social validation. First, because as will be shown in the chapters that follow, foundational doctrines and argumentative techniques are themselves very unstable, controversial, contested and the object of very diverging interpretations and practices. Moreover, the unprecedented growth of the community of international lawyers witnessed in the second half of the twentieth century[87] as well as the turn to pragmatism and multidisciplinarity – as is witnessed in Anglo-American scholarship[88] – makes validation all the more diffuse. It remains that, albeit more diffuse, the validation of legal argumentation remains primarily based on acceptance by the community of socialized international lawyers.

Claiming that validation of argumentation is social and hinges on acceptance by the community directly bears upon the nature of legal argumentation – and hence on the way foundational doctrines and argumentative techniques discussed in this book are designed and deployed. Indeed, those arguments are validated by virtue of their acceptance makes the operation of foundational doctrines and argumentative techniques essentially confrontational.[89] Arguments are weapons[90]

---

[86] See e.g. C. Perelman, *Justice, Law and Argument* (D. Reidel Synthese Library, 1980).

[87] See the comments of J. d'Aspremont, "Wording in International Law" 25 *Leiden Journal of International Law* (2012), pp. 575–602.

[88] For some critical remarks, see J. d'Aspremont, "Send Back the Lifeboats: Confronting the Project of Saving of International Law", 108 *American Journal of International Law* (2014) (forthcoming).

[89] On the adversarial character of the legal arena and the extent to which such adversarial setting is determinative of the linguistic dynamics, see gen. D. Kennedy, "Theses about International Legal Discourse", 23 *German Yearbook of International Law* 353 (1980); M. Koskenniemi, "International Law and Hegemony: A Reconfiguration" (2004) 17 *Cambridge Rev. Int'l Affairs* 197 at 199. See also the remarks by I. Venzke, "Legal Contestation about 'Enemy Combatants' on the Exercise of Power in Legal Interpretation", 5 *Journal of International Law and International Relations* 155 (2009).

[90] See A. MacIntyre, *Whose Justice? Which Rationality*, Duckworth, 1988, at 5.

and words are ammunition.[91] Confrontation means that international lawyers are inextricably engaged in a struggle for persuasiveness.[92] This confrontation pits groups against groups, schools against schools, generations against generations,[93] and ultimately international lawyers against international lawyers. International law is thus a battle-ground where the international lawyer – even the nihilist – is necessarily an activist advocating a certain vision of the law and, hence, a given way to make sense of the world. According to this view, international law is a perpetual site of competition for persuasiveness in legal argumentation.[94] In that sense, although the confrontational nature of international law is often disguised by a rhetoric of consensus,[95] confrontation is the fate of international lawyers.[96]

---

[91] This whole process is why I have referred elsewhere to this confrontational dimension of legal argumentation through the idea of "wordfare". See J. d'Aspremont, "Wording in International Law" 25 *Leiden Journal of International Law* (2012) pp. 575–602.

[92] P. Bourdieu: "The Force of Law: Toward a Sociology of the Juridical Field" (1987) 38 *Hastings Law Journal* 814–53, p. 838: "Law is the quintessential form of symbolic power of naming that creates the things named"; see also p. 837: "What is at stake in this struggle is monopoly of power to impose a universally recognized principle of knowledge of the social world".

[93] This particular aspect of the confrontation has led A. Rasulov to claim that each generation comes to commit a certain kind of injustice against the preceding generation which is no longer there to defend its contentions. A. Rasulov, "New Approaches to International Law: Images of a Genealogy", in J.M. Beneyto and D. Kennedy (eds), *New Approaches to International Law: the European and the American Experiences* (TMC Asser-Springer, 2012), pp. 151–91, 156. See also D. Kennedy who says that "Each generation considers the previous one naïve". See D. Kennedy, "Primitive Legal Scholarship", 27 *Harvard Journal International Law Journal* (1986), 1, at 7.

[94] This does not mean that social validation and persuasiveness cannot work independently of one another. This is a point which I owe to I. Venzke.

[95] This is not a phenomenon inherent in international law. See A. MacIntyre, *Whose Justice? Which Rationality*, Duckworth, 1988, p. 2.

[96] J. d'Aspremont, "Wording in International Law" 25 *Leiden Journal of International Law* (2012) 575–602. See also S. Singh, "International Law as a Technical Discipline: Critical Perspectives on the Narrative Structure of a Theory" in J. d'Aspremont, *Formalism and the Sources of International Law: A Theory of the Ascertainment of Legal Rules* (2nd ed. OUP, 2013) 236–61; see also M. Koskenniemi who claims that international law "revels in adversity, not in consensus". M. Koskenniemi, "The Mystery of Legal Obligation", 3 *International Theory* (2011), 319–25, at 321. See also Koskenniemi: *International Law in the World of Ideas* (47 ff) at 47.

It will not come as a surprise that, in this confrontational setting, social validation is very contingent upon a great variety of parameters: credentials, profession, nationality, origin, reputation, training, affiliation, repetition, proliferation, intense dissemination, footnoting, peer-referencing, moment of production, and linguistic aptitudes. These are usually among the criteria that determine whether an argument gains authority (and thus generates knowledge) or evanesces. As a result, it remains difficult to predict which idea will eventually survive and which international lawyer will be accordingly empowered with persuasiveness and semantic authority. The outcome of the struggle is uncertain and open-ended. It is true that institutional structures come to mitigate this open-endedness of the social validating process[97] as confrontation unfolds in a strongly organized and hierarchical semantic and social system which is far from being egalitarian. There are hierarchies which are rarely acknowledged as such but which fundamentally impinge on how social validation unfolds.[98] This does not suffice, however, to provide any sort of predictability as to which legal arguments will be socially validated.

It is important to note that the idea that the community of socialized international lawyers is essentially confrontational has been contested. It has been said that it puts too much emphasis on the adversarial setting and demotes international legal argumentation to an aggregation of competing claims.[99] In that sense, it is objected that communitarian approaches such as the one put forward here manifest a certain disenchantment about the quest for validity and bring about too radical a move away from the argument itself.[100] It does not leave any justification

---

[97] See gen. A. Rasulov, "New Approaches to International Law: Images of a Genealogy", in J.M. Beneyto and D. Kennedy (eds), *New Approaches to International Law: the European and the American Experiences* (TMC Asser-Springer, 2012), pp. 151–91.

[98] Customary international law and non-formal sources of law offer much more room for projections of power. On this aspect, see J. d'Aspremont, *Formalism and the Sources of International Law* (OUP, 2011), pp. 151–4 and 162–70.

[99] N. Onuf, "Do Rules Say What They Do? From Ordinary Language to International Law", 26 *Harvard International Law Journal* 385 (1985), at 393; see also I. Venzke, "Multidisciplinary Reflections on the Relationship between Professionals and The(ir) International Law" (December 4, 2013). *ESIL* 2013. 5th Research Forum: International Law as a Profession, Conference Paper No. 4/2013, p. 8.

[100] I. Venzke, "What Makes for a Valid Legal Argument? (Editorial)", 27 *Leiden Journal of International Law* (2014) pp. 811–16.

as to why international lawyers should continue to argue.[101] Many of these critiques – albeit not exclusively[102] – find support in the work of Habermas who famously tried to qualify the idea that validity is nothing more than acceptance by testing the validity of arguments in argumentative practice itself.[103]

These weighty criticisms call for a remark with a view to nuancing the idea that validation of legal arguments is social. Indeed, it should be made clear that emphasizing the adversarial dynamics of the social validation of legal argument does not mean that there are no reference points other than social to assess the validity of argument.[104] Nor does it entail an abandonment of internal determinants of legality.[105] Securing persuasiveness and semantic authority lies primarily in the fluctuating balance of powers of the international legal scholarship. This does not exclude, however, that internal consistency of the argument plays a significant role in the validation process. This is precisely why this book focuses both on foundational doctrines and the argumentative techniques (including dissemination techniques). It is true that, as was already highlighted above, securing persuasiveness that is necessary for social validation is not only a matter of argumentation and debate. It is also a question of (the quality of) the substantive doctrines that are relied upon. In that sense, securing validation within the community of socialized international lawyers depends on both argumentation per se and, albeit to a lesser extent, the substance of the argument. It remains that, for the

---

[101] Ibid.

[102] It is worth noting that not all of this critique has been Habermasian. Some critique has been formulated by the so-called "Strukturierende Rechtslehre" on the basis of interdisciplinary research between jurisprudence and linguistics. See F. Müller/R. Christensen, *Juristische Methodik*, 2 Volumes, 9th ed., Berlin 2004 and F. Müller, *Syntagma*, Berlin, 2012. This was brought to my attention by V. Priuli.

[103] It is interesting to note that Habermas has continued to enjoy a very solid appeal among German international lawyers. See more generally, I. Venzke, *How Interpretation Makes International Law – On Semantic Change and Normative Twists* (OUP, 2012). See also I. Venzke, "What Makes for a Valid Legal Argument? (Editorial)", 27 *Leiden Journal of International Law* (2014) (forthcoming). See M. Goldmann, "Principles in International Law as Rational Reconstructions. A Taxonomy" (November 13, 2013), available at SSRN: http://ssrn.com/abstract=2442027.

[104] Contra I. Venzke, "What Makes for a Valid Legal Argument? (Editorial)", 27 *Leiden Journal of International Law* (2014) pp. 811–16.

[105] For an attempt to preserve internal determinants of legality while acknowledging the role of external dynamics, see J. d'Aspremont, *Formalism and the Sources of International Law* (OUP, 2011).

chapters that follow, what is perceived as internally consistent is itself a matter of perception by the community concerned.

## VI. STRUCTURE OF THIS VOLUME

This book is structured after the two-pronged and dialectical line spelled out above. It primarily examines the internal social arrangements sought by socialized international lawyers when they design and deploy the *foundational doctrines* and the *argumentative techniques* around which international law, as an argumentative practice, articulates itself. Needless to say that in its attempt to functionally and internally situate the design and deployment of foundational doctrines and argumentative techniques, this book cannot be comprehensive, let alone exhaustive. It only seeks to functionally and internally situate a carefully selected number of doctrines and argumentative techniques of international law.

The selection thereof is not entirely arbitrary, for it zeroes in on those foundational doctrines and argumentative techniques that are deemed, for the present author, the most prominent for both the socialization of international lawyers and the social validation of legal arguments. In other words, the selection of foundational doctrines and argumentative techniques has been carried out on the basis of the role which each of them plays both in terms of membership of the community of international lawyers (their mastery being an essential part of the socialization process) and in terms of their validating impact (a convincing argument requiring their deployment).

It should also be emphasized that the selection of foundational doctrines and argumentative techniques under examination has also been informed by a search for aesthetics. Too often, aesthetics of legal arguments are denied despite them being extremely conducive to social validation. This book does not conceal the role played by aesthetics in the choice of an equal number of foundational doctrines and argumentative techniques, each of them representing a distinct part of the book. The five foundational doctrines discussed here are subjects (chapter 1), sources (chapter 2), law-making (chapter 3), institutions (chapter 4) and effectivity (chapter 5). The five argumentative techniques examined here are methodology (chapter 6), interpretation (chapter 7), academic writing (chapter 8), dissemination (chapter 9) and expert blogging (chapter 10). It is noteworthy that the discussions on argumentative techniques include reflections on dissemination techniques as well. Although argumentation and dissemination must be distinguished, the two are sometimes so closely intertwined that it does not always seem possible to separate the two. This is why the discussions on the argumentative techniques in Part II include reflections on dissemination, academic writing and expert blogging.

It is conspicuous that many of these chapters are intertwined. Overlaps should certainly not be excluded or denied. For instance, all foundational doctrines have been designed as a result of certain methodological moves or have been generated through interpretive processes. Foundational doctrines have also established themselves as a result of writing and disseminating tactics. Foundational doctrines also overlap with one another. Law-making and sources are – respectively dynamic and static – modes of cognition of the same phenomenon. Likewise, the doctrine of subject has always been informed by (and constituted an offspring of) the doctrine of effectivity. Interconnections and overlaps exist between argumentative techniques as well. It suffices to mention methodology and interpretation or writing and dissemination. Examples of overlaps could be multiplied *ad infinitum* and it does not seem necessary to elaborate on that. It seems more noteworthy to emphasize that such interconnections underpin the idea – on which this book is premised – that all these foundational doctrines and argumentative techniques contribute to the very same socialization process.

It is true that it is not always possible to distinguish between techniques and foundational doctrines. There may be a thin line, especially in the eyes of practitioners. Such hesitations could arise in the sources of international law (which is here examined as a foundational doctrine) or interpretation (which is here examined as an argumentative technique).[106] In that sense, there is an inevitably normative choice behind the branding of each of the ten following areas of legal argumentation as either a foundational doctrine or an argumentative technique. It is accordingly important to stress that foundational doctrines are understood here in the sense in which German scholars use their term "Dogmatic", that is, a coherent set of propositions articulated around rules and case-law which are produced by discourses involving both practice and legal scholarship.[107] Argumentative techniques, for

---

[106] The following branding of interpretation as a technique concurs with that of D. Bederman. See D. Bederman, *The Spirit of International Law*, The University of Georgia Press, 2002, at 70.

[107] On the idea of Dogmatic see M. Goldmann, "Principles in International Law as Rational Reconstructions. A Taxonomy" (November 13, 2013), available at SSRN: http://ssrn.com/abstract=2442027) who relies on the definition by R. Alexy. R. Alexy defines Dogmatic as "(1) a set of propositions; (2) which refer to legal rules or case law, but which are not identical with them; (3) which are

their part, are understood as sets of craftmanship which are deployed by international lawyers when building and communicating their legal arguments.

The foundational doctrines under examination which are deemed to be most instrumental in the social validation of legal arguments as well as the socialization of scholars are statehood, sources, law-making, organization and effectivity. We could discuss at length this choice. It probably is self-evident that this choice is much informed by a continental approach to international law. From an Anglo-American perspective, the emphasis would probably have been given to other doctrines, like legitimacy or compliance.[108] Even from a continental perspective, other foundational doctrines could have obviously been included. One may think of responsibility, territory, personality or jurisdiction.[109] The exercise attempted here could thus be pursued in connection with other doctrines. However, such an obvious finding is certainly not alien to the agenda of the author of the chapters that follow. It seems that there still is much critical reflection necessary when it comes to internal functional situationalism in international law. Albeit to a lesser extent, the foregoing also holds for the choice of the argumentative techniques examined here.

Notwithstanding the normative choices informing how foundational doctrines and argumentative techniques are distinguished, it is true that there seems to be a certain agreement across all traditions of international law as to what the main argumentative techniques of international law are. That methodology, interpretation, writing, dissemination, and – more recently – blogging, boil down to core techniques of argumentation does not seem contested. This even seems to reflect some cross-cutting

---

coherent with each other; (4) which are constructed and administered by a professional elite including judges, public servants and legal scholars; (5) and which have a normative character" (p. 5) (R. Alexy, *Theorie juristischen Argumentation* (2d ed., Suhrkamp Verlag Gmbh, 1991), 314.

[108] On the turn to legitimacy and compliance in the Anglo-American legal scholarship see J. d'Aspremont, "Send Back the Lifeboats: Confronting the Project of Saving of International Law", 108 *American Journal of International Law* (2014) (forthcoming).

[109] As far as jurisdiction is concerned, I must confess that I have never understood how, in mainstream international legal scholarship, this came to be elevated into a doctrine in the first place. First, because what international lawyers identify as grounds of jurisdiction are nothing more than convergences of practices of domestic judges. Second, and more fundamentally, it does not seem that, in the mainstream understanding of international law, there is room for any allocation of competences by international law to domestic authorities. This conceptual contradiction in mainstream scholarship seems to go unnoticed.

consensus in social sciences regarding what it means to build knowledge. It remains that the distinctions made here rest on some normative choices which should not be denied and which peers and colleagues will certainly relish deciphering, deconstructing and critiquing.

# PART I

# The foundational doctrines

# 1. Subjects

This chapter discusses the doctrine of subjects in relation to the state. This part of the doctrine of subject is sometimes called "the law of statehood". The choice to focus on the law of statehood – rather than on those discourses and practices pertaining to other actors of international law – should not be read as manifesting any state-centricism. This is a debate that is not tackled here but that will re-surface in chapter 3 on law-making. This chapter is solely concerned with those academic projects that have shaped the design and deployment of the law of statehood.

The international law of statehood epitomizes the scholarly hunger for doctrinal domestication of the rise and fall of states in the international legal order. Indeed, as it is argued here, the sophisticated constructions behind the international law of statehood have been aptly deployed by a group of professionals seeking to secure a grasp on a subject-matter, that is, state creation. According to the view defended here, the law of statehood is best construed as a delicate elixir which allows international lawyers, not only to make state creation a legal phenomenon worthy of legal investigation, but also to claim control of the volatile phenomenon of births and deaths in the international society. In the pursuit of this project, international lawyers have been guided by the aspiration to control an entire chain of manufacture of international law. In spelling out this argument, this chapter will seek to expose the main methodological moves unfolding in the international law scholarship devoted to the law of statehood and speculate about the specific rationales behind them. It will show that the law of statehood is informed not only by a regulatory and explanatory agenda but also by a few intra- and extra-professional dynamics.

This argument will develop in the following sequence. First, a few remarks are formulated about the main methodological moves – and the corresponding epistemological tensions – witnessed in the mainstream contemporary international legal scholarship on issues of statehood. Reference will be made to the tensions between the facticists and

*33*

legalists on the one hand and those between the subjectivists and the objectivists on the other (I). Second, the chapter will shed light on the main projects pursued by the advocates of a law of statehood (II). Attention will be paid to the regulatory, explanatory and epistemological agendas of the law of statehood. This chapter will conclude with a few final remarks (III).

Before substantiating this argument further, a few caveats are necessary. Preliminarily, this chapter is neither a critique nor a deconstruction of the law of statehood. What this chapter pursues is more elementary. The following merely speculates about the rationales behind the impressive ingeniousness of international lawyers to construct a law of statehood. Certainly, the point made is unorthodox. Yet, it is not unheard of. Similar critiques of other foundational branches of international law exist in the literature. For instance, the theoretical, political, sociological and epistemological moves behind the doctrines of the sources of international law[1] or the international law of responsibility[2] have long been exposed to similar critiques. Those rules and practices that explain, regulate or feed the emergence of states on the international plane have been spared from a comprehensive, foundational exploration. It is particularly astounding that so few self-critical and reflexive studies by international lawyers on the international law of statehood exist in the legal scholarship.[3] The reasons for such scholarly clemency towards the construction behind the law of statehood are mysterious. It is not the

---

[1] M. Koskenniemi, "The normative force of habit: international custom and social theory", 1 *Finnish Y.B. Int'l L.* 77 (1990); D. Kennedy, "When renewal repeats: thinking against the box", 32 *N.Y.U. J. Int'l L. & Pol.* 335 (2000); J. d'Aspremont, "The politics of deformalization in international law", 3 *Goettingen J. Int'l L.* 503 (2011); S. Singh, "International law as a technical discipline: critical perspectives on the narrative structure of a theory", in *Formalism and the Sources of International Law: A Theory of the Ascertainment of Legal Rules*, app. 2 at 236–61 (2013).

[2] P. Allott, "State responsibility and the unmaking of international law", 29 *Harv. Int'l L.J.* 1 (1988); G. Nolte, "From Dionisio Anzilotti to Roberto Ago: The classical international law of state responsibility and the traditional primacy of a bilateral conception of inter-state relations", 13 *Eur. J. Int'l L.* 1083 (2002).

[3] See M. Fabry, "International legal theory of state recognition: a critique" (on file with author); see also G. Simpson, "Great powers and outlaw states: unequal sovereigns in the international legal order" (2004). But see M. Koskenniemi, "National self-determination today: problems of legal theory and practice", 43 *Int'l & Comp. L.Q.* 241 (1994).

purpose of this chapter to solve such a mystery,[4] but rather to allay this lack of foundational inquiry.

## I. CARTOGRAPHIC OVERVIEW OF THE CONTEMPORARY LEGAL SCHOLARSHIP ON THE LAW OF STATEHOOD: A TWOFOLD COGNITIVE TENSION

The following observations shed light on some of the fundamental tensions that drive the international legal scholarship on the law of statehood. The international legal scholarship can be read as the scene of a compound pitted epistemological battle. On the one hand, international lawyers have been divided between the *facticists* and the *legalists*, that is, between those arguing that statehood is a fact and those arguing that statehood is a legal construction. On the other hand, and at a different level of their scholarly inquiries, the law of statehood has been the battleground between the *objectivists* and the *subjectivists*, that is, between those contending that statehood is objectively ascertained by international law and those arguing that international law accommodates inter-subjectivity in the determination of statehood.

It is of the utmost importance to clearly demarcate the two aforementioned epistemological divides. Indeed, these two epistemological battles take place at different levels and in very different terms.[5] The debate between the *legalists* and the *facticists* pertains to the capture of statehood by international law whereas the debate between the *objectivists* and the *subjectivists* relates to the operation of statehood within the system of international law. Said differently, the first debate takes place at the fringe of the international legal system whereas the second one rages within it, that is, once the phenomenon of state creation has been apprehended by international law.

---

[4] For further discussion, see M. Koskenniemi, *From Apology to Utopia: The Structure of International Legal Argument* (CUP, 2005). The same probably explains why voluntarism has remained such a vivid idea.

[5] M. Forteau, "L'Etat selon le droit international: une figure à géométrie variable", 4 *Revue Générale de Droit International Public* 737, 739–42 (2007).

## 1. Epistemological Battle: Penetrating the Legal System as a Fact or as a Legal Institution

The pitted battle between facticists and legalists is an old one. It is also very well known and it does not seem to require much attention here. It opposes those who claim that the state exists inherently as a factual matter[6] and those who contend that it is a legal construction.[7] The first view argues that the state pre-exists as a fact before its capture by international law. According to that view, the yardstick to determine statehood is "success or failure".[8] This facticist view expresses an attempt to consign state creation "to exogeneity in the sense of their surpassing international legal grasp or comprehension".[9] The facticist approach has been deemed reminiscent of Carl Schmitt's idea of sovereignty as external to international law.[10] Opposite to the facticist approach, the legalists contend that the state is a creation of international law.[11] They argue that statehood is constructed and recognized by international law and does not have an autonomous existence outside international law.

To a large extent, the debate between facticists and legalists has become moot and a belated consensus seems to have emerged among international lawyers.[12] Contemporary mainstream scholarship seems to

---

[6] L. Oppenheim, *International Law: A Treatise*, 264 (1905); see also G. Arangio-Ruiz, *L'Etat dans le sens du droit des gens et la notion de droit international*, 3–63, 265–406 (1975); J. Crawford, *The Creation of States in International Law* 23 (1979); "The opinions of the Badinter arbitration committee", Opinion n.1, reprinted in A. Pellet, "The Opinions of the Badinter Arbitration Committee: A Second Breath for the Self-Determination of Peoples", 3 *Eur. J. Int'l L* 178, 182–3 (1992).

[7] See H. Kelsen, *General Theory of Law and State* (1949); R. Ago, "Second report on state responsibility", 2 *Y.B. Int'l L. Comm'n* 177 (1970), U.N. Doc. A/CN.4/233, 202–203, pp. 38–9; A. Peters, "Statehood after 1989: effectivités between legality and virtuality", in 3 *Select Proceedings of the European Society of International Law* 171 (J. Crawford and S. Nouwen (eds) 2012).

[8] D. Anzilotti, "Corso di diritto internazionale: lezioni tenute nell' Universita Di Roma Nell'anno Scolastico 1922–23", 154–5 (Working Paper, 1923) (on file with author).

[9] F. Johns, *Non-Legality in International Law: Unruly Law* 10 (2013).

[10] Koskenniemi, *supra* note 4, at 231.

[11] For an illustration of that approach, see the authors cited by M. Koskenniemi, *supra* note 4, at 229–30.

[12] For M. Koskenniemi, the disagreement between legalists and factualists has lost its contradictory character as each of these arguments comes to rely on each other in a way which makes preferring either one impossible. See Koskenniemi, *supra* note 4, at 272.

simultaneously vindicate both positions in a way that reconciles them. According to this conciliatory view, state creation is a factual process[13] but the state itself is a legal construct.[14] The state is seen as having first emerged as a social reality before being apprehended by the law.[15]

There certainly is some merit to this conciliatory approach. Indeed, it seems difficult to deny that apprehension of a fact by the law necessarily entails a legal construction. Said differently, capturing a fact boils down to reconstructing it in legal terms for there cannot be apprehension of any phenomenon without reconstruction of such a phenomenon according to pre-existing legal categories. Recognizing the virtue of this conciliatory approach does not mean, however, that such a scholarly consensus is exempt from fundamental epistemological flaws, especially because facts themselves do not exist independently of any descriptive framework through which they are constructed.[16] This chapter is certainly not the place to fault the epistemological moves behind the contemporary mainstream conciliatory position. It matters more to highlight here that, as a result of the compromise reached between legalists and facticists, the epistemological struggle within the law of statehood has moved to another level. It is argued here that the divide in the law of statehood is no longer about whether statehood is received as a fact or constructed by the law but, rather, *how* it is received and constructed by international law.

---

[13] See C. de Visscher, *Les effectivitiv du droit international public* 34 (1968); G. Abi-Saab, "Cours général de droit international public", in 207 *Recueil des cours: Collected Courses Hague Academy Int'l L.* 9, 68 (1987); Crawford, *supra* note 6; see *The Opinions of the Badinter Arbitration Committee*, *supra* note 6 ("[T]he existence or disappearance of a state is a question of fact.").

[14] See Peters, *supra* note 7; J. Vidmar, *Democratic Statehood in International Law: The Emergence of New States in Post-Cold War Practice*, 49 (Hart, 2013); Crawford, *supra* note 6, at 15.

[15] Forteau, *supra* note 5, at 736–69; see also id., at 739 ("[A] tout le moins, puisqu'il en est pour douter de l'existence d'un phénomène étatique en dehors du monde du droit, existe-t-il une réalité sociologique, quelle que soit l'idée que l'on s'en fait, à laquelle le droit international va s'intéresser"). For a historical overview of the state as social reality, see A. Cassese, "States: rise and decline of the primary subjects of the international community", in *The Oxford Handbook of the History of International Law* 49 (B. Fassbender and A. Peters eds, 2012).

[16] A. MacIntyre, *Whose Justice? Which Rationality?* 333 (1988).

## 2. Epistemological Battle: Deploying Statehood in the Legal System in Absolute or Relative Terms

The main conceptual controversy permeating the international legal scholarship on statehood is probably not the ontological nature of statehood prior to its capture by international law but about how it operates *within* international law once it has been apprehended. In this respect, international lawyers seem to be divided into two camps, which, contrary to the clash between facticists and legalists, appear more irreconcilable. These two positions rest much more on fundamental and paradigmatic tensions in international law. The purpose of this section is certainly not to revisit the theoretical foundations of such discrepancies but rather to delineate the elementary manifestation of this scholarly rift in the law of statehood when it comes to determining how statehood operates within the legal system.

The way in which mainstream legal scholarship captures, constructs and explains statehood is well-known and does not need exhaustive recapitulation. Among international lawyers, it is traditionally accepted that a number of criteria must be fulfilled for an entity to qualify as a state – without such criteria necessarily being legal criteria. According to the mainstream way of apprehending statehood which emerged in the nineteenth century after Georg Jellinek developed the so-called doctrine of three elements and which came to be embedded in Article 1 of the 1933 Montevideo Convention on Rights and Duties of States.[17] The effectiveness (or *effectivité*) of the entity becomes the linchpin of statehood-determination.[18] Such *effectivité* was subsequently systematized, into two dimensions, namely an *internal* and an *external* one.[19] The internal dimension of *effectivité* pertains to the ability of the authority that claims a monopoly on the exercise of public authority on a piece of territory to actually impose its will – and enforce its decisions – on the people living on that territory. For its part, the external dimension

---

[17] Montevideo Convention on the Rights and Duties of States, Dec. 26, 1933, 49 Stat. 3097, 165 L.N.T.S. 19.

[18] In the following paragraphs, we will use the term *effectivité*, which is the terminology used by the ICJ.

[19] On this distinction, see J. d'Aspremont, "Regulating statehood: the Kosovo status settlement", 20 *Leiden J. Int'l L.* 649, 654 (2007).

of *effectivité* relates to the ability of that entity to enter into inter-state relations and claim state-like existence in the international arena of states.[20]

This nineteenth-century doctrine has been resilient and remains dominant in contemporary scholarship, albeit not without controversy. While international lawyers agree on the criteria of capture put forward by this mainstream construction, they disagree on what do with the object of their capture. On the one hand, there are international legal scholars who believe that once statehood has been captured by international law it becomes objective and universally opposable data within the whole international legal system. For them, once a state has penetrated the international legal system it becomes opposable to all parts of that system and to all stakeholders. In that sense, a state captured by international law is objectivized by the latter and statehood has a community-bestowed character.[21] The objectivation is made possible by the "Montevideo mirage"[22] meant to provide a formal yardstick to ascertain states, and supposedly constituting a rule of customary international law.[23] On the other hand, there are international legal scholars for whom the state enters the international legal system in relative terms only, existing within that system only to the extent those stakeholders are ready to accept it. For them, the concept of statehood operates within the system of international law inter-subjectively, thereby generating legal effects only in relation to those actors or regimes that are ready to give it some legal significance.[24] In other words, the fundamental difference between objectivists and subjectivists is as follows: the objectivists project stability in

---

[20] Note in particular that the external *effectivité* of an entity hinges primarily on its recognition by other states. Id. at 655.

[21] T.M. Franck, *The Power of Legitimacy Among Nations* 190 (1990).

[22] By reference to the famous 1933 Montevideo Convention on the Rights and Duties of States, which, for the sake of the Convention, elaborates on the criteria an entity should satisfy to be considered a state.

[23] C. Ryngaert and S. Sobrie, "Recognition of states: international law or realpolitik? The practice of recognition in the wake of Kosovo, South Ossetia, and Abkhazia", 24 *Leiden J. Int'l L.* 467 (2011); see also D. Bederman, *The Spirit of International Law* 49 (University of Georgia Press, 2002) (arguing that clear rules for what are the subjects of international law are felt essential for the construction of an international legal system).

[24] Accordance with International Law of the Unilateral Declaration of Independence by the Provisional Institutions of Self-Government of Kosovo (Req. for Advisory Op.), at 60 (Dec. 8), available at http://www.icj-cij.org/docket/files/141/15726.pdf ("Again, it is the factual context that should decide which value should weigh heaviest."); Accordance with International Law of the

state-identification whereas inter-subjectivists accept that the notion, even within the legal system, remains in constant flux according to inter-subjective dynamics. While the tension between subjectivists and objectivists is of a paradigmatic nature, it is noteworthy that, from a historical point of view, the inter-subjectivist perspective predates the objectivist approach.[25] It is also interesting to note that the inter-subjectivist perspective has been called "positivist", despite the latter having scarcely anything to do with voluntarism and state will.[26]

Arguably, most of the controversies witnessed in connection to statehood in the contemporary international legal scholarship revolve around these structural tensions between objectivism and intersubjectivism.[27] It suffices here to provide a few examples.

For instance, the old debate on the nature of recognition[28] that has been unfolding for the last century can be understood as unfolding along the lines of the above-mentioned conflict.[29] Proponents of the declaratory theory affiliate themselves with an objectivist approach to statehood whereas advocates of the constitutive theory have been embracing a

---

Unilateral Declaration of Independence in Respect of Kosovo, Advisory Opinion, 2010 ICJ 404 (July 22); *Oppenheim's International Law* § 12, at 17, § 71, at 108 (1st ed., 1945); para. 71; see also *Oppenheim's International Law* § 5, at 14, § 39, at 128 (R. Jennings and A. Watts (eds), Oxford Univ. Press 9th ed. 2008). Lauterpacht himself came to terms with this inter-subjectivism but found it an anomaly. It is this anomaly that led him to put forward his idea of a duty to recognize. See H. Lauterpacht, *Recognition in International Law* 87 (1947).

[25] This evolution is discussed in Crawford, *supra* note 6, at 14–19.

[26] *Id.* at 17.

[27] This chapter leaves aside the tensions between sovereign equality and anti-pluralism as well as legalized hegemony that may be operating in the law of statehood. For a study of those tensions in international law since 1815, see G. Simpson, *Great Powers and Outlaw States: Unequal Sovereigns in the International Legal Order* (2004).

[28] J. d'Aspremont, "Recognition", *Oxford Bibliographies Online*, (Nov. 21, 2012), http://www.oxfordbibliographies.com/view/document/obo-9780199796953/obo-9780199796953-0009.xml.

[29] In the same vein, see Koskenniemi, *supra* note 4, at 272. Some authors propose a "third way" to bridge this gap, in which recognition is neither merely constitutive nor merely declaratory but is more simply conducive to the effectiveness of the entity. See D.J. Bederman, *The Spirit of International Law* 83 (2002); J. Verhoeven, *La Reconnaissance Internationale dans la Pratique Contemporaine* 679 (1975); d'Aspremont, *supra* note 19, at 655. For the remarks on this approach made by Ryngaert and Sobrie, see *supra* note 23, at 471.

subjectivist approach.[30] The declaratory theory is probably more dominant in mainstream legal scholarship.[31] The reason this happens is precisely because recognition is thought of as objectivizing the birth of new states, conveying the impression that state creation is, within the legal system, not subject to "political arbitrariness",[32] the inter-subjective posture being deemed "counter-intuitive".[33]

The profound cleavage witnessed in the international legal scholarship during Kosovo's declaration of independence manifested a similar oscillation between objectivism and inter-subjectivism. The dominant positions which emerged during the controversy shrouding the advisory opinion can also be understood in the light of this dichotomy. Indeed, both those arguing that Kosovo could not qualify as a state by virtue of some allegedly wrongful origins and those conversely saying that Kosovo had mustered enough recognition and effectiveness to qualify as a state expressed positions informed by objectivism.[34] On the contrary, those arguing that Kosovo constituted a state only in its relation with those recognizing the entity as a state can be seen as proponents of an inter-subjective approach.[35]

A last controversy that proves illustrative of the ubiquitous tension between inter-subjectivism and objectivism is the one that arose in connection to the entitlement of Palestine to seize the Prosecutor of the International Criminal Court.[36] In that case, the divisive point for

---

[30] For a similar reading of these two approaches, see Crawford, *supra* note 6, at 21; K. Marek, *Identity and Continuity of States in Public International Law* 132 (1968); Ryngaert and Sobrie, *supra* note 23, at 467–90.

[31] Crawford, *supra* note 6, at 23, 25; *Deutsche Continental Gas-Gesellschaft v. Polish State*, 5 Ann. Dig. I.L.C. 11 at 13 (Germano-Polish Mixed Arb. Trib. 1929); "Opinions of the arbitration committee of the peace conference on Yugoslavia, opinion no. 1", reprinted in A. Pellet, "The opinions of the Badinter Arbitration Committee. A second breath for the self-determination of peoples", 3 *Eur. J. Int'l L.* 178, 182 (1992); "Opinions no. 10 of the arbitration commission of the international conference on Yugoslavia", reprinted in D. Turk, "Recognition of States: A Comment", 4 *Eur. J. Int'l L.* 66, 90 (1993).

[32] Ryngaert and Sobrie, *supra* note 23, at 470 ("An important aspect of its success lies in the fact that it deprives states of the prerogative of deciding on statehood based on political arbitrariness, in favour of objective legal norms.").

[33] *Id.* at 467–90.

[34] *Id.*

[35] "J. d'Aspremont and T. Liefländer, "Consolidating the statehood of Kosovo: leaving the international law narrative behind", 1 *J. Euro. Int'l Aff.* 8, 13 (2013).

[36] A. Zimmermann, "Palestine and the international criminal court *quo vadis*? Reach and limits of declarations under article 12(3)", 11 *J. Int'l Crim. Jus.*

international lawyers was the nature of the determination of Palestine as a state. For some international lawyers, the status of Palestine – whether as a state or as a non-state entity – was objectively ascertained by international law in a way that binds the ICC. For others, the treatment given to Palestine was regime-specific in that the ICC can determine for itself whether Palestine is a state for the sake of the application of its statute.

While illustrations could be multiplied *ad infinitum*, these examples suffice to show the structural importance of the divide with respect to the way statehood operates within the legal system once it has been captured. The above-mentioned examples show how much scholarship on the law on statehood is fragmented between these two paradigmatic poles.[37] It is not necessary to discuss this structural divide any longer. Nor is it necessary to evaluate any of them. Instead, the next section tries to show that whatever side of these epistemological fences scholars have put themselves – legalism vs. facticism or objectivism vs. inter-subjectivism – they have all been part of the same enterprise, that is, the establishment of a law of statehood. It is the agenda behind this scholarly project that the following sections will critically review.

## II. THE AGENDA OF THE INTERNATIONAL LAW OF STATEHOOD AND THE MODERN ADVANCEMENT OF INTERNATIONAL LAW

This chapter argues that irrespective of their ultimate paradigmatic positions (that is irrespective of whether they are facticist, legalist, objectivist or subjectivist) experts of the law of statehood have been involved in a common project for the advancement of international law. Indeed, however they understand the apprehension of the volatile practice of state creation by the legal system and the effects of statehood within the legal system, experts have – consciously or unconsciously – been partaking in an explanatory, regulatory and epistemological quest whose contours are described here. It is the aim of this section to speculate on

---

303 (2013); J. Vidmar, "Palestine and the conceptual problem of implicit statehood", 12 *Chinese J. Int'l L.* 1 (2013).

[37] Note that Bederman identifies another dialectical move in the literature, namely between "neomedievalism" (centered on an unequivocal break of states' authority and the rise of new actors) and "globalism" (based on the idea of an explosion of new and legitimate topics of international legal regulation). See Bederman, *supra* note 29, at 92–3.

the various motives that have informed the scholarly quest for an international law of statehood. According to the argument made here, the various agendas behind the idea of a law of statehood generally follow three specific dynamics: explanatory, regulatory and epistemological. These dynamics are *explanatory* in the sense that the law of statehood constructed by international legal scholars seeks to make sense of the intricate and volatile practice of state creation. They are *regulatory* in the sense that the law of statehood seeks to order the intricate and volatile practice of state creation. They are *epistemological* in the sense that they manifest the pursuit by one group of professionals of ownership on the intricate and volatile practice of state creation.

## 1. Explanatory and Elucidatory Ambitions

The first dimension of the project of the law of statehood is explanatory and elucidatory. It is geared towards generating intelligibility of an otherwise unintelligible phenomenon. The explanatory project behind the law of statehood is multifold. It includes a penchant for disentanglement through law of law-created problems (1.1) while also being anthropomorphic (1.2). Each of these inclinations is briefly reviewed and illustrated. Mention is then made of two of the main instruments by which the explanatory virtues of the law of statehood are maintained: proceduralization and territorialization (1.3).

### 1.1 Disentanglement of self-generated entanglements

The law of statehood is a self-nourishing prophecy. It provides a cognitive structure to look at the world. This cognitive structure is necessarily restricting. It comes to generate a certain type of complexity that only the law of statehood can solve. Said differently, the law of statehood creates entanglement which needs to be disentangled according to the paradigms in which the entanglement originated. It is noteworthy that the self-nourishing and self-referential law of statehood grows unabated as the international life continues to generate practice that does not fit in the growingly complex law of statehood paradigms, thereby constantly calling for adjustments and further sophistication. In that sense, the sophisticated modeling put forward by the law of statehood constantly generates cognitive insufficiency and the need for refinement to preserve its ability to explain the practice.[38] As a result, there is a

---

[38] J. Vidmar, *Democratic Statehood in International Law: The Emergence of New States in Post-Cold War Practice* 11 (2013).

sense of need among experts of the law of statehood that the latter yields problems that are "insufficiently explored",[39] thereby generating calls to "take the international law of statehood further".[40] This undoubtedly situates the law of statehood in the unbound hamster wheel of the constant disciplinary need for renewal witnessed in international law.[41]

The self-referential dynamic behind the law of statehood can be easily illustrated. For instance, international legal scholars have felt that it behooves them to explain why some effective entities cannot become states even while satisfying the criteria of statehood.[42] A disconnect between the law of statehood and the practice of non-recognized entities has itself spawned calls for new modeling and theorization. In the same vein, it has been claimed that the post-1990 developments were marked by an entanglement of the process of democratization and state creation. It has accordingly been contended that the status of democracy in the international law of statehood still is in need of scholarly clarification and ordering.[43] Another traditional example of such need for the disentanglement of a self-created entanglement is the common idea that neither the declaratory nor constitutive theories of recognition are satisfactory to explain the modern practice of recognition.[44] The famous duty to recognize designed by Lauterpacht can also be read in this light, for it was meant to correct the "anomaly" created by the constitutive character of recognition.[45]

---

[39] *Id.* at 6–8.
[40] *Id.* at 11.
[41] Kennedy, *supra* note 1, at 335, 407.
[42] Vidmar, *supra* note 38, at 5.
[43] *Id.* at 3, 63–5.
[44] Crawford *supra* note 6, at 5. This is also a criticism made by Brownlie with respect to recognition:

> [T]heory has not only failed to enhance the subject but has created a *teritum quid* which stands, like a bank of fog on a still day, between the observer and the contours of the ground which calls for investigation. With rare exceptions the theories on recognition have not only failed to improve the quality of thought but have deflected lawyers from the application of ordinary methods of legal analysis.

I. Brownlie, "Recognition in theory and practice", in *The Structure and Process of International Law: Modern Essays in Legal Philosophy, Doctrine and Theory* 197, 197 (R. St. J. Macdonald and D. Johnston (eds), 1983).

[45] Lauterpacht, *supra* note 24, at 65–7.

## 1.2 Anthropomorphism

Although this is not without paradox, the world often seems more intelligible if constructed and analyzed through models inspired by human nature. Thus, it is not surprising that anthropomorphism – this inclination, in the course of a descriptive exercise, to ascribe human forms or attributes to constructs, phenomena, practices or dynamics which are not necessarily themselves human – is omnipresent in the international law of statehood. It is argued here that the mainstream statehood doctrine manifests a clear anthropomorphist calling as access to the Eden of non-interference, immunity, sovereign equality, and territorial integrity – to name only a few of the privileges inherent in the recognition of a legal being in the international legal order – is reserved for privileged holders of the three or four keys prescribed by the famous criteria of statehood.[46] The famous doctrine of "fundamental rights of the states" is also a manifestation of the inclination of thinkers to transpose a human blueprint on their prescriptive and normative constructions of inter-state relations.[47]

This – surprisingly unchallenged – common understanding of the law of statehood often constitutes a mechanical transposition, without attention to the specificities of states and the dynamics of the international legal order, and of how the legal condition of individuals is understood under domestic law.

The anthropomorphic move behind the law of statehood should certainly not be seen as singular or extraordinary. Anthropomorphism is rather commonplace in the social sciences. In the thinking about international law, it occurs more often than not. In fact, anthropomorphism has been with international legal thinking since the early natural law manifestations of international law. It is, for instance, very present in the naturalist conceptualizations of international law found in the early scholastic systematizations of international law.[48] Even after

---

[46] I have already made that point elsewhere. See J. d'Aspremont, "The law of recognition: a reply to E. Tourme-Jouannet", 24 *Eur. J. Int'l L.* 691 (2013).

[47] See generally F. Poirat, "La doctrine des droits fondamentaux de l'etat", 16 *Droits: Revue Française de Theorie Juridique* 83 (1992).

[48] See, e.g. A. Gentili, *On the Law of War* (J.C. Rolfe trans., 1933); F. de Vitoria, *Political Writings* (A. Pagden and J. Lawrance (eds), 1991). On Gentili, see generally *The Roman Foundations of the Law of Nations: Alberico Gentili and the Justice of Empire* (Benedict Kingsbury and Benjamin Straumann (eds), 2011).

the estrangement of international law from natural law thinking,[49] international legal scholarship remained replete with anthropomorphic moves.[50]

Although not unprecedented, the anthropomorphist moves behind the law of statehood reinforce its elucidatory virtues and its overall appeal to international lawyers. Accordingly, it contributes to the explanatory project behind the law of statehood.

### 1.3 Elucidatory instruments of the law of statehood

Two aspects of the law of statehood seem to serve best its explanatory agenda: proceduralization and territorialization. These tools are instrumental in the elucidatory agenda of the law of statehood. Each deserves attention.

*1.3.1 Proceduralization* For lawyers, probably more than for international relations scholars, procedures can be more easily captured than eclectic and multi-layered processes whose intricacies are more difficult to understand. More precisely, for international lawyers, procedures constitute a way to make sense of complex processes by constraining them within formal walls. This is why the international law of statehood comes with a high degree of proceduralization of state creation. A good example of this is the proceduralization inherent in the right of self-determination whereby the exercise of that right must follow certain procedural patterns.[51] Proceduralization also resides in the voluminous literature dedicated to collective recognition processes[52] and collective creations of states.[53] Proceduralization is omnipresent in contentions that

---

[49] See E. Jouannet, *Vattel and the Emergence of Classic International Law* (Hart Publishing, 2015).

[50] For a critical exploration of the anthropomorphic foundations of human rights law through the lens of modern communications theory, see W.P. Nagan and C. Hammer, "Communications theory and world public order: the anthropomorphic, jurisprudential foundations of international human rights", 47 *Va. J. Int'l L.* 725 (2007).

[51] *Western Sahara*, Advisory Opinion, 1975 ICJ 12 (Oct. 16) available at http://www.icj-cij.org/docket/files/61/6195.pdf. On the democratic dimension of the exercise of the right to self-determination, see J. d'Aspremont, "La création internationale d'etats démocratiques", 4 *Revue Generale de Droit International Public*, 2005, at 889.

[52] See, e.g., J. Dugard, *Recognition and the United Nations* (1987).

[53] See, e.g., J. d'Aspremont, "Post-conflict administrations as democracy-building instruments", 9 *Chi. J. Int'l L.* 1, 1 (2008); d'Aspremont, *supra* note 51, at 889–908.

state creation is an "international law-governed process of overcoming an applicable counterclaim to territorial integrity"[54] or in the idea that secession is "a regulated process which prescribes peaceful and democratic procedures"[55] and which can be null or invalid.[56] There eventually are other forms of proceduralization which emphasize formal international acceptance[57] or "a grant of legal authority".[58]

It is argued here that the success of the law of statehood can be traced back to its cognitive and explanatory virtues and the proceduralization that it makes possible. The proceduralization found in the law of statehood provides international lawyers with an elucidatory tool that can prove instrumental in the recognition of what is otherwise a volatile process. It is interesting to note, however, that proceduralization has become both a reason for the success of the law of statehood as well as a goal in itself. Indeed, in the recent literature, proceduralization is seen as an ideal towards which the law of statehood must lean.[59]

---

[54] Vidmar, *supra* note 14, at 3–11 (state creation is an "international law-governed process of overcoming an applicable counterclaim to territorial integrity. This process is influenced by the statehood criteria, among other factors. The process prescribes certain democratic procedures and may even result in the international imposition of "democratic institutions"; he seeks to "demonstrate that the act of recognition was not crucial for the emergence of new states in the territory of the federation (of SFRY)", arguing that it "was rather that the international involvement led to an internationalized extinguishing of the SFRY's personality which made its claim to territorial integrity inapplicable").

[55] A. Peters, "Does Kosovo lie in the lotus-land of freedom?", 24 *Leiden J. Int'l L.* 95, 107 (2011) ("Any extraordinary allowance to secede has to be realized in the appropriate procedures, notably under recourse to free and fair referendum on independence or after democratic elections, ideally under international supervision.").

[56] T. Christakis, "The ICJ advisory opinion on Kosovo: has international law something to say about secession?", 24 *Leiden J. Int'l L.* 73, 73–86 (2011); see Peters, *supra* note 55, at 95–108. But see J. d'Aspremont, "Kosovo and international law: a divided international legal scholarship" (2008), available at http://igps.files.wordpress.com/2008/03/kosovo-and-international-law-daspremont.pdf; see also *Maritime Dispute* (Peru v. Chile), Verbatim Record, (Dec. 4, 2012), www.icj-cij.org/docket/files/137/17206.pdf#view=FitH&pagemode=none&search=%22December%204%202012%22.

[57] Lauterpacht, *supra* note 24, at 66.

[58] M. Weiler, "Modesty can be a virtue: judicial economy in the ICJ Kosovo opinion?", 24 *Leiden J. Int'l L.* (2011), 127, 129.

[59] Vidmar, *supra* note 38, at 8.

*1.3.2 Territorialization* It will not come as a surprise that international life seems a much more intelligible process when constructed in territorial units. The law of statehood – and some of its affiliates like sovereignty and territorial integrity – comes with models that recognize the world in territorial terms. For instance, the effectiveness found behind the so-called criteria of statehood is territorial effectiveness.[60] Likewise, the "ineradicable"[61] catchwords constantly referred to by international legal scholars in this context – like sovereignty and territorial integrity[62] – bring about, if not a structuring of the world along territorial lines,[63] at least a territory-based narrative. It is in this sense that the law of statehood can be seen as conveying a territorialization of the world that, in turn, enhances the explanatory appeal of the law of statehood. Territorialization facilitates understanding of the world and that of international law, which it makes more intelligible and operable.

An important remark logically follows this point. Certainly, the structuring of the world along territorial lines which comes with the law of statehood is not surprising. It could even be seen as tautological, for the law of statehood is primarily about defining territorial units. Yet, at least from a theoretical perspective, the territorialization of international law should not be taken for granted. First, there are now a growing number of actors whose behaviors have been incorporated in the ambit of international law without these actors being recognized in territorial terms.[64] Second, it must be acknowledged that the central subjects of the system of international law could well be defined according to non-territorial categories. The day the oceans expunge some states from the map, international lawyers may be forced to rethink the world on a non-territorial basis.[65] For the time being, territorialization and the law of statehood remain linked, the former consolidates the success of the latter because of its powerful explanatory virtues.

---

[60] For a critical review of these criteria, see Crawford, *supra* note 6, at 95.
[61] *Id.* at 32.
[62] For a critical analysis of some of these common catchwords, see G. Simpson, *Great Powers and Outlaw States: Unequal Sovereigns in the International Legal Order* (2004), 25–61.
[63] Sovereignty is "a somewhat unhelpful, but firmly established, description of statehood; a brief term for the State's attribute of more-or-less plenary competence". Crawford, *supra* note 6, at 32.
[64] See generally J. d'Aspremont, *Participants in the International Legal Systems: Multiple Perspectives on Non-State Actors in International Law* (2011).
[65] R. Rayfuse and S.V. Scott, *International law in the Era of Climate Change* (2012); D. Badrinarayana, "Global warming: a second coming for international law?", 85 *Wash. L. Rev.* (2010) 253, 255.

## 2. Regulatory Ambitions

The second driving force behind the law of statehood is more managerial, in that the law of statehood has a proclivity to expand its control on the volatile phenomenon of state creation. The legalization of the state creation inherent in the law of statehood and the proceduralization discussed above can simultaneously be understood as an endeavor to regulate political power. In that sense, the last fifty years of international legal scholarship dedicated to the question of statehood has constituted a heroic conquest, led by international lawyers, to secure a voice in one aspect of international life. The production of scholarly work on the matter can thus be construed as the attempted rise to power of an academic aristocracy on questions that were previously reserved for chancelleries.

Such a regulatory agenda can be delineated in several versions. There is first a general undertaking to control and program the births and deaths in the international society. One also witnesses a quest for a completeness of the international legal system. Each of these inclinations is briefly reviewed and illustrated. This section then turns to two of the main tools by which the regulatory virtues of the law of statehood are maintained: legalism and, again, proceduralization.

### 2.1 Control (and programming) of the death and birth of states

Controlling membership of the international legal system has long been a pipe dream of international lawyers. This is a fantasy about gaining power to determine the happy few, who will enjoy the privileges attached to membership in the international legal system as well as an ability to filter out the many who do not deserve entry into the elite club. As part of this regulatory agenda, scholars seek a certain type of ordering that, at least on the surface, guarantees formal equality between the members admitted to the club.[66] This yearning for controlling entry into the international legal system even seems a natural and intuitive penchant among international lawyers.[67] Accordingly, it is not surprising that the law of statehood is not the only manifestation of such a pursuit of control

---

[66] For a critical and illuminating examination of this question outside the law of statehood, see G. Simpson, *Great Powers and Outlaw States* (2004). For the anti-pluralistic moves found in the law of statehood in connection with democracy, see generally J. d'Aspremont, *L'Etat Non Démocratique en Droit International. Étude Critique du Droit International Positif et de la Pratique Contemporaine* (2008).

[67] Ryngaert and Sobrie, *supra* note 23, at 469.

over the composition of the international society found in international legal scholarship and practice. The international law of succession is another good example.[68] Whether such a pursuit will ever succeed is a different question, one which does not need to be addressed here.

## 2.2 Completeness of international law

It is argued here that the law of statehood also is an attempt within the larger quest of international lawyers for a comprehensive paradigm in which they seek a normative order regulating all aspects of the international life. This endeavor is often premised on the idea that international law cannot qualify as a legal system properly if it does not regulate all the important aspects of international life, including births and deaths of its most important actors.[69] From this perspective, there is no place for black holes in the international legal space as they would create the risk of absorbing the whole legal universe and the profession organized around it. This "fear of the dark" and the thirst for completeness to the international legal system that comes with it are, according to the argument made here, strong underpinnings of the law of statehood. Indeed, the law of statehood can be understood as an indispensable element to allow and realize the completeness to the international legal system and the ability of such a system to control the main aspects of international life. It is noteworthy that international lawyers and experts in the law of statehood are sometimes completely transparent about this dimension of the law of statehood. For example, James Crawford, who

---

[68] It is interesting to note that, read as a project for the control of the births and deaths in the international society, the project of the international law of succession has been the object of severe criticism, notably because of its denial of the political question of identity of states inevitably preceding the formal determination of the consequences of identity changes. Many would contend that there simply is no possibility to locate the notion of continuity or succession in advance. See M. Craven, "The problem of state succession and the identity of states under international law", 9 *Eur. J. Int'l L.* 142, 152–62 (1998) (defining considerations about whether or not the state concerned retains its legal identity in each case); M. Koskenniemi, "Report of the director of studies of the English-speaking section of the centre", in 1 *State Succession: Codification Tested Against the Facts* 65, 122–4 (1997). But see d'Aspremont, *supra* note 53, at 1–16 (2008).

[69] Crawford, *supra* note 6, at 5 ("Fundamentally, the question is whether international law is itself, in one of its most important aspects, a coherent or complete system of law."); see also Ti-Chiang Chen, *The International Law of Recognition: With Special Reference to Practice in Great Britain and the United States* 18–19 (L.C. Green ed., 1951).

has been very open about this aspect of his scholarship on statehood, describes his work as an "attempt to defend formal coherence and completeness of international law as a system of law."[70]

## 2.3 Regulatory instruments of the law of statehood

The two aspects of the law of statehood that are the most conducive to the regulatory project of the law of statehood are legalism and proceduralization. The last fifty years of international legal scholarship can even be read as an attempt to shore up these two features of the law of statehood with an eye towards maximizing the regulatory grip that international lawyers can claim on the international life.

*2.3.1 Legalism* The turn to legalism is the most common tactic to which international lawyers have resorted in order to give weight to the regulatory project behind the law of statehood. Here, legalism is not merely meant as a turn to the narrative of law.[71] In this context, legalism more specifically constitutes the attempt by some international lawyers to legalize state creation and to define statehood by criteria of legality rather than effectiveness. Such a legalism comes to confer upon the law of statehood "some defined time, space and subject matter for its 'proper' (albeit not autonomous) operation",[72] without which it could not perform its regulatory function.

Such an endeavor is particularly present among those international lawyers with objectivist inclinations, that is, those who affirm, as was explained above, that statehood, once captured by the international legal system, is opposable in all parts of that system and to all stakeholders.[73] If statehood operates objectively within the legal system, the legal system in turn can objectively regulate statehood. This is where the strong support for the idea of legality-based criteria of statehood finds its roots.

The way such a legalism operates and manifests itself can be succinctly described as follows. According to that legalist view, "success or failure"[74] can no longer be the determinative factor. A whole series of criteria come to supplement or even overwrite the traditional

---

[70] See F. Johns, *Non-legality in International Law: Unruly Law* (2013).
[71] See generally M. Koskenniemi, "What is international law for?", in *The Politics of International Law* (2011), 241.
[72] Johns, *supra* note 9, at 8.
[73] Cf. *supra* 1.2.
[74] Anzilotti, *supra* note 8, at 154.

effectiveness-based criteria of statehood and can bar statehood.[75] If one of these conditions is disregarded, access to the international legal system, is denied. Denial takes the form of nullifying statehood[76] – envisaged as a legal act.[77] Some other criteria can even offset the absence of effectiveness[78] and provide a direct access to the international legal system. Such a legalism usually comes with a compelling narrative built on a wide variety of concepts and principles, like *ex injuria jus non oritur*,[79] principle of territorial integrity,[80] the concepts of *ius cogens*, the prohibition to use force,[81] self-determination,[82] democracy,[83] and the

---

[75] Peters, *supra* note 7 ("[A] middle ground. Effectiveness and legality are not simple opposites, because, as explained, effectiveness is itself a legal principle which performs normative functions. But to the extent that effectiveness has an a-legal quality, considerations of effectiveness and of legality form a system of communicating vessels. Put differently, there is a dialectics of 'might' and 'right'. A relative weakness of effective government can be compensated by a surplus of legality/legitimacy. Effectiveness is a necessary, but no sufficient criterion of statehood. It must be complemented by criteria of legality and of legitimacy. Still, effectiveness remains indispensable. It must not be substituted by indices of legality or legitimacy, because such an approach would transform the international legal system into a purely virtual one which could not perform its ordering function. However, because effectiveness is a relative concept, it is difficult to call a government arrangement completely non-effective.").

[76] *Id.*

[77] For a rejection of this approach, see "On the Accordance with International Law of the Unilateral Declaration of Independence by the Provisional Institutions of Self-Government of Kosovo" (Req. for Advisory Op.) (Dec. 4), www.icj-cij.org/docket/files/141/15718.pdf#view=FitH&pagemode=none&search = %22Burundi%22.

[78] Peters, *supra* note 7; see also Crawford, *supra* note 6, at 97–9.

[79] T. Christakis, "The state as a primary fact: some thoughts on the principle of effectiveness", in *Secession: International Law Perspectives* 138, 139 (Marcelo G. Kohen (ed.), 2006).

[80] O. Corten, "Territorial integrity narrowly interpreted: reasserting the classical inter-state paradigm of international law", 24 *Leiden J. Int'l L.* (2011), 87, 87–94.

[81] Crawford, *supra* note 6, at 107; see also A. Peters, "Membership in the global constitutional community", in *The Constitutionalization of International Law* 153, 180–81 (J. Klabbers et al. eds, 2009) (arguing that the same effect should be granted to all peremptory norms).

[82] R. Wilde, "Self-determination, secession and dispute settlement after the Kosovo advisory opinion", 24 *Leiden J. Int'l L.* (2011), 149, 149–54; see generally Theodore Christakis, *Le droit à l'autodétermination en dehors des situations de décolonisation* (1999), 253–6.

[83] See Peters, *supra* note 7, at 171.

obligation not to recognize. Legality criteria are also said to originate in special regimes.[84] Legalism also manifests itself in the vindication of primary obligations, like the right to a name.[85]

Although subject to strong objections,[86] this legalism has been one of the dominant features of the last fifty years of scholarship. The idea that criteria of legality impact statehood is now widely accepted among scholars.[87] It is argued here that this approach is the best manifestation of the regulatory project which undergirds the law of statehood. This is openly acknowledged by the proponents of the legalist approach to statehood.[88]

---

[84] See M.G. Kohen and K. Del Mar, "The Kosovo Advisory Opinion and UNSCR 2144 (1999): A declaration of 'independence from international law'?", 24 *Leiden J. Int'l L.* 109 (2011) (discussing the legality of the declaration of the independence of Kosovo in the light of Security Council Resolution 1244 (1999)). For a different opinion, see Wilde, *supra* note 82 at 149–54; M. Weller, "Modesty can be a virtue: judicial economy in the ICJ Kosovo opinion?", 24 *Leiden J. Int'l L.* (2011), 127.

[85] *Application of the Interim Accord of 13 September 1995* (Maced. v. Greece), Judgment, 2011 I.C.J. 644 (Dec. 5); I. Bantekas, "The authority of states to use names in international law and the Macedonian affair: unilateral entitlements, historic title, and trademark analogies", 22 *Leiden J. Int'l L.* 563 (2009); F. Messineo, "Maps of ephemeral empires: the ICJ and the Macedonian name dispute", 1 *Cambridge J. Int'l & Comp. L.* (2012), 169.

[86] See B. Roth, "Secessions, coups and the international rule of law: assessing the decline of the effective control doctrine", 11 *Melb. J. Int'l L.* (2010) 393; Accordance with International Law of the Unilateral Declaration of Independence by the Provisional Institutions of Self-Government of Kosovo (Request for Advisory Op.) at 58 (Dec. 8), available at http://www.icj-cij.org/docket/files/141/15726.pdf ("Now, Serbia and its supporters claim that the rule of territorial integrity and consent of the parent State regulate the process of independence. But surely this is both conceptually and historically wrong? Was the United States born out of a legal process that peaked in the consent of Britain? Or Russia or Germany? Venezuela, Algeria or Bangladesh or indeed Serbia? Did any of the republics formerly part of the SFRY emerge from a process that respected the integrity of the mother State or out of the consent of the latter? They did not."); see also Accordance with International Law of the Unilateral Declaration of Independence by the Provisional Institutions of Self-Government of Kosovo (Request for Advisory Op.) (Dec. 4), available at http://www.icj-cij.org/docket/files/141/15738.pdf [hereinafter Verbatim Record CR 2009/28].

[87] Crawford, *supra* note 6, at 97–173. According to Crawford, "there is nothing incoherent about the legal regulation of statehood on a basis other than that of effectiveness" and "there is now a considerable amount of practice in favour of regulations of this type." *Id.* at 106.

[88] This is expressly acknowledged by Crawford, *supra* note 6, at 99.

*2.3.2 Proceduralization (bis)* Mention has already been made of the proceduralization that is instrumental in the performance of explanatory functions by the law of statehood. Interestingly, the proceduralization witnessed in the law of statehood is also valued for the regulatory tools it provides to international lawyers. Indeed, elevated into a procedure, state creation lends itself more easily to regulation. For instance, a proceduralized law can be subjected to democratization.[89] Likewise, a reading of the creation of states – and especially for secession processes[90] – as being that of a formal procedure that can be null or invalid provides a great sense of control over the process of disintegration of states. It is no surprise that this reading of the Kosovo advisory opinion delivered by the International Court of Justice[91] has gathered strong support among scholars.[92]

## 3. Epistemological Self-rehabilitating Ambitions

The explanatory and regulatory agendas behind the law of statehood described above are probably more conspicuous than controversial. Other epistemological moves behind the construction at the heart of the law of statehood are less perceptible. They pertain to the internal dynamics of groups of professionals who dedicate their lives to the study (and construction) of international law. Most of such driving forces are geared towards the rehabilitation of the profession of international lawyers. They must now be briefly described. Special attention is paid to the search for sophistication (3.1), the obfuscation of interdisciplinary study (3.2), the production of new materials of study (3.3) and the quest for the ubiquity of international law as a discipline (3.4).

---

[89] Vidmar, *supra* note 38.

[90] See generally T. Christakis, "The state as a primary fact: some thoughts on the principle of effectiveness", in *Secession: International Law Perspectives* 138 (M.G. Kohen (ed.), 2006); A. Tancredi, "A normative due process in the creation of states through secession", in *Secession: International Law Perspectives* 171 (M.G. Kohen ed., 2006).

[91] See Accordance with International Law of the Unilateral Declaration of Independence in Respect of Kosovo, Advisory Opinion, 2010 I.C.J. 437 (July 22).

[92] Christakis, *supra* note 56, at 73–86; see also A. Peters, "Does Kosovo lie in the lotus-land of freedom?", 24 *Leiden J. Int'l L.* 95, (2011), 105–7; but see J. d'Aspremont, *supra* note 53; see also Verbatim Record CR 2009/28, *supra* note 86 (statements from the Republic of Burundi).

## 3.1 Sophistication as redemption

Within the law of statehood, sophistication often constitutes a self-indulging scholarly ambition. It is cherished and generated by international legal scholars themselves. Sophistication is not only sought after for the above-mentioned potentially greater explanatory force it conveys. It is now common for international lawyers to seek sophistication for its salutary character. Sophistication is now elevated as the indicator of the value and intellect of international lawyers. It is through sophistication that the international lawyer secures intellectual and communitarian salvation.

In the particular context of the law of statehood, sophistication is mostly definitional, or procedural. It is definitional when it manifests itself through multiplication of the criteria of statehood,[93] for example by elevating democracy in a criterion of statehood.[94] Definitional sophistication is similarly found in attempts to design subtle taxonomy, like those distinguishing states from para-states,[95] de facto states,[96] state-like entities[97] or de facto regimes.[98] Sophistication is procedural when, as mentioned above, state creation is construed as an "international law-governed process of overcoming an applicable counterclaim to territorial integrity"[99] or when secession is thought of as "a regulated process which

---

[93] See Crawford, *supra* note 6, at 96–173 (discussing the possibility of additional criteria for Statehood).

[94] See A. Peters, "Statehood after 1989: effectivités between legality and virtuality", in *Select Proceedings of the European Society of International Law* 171 (J. Crawford and S. Nouwen (eds), 2012) (discussing the possibility for democracy to be a new criterion for statehood).

[95] K. Pelczyinska-Nalecz, K. Strachota and M. Falkowski, "Para-states in the post-Soviet area from 1991 to 2007", 10 *Int'l Stud. Rev.* (2008), 370.

[96] S. Pegg, *International Society and the De Facto State* (1998).

[97] "Independent international fact-finding mission on the conflict in Georgia, report" *("Tagliavini-Report")* of September 2009, vol. 2, at 134, available at http://www.ceiig.ch/pdf/IIFFMCG_Volume_II.pdf.

[98] J.A. Frowein, "De facto regime", in *Max Planck Encyclopedia of Public International Law* 4–5 (online ed., Mar. 2009); R. Kolb, *Ius contra bellum: Le droit international relatif au maintien de la paix*, (2003), 247–50.

[99] Vidmar, *supra* note 38, at 3–11 (seeking to "demonstrate that the act of recognition was not crucial for the emergence of new states in the territory of the federation (of SFRY)", arguing that it "was rather that the international involvement led to an internationalized extinguishing of the SFRY's personality which made its claim to territorial integrity inapplicable"; state creation is "international law-governed process of overcoming an applicable counterclaim to territorial integrity. This process is influenced by the statehood criteria, among other

prescribes peaceful and democratic procedures"[100] and which can potentially be null or invalid.[101]

This is certainly not the place to gauge the epistemological value of sophistication. However, as I have contended elsewhere,[102] sophistication can often reveal itself to be counter-productive when assessed in the light of its assigned objectives. In the context of the law of statehood, sophistication may be seen as increasing the explanatory deficiency of the law of statehood and undermining its regulatory power. The inextricable and growing disconnection between the sophisticated modeling of the law of statehood and an incongruous practice often frustrates the ability of the law of statehood to explain and regulate such a practice.

### 3.2 Camouflaged interdisciplinarity

As was mentioned above, legalism has been one of the main tools to promote and implement the regulatory agenda of the law of statehood. Legalism, however, has also been serving another aspect of the agenda behind the law of statehood. Indeed, through the above-mentioned legalism, international lawyers have been able to camouflage their craving for interdisciplinarity. Indeed, through the law of statehood, international lawyers interact with a wild international arena already patrolled by the experts of international relations and political theory.[103]

---

factors. The process prescribes certain democratic procedures and may even result in the international imposition of democratic institutions").

[100] Peters, *supra* note 92, at 107 ("Any extraordinary allowance to secede has to be realized in the appropriate procedures, notably under recourse to free and fair referendum on independence or after democratic elections, ideally under international supervision.").

[101] Christakis, *supra* note 56, at 73–86; see Peters, *supra* note 92, at 105–7. But see d'Aspremont, *supra* note 56.

[102] J. d'Aspremont, "Wording in International Law", 25 *Leiden J. Int'l L.* (2012), 575.

[103] Referring to the Kosovo Advisory Opinion, Koskenniemi writes:

[I]t was impossible to argue about the lawfulness of the unilateral declaration of independence without a general view of the significance of nationhood and sovereignty today, the role of international institutions and the experience of war and peacemaking in Europe and more widely. The (universal) legal concepts and the specific histories were then woven together by the legal "teams" in a proposal to decide the case one way or another. At the same time, the available legal concepts enabled the understanding of the differences in genuinely political terms – as differences about how to understand Balkan history and the relations of the several communities there – and the assessment of them through a vocabulary that, although it was open-ended,

In that context, the law of statehood is what allows international lawyers to enter into a new universe and to toy, on the basis of their own techniques and methods, with phenomena recognized and analyzed by other disciplines and inject therein their own dose of legalism.

The foregoing calls for an important remark. It seems no longer disputed that interdisciplinarity is relative in at least two senses. First, there is as much interdisciplinarity as the (relative and self-defined) boundaries of the involved disciplines allow. This is why interdisciplinarity often carries with it dubious politics.[104] Second, law, as an argumentative practice, necessarily seeks the design of universal standards applicable in the international world.[105] Importantly, for the sake of this argument, it is noteworthy that international lawyers often try to bridge law and politics, before taking a plunge into – and seeking to exert their influence on – the latter. As I noted elsewhere,[106] international legal scholars are uneasy when grappling with a given question without including it in the realm of international law. It is as if international legal scholars cannot zero-in on non-legal phenomena without feeling a need to label them as law. The law of statehood seems to epitomize this penchant of international legal scholars. One continues to wonder,

---

reaffirmed the need to obtain some minimal agreement from the populations themselves about how to live together in the future.

M. Koskenniemi, "Law, teleology and international relations: an essay in counterdisciplinarity", 26 *Int'l Rel.* (2012), 3, 25.

[104] See J. Klabbers, "The relative autonomy of international law and the forgotten politics of interdisciplinarity", 1 *J. Int'l L. & Int'l Rel.* (2005), 355.

[105] As Koskenniemi wrote:

Much of the debate concerning the relation between international law and politics has focused on the applicability of universal standards in the international world. From Hans Morgenthau's Frankfurt doctoral thesis, to Hersch Lauterpacht's views of the completeness of the international legal system, to Julius Stone's defense of politics in a fragmented world and Thomas M. Franck's exploration of the "political questions" doctrine, lawyers have debated the wisdom of generalizing about the facts of the international world, supposedly the realm of the singular, the extreme, the historically specific. There are not many cases from international practice (in contrast to academic writing), however, where lawyers would have raised their hands in deference to "the political".

Koskenniemi, *supra* note 103, at 22.

[106] J. d'Aspremont, "From a pluralization of international norm-making process to a pluralization of the concept of international law", in *Informal International Lawmaking* (J. Pauwelyn, R. Wessel and J. Wouters. (eds), 2012).

however, why international legal scholars cannot study the phenomenon without portraying it as a legal phenomenon.

### 3.3 Epistemological ownership and quest for new legal materials

Another set of professional dynamics that sustain the development of a law of statehood is an epistemological move I have already examined elsewhere. Indeed, the law of statehood brings to existence a new scholarly field. It allows the legalization of world politics and the elevation of the volatile phenomenon of state-creation as a rich muse for scholarly study. It is a treasure trove that helps scholars find new research materials and open new avenues for legal research.[107] It is simultaneously a tactic to deprive other social sciences of any monopoly on this aspect of the international life. Said differently, it not only feeds international lawyers' appetite for new subjects, but also allows them to claim ownership of a phenomenon that would otherwise fall exclusively in the ambit of other areas of study.[108] If it is construed, the law of statehood seems to be rich soil for future scholarly mushrooming. Practice, at least when constructed and deciphered through the categories of the law of statehood, provides abundant materials of study, thereby opening up huge fields of scholarly research.

The development of the law of statehood is, of course, an old scholarly endeavor. Its inception dates back to a time where international legal scholars were few and where imposing one's mark or leaving one's trace on the knowledge about international law was far less arduous than it is today. In that sense, the law of statehood, as an epistemological enterprise, pre-dates the current scholarly gluttony observed in the contemporary era of legal scholarship. This being said, it is hard to deny that contemporary scholarship exhibits an unprecedented investment in the expansion, fine-tuning and sophistication of the law of statehood. Such devotion has turned pathological, for the scholarly gluttony is currently exacerbated by the unabated difficulty for everyone to find a niche, the aggressive competition igniting a feeling of constriction.[109] Such a

---

[107] For an illustration of that phenomenon, see D. Johnston, "Theory, consent and the law of treaties: a cross-disciplinary perspective", 12 *Aust. Y.B. Int'l L.* (1988–89), 109.

[108] On the battle for controlling the production of discourse, see M. Foucault, "The order of discourse", in *Untying the Text: A Post-Structuralist Reader* (R. Young (ed.), 1981), 48, 52.

[109] For more on this argument, see J. d'Aspremont, "Softness in international law: a self-serving quest for new legal materials", 19 *Eur. J. Int'l L.* (2008), 1075.

regulatory gluttony is certainly not unique and has been observed in other areas.[110] It would be of no avail to dwell on it here.

### 3.4 The dream of ubiquity of the discipline of international law

As the above-mentioned legalist tactics to which experts of the law of statehood have been resorting illustrate, the quest for universal standards in the international world is, from the perspective of international lawyers, a quest for ubiquity of international law. Indeed, it is the pursuit of the dream of having all aspects of international life, including the most volatile of them like births and deaths, regulated by international law. This enterprise is not only a regulatory one as was described above.[111] It is also an epistemological one, in that it is a way to ensure the omnipresence of the discipline of international law. In that sense, the law of statehood is a hegemonic disciplinary enterprise at the service of professionals who seek to make their expertise omnipresent in (the study of) international life.

## III. CONCLUDING REMARKS

All the scholars engaged in the law of statehood make different methodological moves and pursue different agendas. In that sense, the scholarship on the law of statehood is pluralistic in its nature and its ambitions. This chapter has attempted to expose such a plurality. Whether experts of the law of statehood are facticist, legalist, objectivists, or inter-subjectivists (as described in section I) and whether they pursue a regulatory, explanatory or epistemological agenda (as described in section II) matter little for the purpose of this chapter. There is no meta-criterion that elevates one approach or one agenda over the others. More fundamentally, there is no meta-criterion that can (in)validate the law of statehood altogether but the fact that the law of statehood is a social reality. It seems uncontroversial that a large majority of international lawyers write on the law of statehood, use its narratives and construct the world according to its cognitive paradigms.

As was already mentioned above, the law of statehood has been with international lawyers since the nineteenth century. The law of statehood, in its more than 100 years of existence, has offered a unique tool to make a (certain) sense of the international world. It has simultaneously

---

[110] See id.; J. d'Aspremont, "The politics of deformalization in international law", 3 *Goettingen J. Int'l L.* (2011), 503.
[111] See *supra* section II.3.

provided a confidence-building framework for the moments of crisis or turbulences that inevitably follow attempts to apply law to the volatile phenomenon of state-creation. It is true that the success of the law of statehood has often been tempered by the self-created unintelligibility it has generated, as well as the limited grip it has offered on international life. However, the floundering of the regulatory and explanatory projects of the law of statehood should not alter the luster of this social reality. Indeed, the law of statehood remains an admirable and impressive enterprise of craftsmanship. By virtue of the level of sophistication it has reached in contemporary legal thinking, the scholarship on the law of statehood is closer to art than to a banal, naïve, managerialist and descriptive project. As in any art, fundamental discrepancies are observed in the techniques and the skills of professionals fluent in the law of statehood. After all, more than the aesthetics, variations of techniques and normative ambitions constitute the very reason why art is so fascinating.

# 2. Sources

The sources of international law are often seen as the most cardinal doctrine of international law. This is not surprising. In the modern international law designed at the end of the nineteenth century and the beginning of the twentieth century, the doctrine of sources was not only what allowed international law to emancipate itself from the arbitrariness of both metaphysical consideration or voluntarism. It also was the tool by virtue of which international law takes control of the identification of its own rules.[1] Needless to say that this modernist institution has been the object of various attacks throughout the last century. Albeit weakened and contested, the doctrine of sources has nonetheless survived such broadsides and maintained itself as one of the most foundational doctrines of international law.

From the communitarian perspective of this book, it is interesting to note that the centrality of the doctrine of sources is reinforced by its prominent role in the socialization of international lawyers. Being socialized as an international lawyer,[2] often means, being trained to identify international law according to the criteria provided by the doctrine of sources. In that sense, it is no coincidence that in certain parts of the world, textbooks[3] always begin with an exposition of the doctrine of sources even before looking at the identification of the subjects. It suffices to take English-speaking textbooks of international law, which, subject to a few exceptions,[4] make the study of sources precede that of

---

[1] On the extent to which Article 38 of the Statute of the ICJ has been held as a canonical provision, see J. Crawford and M. Koskenniemi, "Introduction", in J. Crawford and M. Koskenniemi (eds), *Cambridge Companion to International Law* (CUP, 2012), at 11. See also the critical remarks by H. Charlesworth, "Law-making and Sources", in J. Crawford and M. Koskenniemi, *Cambridge Companion to International Law* (CUP, 2012), 188.

[2] On the process of socialization of international lawyers, see the *supra* introduction.

[3] On the role of textbook in the socialization of international lawyers, see *supra* introduction.

[4] See A. Cassese, *International Law*, 2nd ed., 2005. It is also interesting to draw attention to the changes introduced by J. Crawford in the 8th ed. of

the subjects of international law.⁵ It is true that, in contrast, many more French-speaking textbooks place the study of the subjects as the gateway to the study of the other dimensions of the international legal order.⁶

For the sake of this chapter, it is important to note that these sequential choices in the tools of socialization of international lawyers are not only of a pedagogical and didactic character but are the expression of paradigmatic and normative choices. A sequence that would give the doctrine of sources a pole position denotes some strong legalist inclinations. More particularly, making the study of the sources preceding the study of the subjects and especially of the law of statehood creates a paradigmatic presupposition that other phenomena are regulated by rules and principles which themselves are formed through (and identified by virtue of) the traditional doctrine of sources. In that sense, the sequence "sources-first" comes with a strong legalist veil.

Legalist attitudes have been examined extensively in chapter 1 in connection with the law of statehood. It is no longer necessary to discuss them here. Nor should this chapter elaborate on textbooks, despite their central role in the socialization of international law. The social arrangements sought by international lawyers in the doctrine of sources are rather to be found in expert scholarship. In this respect, there is a particular phenomenon in the scholarship and expert literature on the sources of international law that seems particularly interesting to examine and situate and which this chapter will focus on. This is the deformalization process that infuses the doctrine of sources.

---

Brownlie's *Public International Law*. Indeed, while the very first chapter was devoted to the sources in the latter, the former has demoted the overview of the sources to a (short) subsection of the Introduction, postponing the examination of the law of treaties to chapter 6. In doing so, the legalism and rule-based approach permeating the first editions of Brownlie have been played down in the 8th ed. prepared by J. Crawford.

⁵ See M. Evans, *International Law*, 2nd ed., 2006, D.J. Harris, *International Law*, 6th ed., 2004, I. Brownlie, *Public International Law*, 6th ed., 2003, J. Crawford, *I. Brownlie's Public International Law*, 8th ed., 2012, A. Clapham, *Brierly's Law of Nations*, 7th ed., 2012, M. Shaw, *International Law*, 5th ed., 2003, Lowe, *International Law*, 2007.

⁶ See D. Carreau, *Droit international*, 8th ed., 2004, J. Verhoeven, *Droit international public*, 2000, P.-M. Dupuy and Y. Kerbat, *Droit international public*, 11th ed., 2012; see contra P. Dailler, M. Forteau and A. Pellet, *Droit international public*, 8th ed., 2009, J. Combacau and S. Sur, *Droit international public*, 5th ed., 2001. This is not the case of all French-speaking textbooks. See P. Dailler, M. Forteau and A. Pellet, *Droit international public*, 8th ed., 2009, J. Combacau and S. Sur, *Droit international public*, 5th ed., 2001.

Deformalization, although far from being a new phenomenon, has proved rampant in the thinking about the sources of international law. In the last decades, international lawyers have found in deformalization an elixir for many of the problems inherent in the current pluralization of the exercises of public authority at the international level. Indeed, deformalization has turned to be perceived as the antidote for many of the anxieties of international lawyers who, in an era where exercise of public authority manifests itself more heterogeneously, have been witnessing the retreat of international law and the proportionally growing resort to other regulatory instruments. It is not that the pluralization of the exercise of public authority is a new development.[7] It is simply that, amidst the explosion of new manifestations of global governance, international law is playing an incrementally reduced role, thereby placing international lawyers on the defensive. In particular, international lawyers have begun to fret about the shrinking importance of their primary material of study and responded with two main, diverging survival strategies. On the one hand, there are international legal scholars who have tried to constitutionalize traditional international law[8] in hopes of enhancing its appeal and promoting its use by global actors.[9] On the other hand, there are scholars who have embarked on a deformalization

---

[7] One of the first studies on transnational regulatory networks (TRNs), see A.-M. Slaughter, *A New World Order* (2004). More recently, see P.-H. Verdier, "Transnational regulatory networks and their limits", 34 *Yale Journal of International Law* (2009) 1, 113.

[8] For some e.g. B. Fassbender, "The meaning of international constitutional law", in N. Tsagourias (ed.), *Transnational Constitutionalism: International and European Perspectives* (2007) 307, 311; C. Tomuschat, "International law: ensuring the survival of mankind on the eve of a new century", 281 *Collected Courses* 9 (1999), 89. It should be noted, however, that constitutionalists do not reject the fragmentation associated with the multiplication of international judicial bodies, for this can constitute a step towards a more systemic implementation of the international rule of law. See A. Peters, "Global constitutionalism revisited", 11 *International Legal Theory* (2005), 39, 65.

[9] On the agenda of constitutionalism, see W. Werner, "The never-ending closure: constitutionalism and international law", in N. Tsagourias (ed.), *Transnational Constitutionalism: International and European Perspectives* (2007), 329; see also J. Klabbers, "Setting the scene", in J. Klabbers, A. Peters and G. Ulfstein (eds) *The Constitutionalization of International Law* (2009) 1, 18; M. Koskenniemi, "The fate of public international law: between technique and politics", 70 *Modern Law Review* (2007) 1, 1.

of international law that has reshaped the lens through which they make sense of reality. For the latter group, legal pluralism has become the key mantra while formalism is castigated as the root of many of the pains of an embattled profession for "constrain[ing] creative thinking.[10]

The constitutionalist attitude has already been extensively discussed in the literature.[11] Deformalization, on the contrary, and despite its current success, has thrived almost unnoticed. This chapter seeks to critically evaluate this second scholarly strategy to the pluralization of the exercise of public authority and its impact on the doctrine of sources.

After sketching a definition of deformalization (I) and providing some contemporary examples (II), the chapter elaborates on the agenda in the international legal scholarship behind deformalization (III). It then argues that, while providing some welcome relief in an era of pluralized normativity, deformalization does not come without some serious costs (IV). The chapter subsequently shows that these costs explain why most of the deformalization strategies in the contemporary legal scholarship always preserve some elementary formalism, in one way or another (V). This will be illustrated by Global Administrative Law, the Heidelberg Project on the Exercise of Public Authority, Martti Koskenniemi's culture of formalism as well as new streams of international legal positivism. The chapter ends with a few critical remarks on the political choice for deformalization (VI).

---

[10] J. Brunnée and S.J. Toope, "International law and constructivism, elements of an international theory of international law", 39 *Columbia Journal of Transnational Law* (2000–2001) 1, 19, 65; *See* also P. Shlag, "Formalism and realism in ruins", 96 *Iowa Law Review* (2009), at 214: "to declare one's self a comprehensive formalist today is thus a bit akin to announcing that one is a monarchist. It is simply not a convincing belief system given our present legal and social conditions".

[11] See e.g. N. Tsagourias (ed.), *Transnational Constitutionalism: International and European Perspectives* (2007); A. von Bogdandy, "Globalization and Europe: how to square democracy, globalization and international law", 15 *European Journal of International Law* (2004) 5, 885. I have myself discussed it as well. See J. d'Aspremont and F. Dopagne, "Two constitutionalisms in Europe: pursuing an articulation of the European and international legal orders", 68 *Heidelberg Journal of International Law* (2009) 4, 939, or see J. d'Aspremont, "The foundations of the international legal order", 18 *Finnish Yearbook of International Law* (2007), 219–55.

# I. THE CONCEPT OF DEFORMALIZATION

## 1. Deformalization of Law-ascertainment

Deformalization – and thus its antithesis: formalism – carry a great variety of meanings and come to represent a wide range of ideas about law. As a result, disagreement arises in connection to what the word means, even before one discusses its role and its impact.[12] There is such variety of opinions on what the concept means and refers to that it is materially impossible to recall them all here. It suffices to say that in general legal theory and jurisprudence, one distinguishes between forms of vulgar formalism and sophisticated forms of formalism, the former one being almost a myth – or a useful straw man – rather than a proper scholarly posture.[13] Whether vulgar or sophisticated, it seems that formalism has always had a bad connotation.[14] Formalism has not enjoyed a more favorable treatment in international legal theory. International legal theory distinguishes itself for its particular attention to the phenomenon of deformalization. Indeed, there has been some – mostly academic – tumult around the idea of deformalization that is understood as referring to these processes "whereby law retreats solely to the provision of procedures or broadly formulated directives to experts and decision-makers for the purpose of administering international problems by means of functionally effective solutions and 'balancing' interests".[15] This has been deemed dismaying, for deformalization – so understood – makes law defer to the politics of expertise and lends support to managerialism.[16] Deformalization is bemoaned as the anti-Kantian shift in the discipline's vocabulary, from institutions to regimes, from rules to

---

[12] See N. Duxbury, *Patterns of American Jurisprudence* (OUP, 1997), at 1.

[13] B. Leiter, "Legal formalism and legal realism: what is the issue?", 16 *Legal Theory* (2010), 111–33, at 111–12.

[14] D. Bederman, *The Spirit of International Law*, The University of Georgia Press (2002), 163 and 171.

[15] M. Koskenniemi, "Constitutionalism as Mindset: Reflections on Kantian Themes about International Law and Globalization", 8 *Theoretical Inquiries in Law* (2006) 9, at 13. See also M. Koskenniemi, "The fate of public international law: between technique and politics", *The Modern Law Review*, 1997, 1–30, at 9–15.

[16] M. Koskenniemi, "The politics of international law – 20 years later", 20 *European Journal of International Law* (2009), pp. 7–19.

regulation, from government to governance, from responsibility to compliance, from legality to legitimacy, from legal expertise to international relations expertise.[17]

In this chapter, the concept of deformalization is construed differently. In that sense, this chapter approaches deformalization in a way that departs from its common meaning in international legal theory literature. It refers here to the move away from formal law-ascertainment and the resort to non-formal indicators to identify legal rules. Deformalization is thus an attitude whereby rules of international law are not identified by virtue of formal criteria. More specifically, it boils down to a rejection of the idea that rules must meet predefined formal standards to qualify as a rule of law. This is tantamount to an abandonment of pedigree as the core benchmark of their ascertainment. Traditionally, the definition of such formal indicators – that is the *ex ante* definition of the pedigree of legal rules – has been a task entrusted to the doctrine of sources. This is why this deformalization often boils down to a movement away from the formal doctrine of sources.[18]

Alternatively, deformalization can materialize itself in a radical rejection of questions of law-ascertainment, ascertainment being seen as a process or a *continuum*.[19] Law, and particularly law-making, are viewed as continuous processes that do not, in themselves, constitute a form of deformalization. A process-based representation of law – which is embodied by descriptive virtues more than by static conceptions[20] – only

---

[17] M. Koskenniemi, "Formalism, fragmentation, freedom", Speech given on Kantian Themes in Today's International Law given in Frankfurt 25 November 2005, 7–17, available at http://www.helsinki.fi/eci/Publications/talks_papers_MK.html (last visited 29 August 2011).

[18] For a similar definition of the doctrine of sources, see D. Bederman, *The Spirit of International Law*, The University of Georgia Press, 2002, 48.

[19] For some famous support to the idea of a normative continuum, see R. Baxter, "International law and her infinite variety", 29 *International and Comparative Law Quarterly* (1980) 4, 549, 563; O. Schachter, "The twilight existence of non-binding international agreements", 71 *American Journal of International Law* (1977) 2, 296; A.E. Boyle, "Some reflections on the relationship of treaties and soft law", 48 *International Law and Comparative Law Quarterly* (1999) 4, 901, 913; C. Chinkin, "The challenge of soft law: development and change in international law", 38 *International Law and Comparative Quarterly* (1989) 4, 850, 866. A. Pellet, "Complementarity of international treaty law, customary law and non-contractual law-making", in R. Wolfrum and V. Röben (eds), *Developments of International Law in Treaty Making* (2005) 409, 415.

[20] J. d'Aspremont, "Non-state actors in international law: oscillating between concepts and dynamics", in J. d'Aspremont (ed.), *Participants in the*

generates deformalization to the extent of the accompanying rejection of formal criteria that distinguish between law and non-law or the total rejection of the necessity to ascertain legal rules, as has been advocated by some scholars affiliated with the New Haven Law School.[21]

The concept of deformalization employed here is thus restrictive and is centered around a rather limited phenomenon: the embrace of informal law-ascertainment criteria or an utter abandonment of a pedigree-based ascertainment theory of law. So defined, deformalization is not used here to refer to norm-making by informal non-territorial networks as is sometimes the case in the literature.[22] That said, while not constituting a catch phrase for these informal non-territorial networks, deformalization of law-ascertainment is not entirely alien to them as this concept is used in this chapter to designate one of these scholarly attitudes that allow the normative practice of these non-territorial networks to be captured by international lawyers. Likewise, deformalization here does not refer to the attempts to lay bare the formal camouflage of legal rationality.[23] Indeed, the legal realist critique[24] – which has raised objections against the "abuse of logic",[25] the "abuse of deduction"[26] and the "mechanical jurisprudence"[27] – and the amplification[28] thereof brought about by

---

*International Legal System – Multiple Perspectives on Non-State Actors in International Law* (2011), 1.

[21] In the same vein, see G.J.H. Van Hoof, *Rethinking the Sources of International Law* (1983), 283. See also one of the grounds of the criticisms of F. Kratochwil, *Rules Norms and Decisions: On the Conditions of Practical and Legal Reasoning in International Relations and Domestic Affairs* (1989), 194–200.

[22] M. Koskenniemi, "Constitutionalism as a mindset: reflections on Kantian themes about international law and globalization", 8 *Theoretical Inquiries in Law* (2007), 1, 9, 13.

[23] This is how formalism is most commonly understood. See e.g. C.C. Goetsch, "The future of legal formalism", 24 *American Journal of Legal History* (1980), 3, 221. See also E.J. Weinrib, "Legal formalism", in D. Patterson (ed.) *A Companion to Philosophy of Law and Legal Theory* (1999), 332–42. See also the remarks of O. Corten, *Méthodologie du droit international public* (2009), 57.

[24] On the realist criticisms of formalism as a theory of legal reasoning in adjudication, see gen. A.J. Sebok, "Misunderstanding positivism", 93 *Michigan Law Review* (1995), 7, 2054, esp. 2071. On the idea that realism and formalism are not necessarily antithetical, see N. Duxbury, *Patterns of American Jurisprudence* (OUP, 1997), at 64.

[25] *Id.*, 2093

[26] D. Kennedy, *The Rise and Fall of Classical Legal Thoughts* (2006), xviii.

[27] This is the famous expression of Roscoe Pound, see. R. Pound, "Mechanical jurisprudence", 8 *Columbia Law Review* (1908), 8, 605.

approaches affiliated with deconstructivism and critical legal studies[29] have long exposed formal legal argumentation as an illusion and thwarted the idea that a formal immanent rationality actually exists. It is under their influence that international lawyers, although not denying its bearing upon legitimacy and authority of judicial decisions,[30] have lost faith in the mathematically formal predictability in the behavior of law-applying authorities. If it were simply to recall this move away from the faith in the immanent rationality of formal legal reasoning, deformalization would be a very banal concept. It is thus not as a forsaking of formal reasoning in legal argumentation that deformalization is associated with here. Albeit the deformalization of the vocabulary of the discipline will often be the reflection of a deformalization of law-identification, deformalization, for the sake of the argument made here, is more simply construed as the rejection of formal indicators to identify international legal rules.

---

[28] For a challenge of the kinship between realism and critical legal studies, see N. Duxbury, *Patterns of American Jurisprudence* (OUP, 1997), at 425.

[29] See e.g. D. Kennedy, "The disciplines of international law and policy", 12 *Leiden Journal of International Law* (1999), 9, 84; D. Kennedy, "When renewal repeats: thinking against the box", 32 *New York University Journal of International Law & Politics* (2000), 2, 335; M. Koskenniemi, *The Gentle Civilizer of Nations: The Rise and Fall of International Law 1870–1960* (2002), 502 [Koskenniemi, *Gentle Civilizer*]; M. Koskenniemi, *From Apology to Utopia: The Structure of International Legal Argument* (2005), 306, [Koskenniemi, *Apology to Utopia*]; N. Purvis, "Critical legal studies in public international law", 32 *Harvard Journal of International Law* (1991), 1, 81; T. Skouteris, "Fin de NAIL: new approaches to international law and its impact on contemporary international legal scholarship", 10 *Leiden Journal of International Law* (1997), 3, 415–20; T. Skouteris, *The Notion of Progress in International Law Discourse* (2008), chapter 3, later published as *The Notion of Progress in International Law Discourse* (2010), [Skouteris, *Notion of Progress*]; for a similar interpretation of formalism from the vantage point of critical legal studies, see I. Scobbie, "Towards the elimination of international law: some radical scepticism about sceptical radicalism", 61 *British Yearbook of International Law* (1990), 339, 345.

[30] See E.J. Weinrib, "Legal formalism: on the immanent rationality of law", 97 *Yale Law Journal* (1988), 6, 949; S.V. Scott, "International law as ideology: theorizing the relationship between international law and international politics", 5 *European Journal of International Law* (1994), 3, 313, esp. 322. See also the remarks of Koskenniemi, "What is international law for?", in M. Evans (ed.), *International Law*, 2nd ed. (2006), 57, 69.

## 2. Deformalization and Traditional Doctrine of Sources of International Law

At this preliminary stage, it is necessary to spell out how the traditional theory of international law accommodates deformalization defined above. The following paragraphs make the somewhat iconoclastic argument that the traditional doctrine of international law's sources has long encompassed informal law-ascertainment mechanisms. In that sense, contrary to mainstream understanding, they argue that the traditional doctrine of sources already encapsulates some forms of deformalization. Thus, the contemporary deformalization that this chapter depicts should not been seen as a radical rupture from traditional sources doctrine.

The idea that international law is grounded in a doctrine of formal sources is an achievement of twentieth-century scholars. Indeed, to a great majority, twentieth-century scholars did not share their nineteenth-century predecessors' belief that international law rests on the consent of states.[31] They posited the theory that the will of the state is the most obvious *material source* of law,[32] and, subject to a few exceptions,[33] agreed that natural law does not constitute a source of law per se, even if the content of rules may reflect principles of morality.[34] The main

---

[31] One of the first most complete expressions of this formal consensual understanding of international law has been offered by D. Anzilotti, *Corso di diritto internazionale* (1923), 27. For a more recent manifestation of the voluntary nature of international law, see P. Weil, "Vers une normativité relative en droit international", 87 *Revue Générale de Droit International Public* (1982), 1, 5.

[32] On the distinction between material and formal sources, see gen. L. Oppenheim, *International Law*, Vol. 1, (1955), 24; G. Fitzmaurice, "Some problems regarding the formal sources of international law", in M. Nijhoff (ed.), *Symbolae Verzijl*, (1958), 153.

[33] See e.g. L. Le Fur, "La théorie du droit naturel depuis le XVIIème siècle et la doctrine moderne", 18 *Collected Courses* (1927), 3, 259–442.

[34] C. Rousseau, *Principes généraux du droit international public* (1944), 32–3; J. Basdevant, "Règles générales du droit de la paix", 58 *Collected Courses* (1936), 4, 477–8. See also A. D'Amato, "What 'counts' as law?", in N.G. Onuf (ed.), *Law-Making in the Global Community* (1982), 83, 90. This idea was not fundamentally challenged in the early twenty-first century. See P.-M. Dupuy, "L'unité de l'odre juridique international: cours général de droit international public", 297 *Collected Courses* (2002), 9, 31–2 and 200–202. See J. Verhoeven, "Considérations sur ce qui est commun", 334 *Collected Courses* (2008), 15, 110; A. Orakhelashvili, *The Interpretation of Acts and Rules in Public International Law* (2008), 51 [Orakhelashvili, *International Law*]; A. Orakhelashvili, "Natural law and justice", *Max Planck Encyclopedia of Public International Law*,

difference between nineteenth-century and twentieth-century international legal scholars lies in the fact that the latter tried to devise formal law-ascertainment criteria with which to capture state consent.[35] This is precisely how twentieth-century scholars ended up basing the recognition of international legal rules in a doctrine of allegedly formal sources[36] – a construction that continues to enjoy a strong support among twenty-first-century scholars.[37] It is true that the terminology of "source" is not always considered adequate to describe how international legal rules are ascertained[38] and a varying terminology – sources *sensu stricto,*[39] formal validation[40] or formal law-creating processes[41] – is found in the literature. Regardless of the terminology's variations, there is little dispute that, despite some occasional but significant exceptions, a great majority of twentieth-century scholars adhered to a formal law-ascertainment blueprint.[42]

---

para. 33, available at http://www.mpepil.com/subscriber_article?script=yes&id=/epil/entries/law9780199231690e730&recno=1&searchType=Quick&query=Orakhela
shvili+Natural+Law+and+Justice (last visited 11 August 2011).

[35] See the refinement of the theory of consent by Elias and Lim, O.A. Elias and C.H. Lim, *The Paradox of Consensualism in International Law* (1998).

[36] See gen. A. Pellet, "Cours général: le droit international entre souveraineté et communauté internationale", 2 *Anuário Brasileiro de Direito Internacional* (2007), 1, 12, esp. 15, 19 and 31; G. Buzzini, "La théorie des sources face au droit international général", 106 *Revue générale de droit international public* (2002), 581, esp. 584–90.

[37] See e.g. Orakhelashvili, *International Law, supra* note 34, 51–60.

[38] See e.g. Buzzini, *supra* note 36, 581; R. Quadri, *Diritto internazionale pubblico* (1968), 107, referred to by H.W. Thirlway, *International Customary Law and Codification: An examinating of the continuing role of custom in the present period of codification of international law* (1972), 40; A.D'Amato, *The Concept of Custom in International Law* (1971), 264; G. Schwarzenberger, *International Law*, Vol. 1, 3rd ed. (1957), 26.

[39] For Condorelli, the term sources remains appropriate even with respect to customary international law. See L. Condorelli, "Custom", in M. Bedjaoui (ed.) *International Law: Achievements and Prospects* (1991), 179, 186; see also G. Abi-Saab, "La Coutume dans tous ses Etats", in *Essays in Honor of Roberto Ago*, Vol. I (1987), 58; Rousseau, *supra* note 34, 108.

[40] See D'Amato, *supra* note 34, 83.

[41] See D.P. O'Connell, *International Law*, Vol. 1, 2nd ed. (1970), 7–8; see Schwarzenberger, *supra* note 38, 25–7; R. Jennings, "Law-making and package deal", in D. Bardonnet (ed.), *Mélanges offerts à Paul Reuter: le droit international: unite′ et diversite′* (1981), 347, 348.

[42] I concur with David Bederman that part of the problem of sources is that the latter has been codified, if not constitutionalized, in a key document of the

Yet, as explained elsewhere in further detail,[43] the idea that international law-ascertainment can be exclusively attributed to formal sources is, to a large extent, fallacious and misleading. Indeed, the doctrine of customary international law and the law-ascertainment criteria concerning international treaties, unilateral promises and other international legal acts give way to deformalization. In other words, it can be argued that the identification of customary rule as well as that of treaties is ultimately dependent entirely upon informal mechanisms. As a result, it can be said that the mainstream doctrine of sources has long accommodated some form of deformalization.

In the particular case of customary international law, it seems difficult to deny that the conceptualization of the ascertainment of customary international law within mainstream scholarship has always rested on informal criteria. Indeed, in the mainstream doctrine of the sources of international law, the ascertainment of customary international law is viewed as *process-based*.[44] More specifically, according to traditional views, customary international rules are identified on the basis of a *bottom-up crystallization process* that rests on a consistent acquiescence by a significant number of states, accompanied by the belief (or intent) that such a process corresponds to an obligation under international law.[45] Yet, it has not been possible to formalize that process's recognition. Neither the behavior of states nor their beliefs can be captured or identified by formal criteria.[46] As a result, ascertainment of customary

---

international order. See D. Bederman, *The Spirit of International Law*, The University of Georgia Press, (2002), at 27.

[43] See J. d'Aspremont, *Formalism and the Sources of International Law* (2011).

[44] For a classical example, see P. Daillier and A. Pellet, *Droit international public*, 6th ed. (1999), 318. On the various conceptualizations of customary international law as a process, see the remarks of R. Kolb, "Selected problems in the theory of customary international law", 50 *Netherlands International Law Review* (2003) 2, 119, 119–50. For a recent state-of-the-art study of customary international law, see H. Thirlway, *The Sources of International Law* (OUP, 2014), 53–92.

[45] On the emergence of the subjective element in the theory of custom in the nineteenth century, see P. Guggenheim, "Contribution à l'histoire des sources du droit des gens", 94 *Collected Courses* (1958), 1, 36–59; D'Amato, *supra* note 38, 44–50.

[46] In the same vein, Koskenniemi, *Apology to Utopia, supra* note 29, 388. See also S. Zamora, "Is there customary international economic law?", 32 *German Yearbook of International Law* (1989), 9, 38; for a classical example of the difficulty of capturing the practice, see ICJ, Case concerning the *Dispute*

international law does not hinge on any standardized and formal pedigree. Like other process-based models of law-identification, custom-identification eschews formal criteria and follows a fundamentally informal pattern of identification.[47] This is why custom-identification has often been deemed an "art"[48] and why some authors have been loath to qualify customary law as a proper "source" of international law.[49] Nonetheless, ambitious attempts to endow custom-ascertainment with formal trappings have resulted in spectacular scholarly efforts to elaborate and streamline the above-mentioned subjective and objective elements of constituting a custom.[50] A fair number of these scholarly attempts have asserted that custom is a formal source of law whose rules are identified on the basis of formal criteria.[51] It is argued here that the extreme

---

*Regarding Navigational and Related Rights* (Costa Rica v. Nicaragua), 13 July 2009, ICJ Reports (2009), para. 141. On the particular difficulty to establish practice of abstention, see PCIJ, *Lotus*, Series A, No. 10 (1927), 28 or ICJ, *Military and Paramilitary Activities in and against Nicaragua* (Nicaragua v. United States of America), Merits, ICJ Reports (1986), para. 188.

[47] M.H. Mendelson, "The Formation of Customary International Law", 272 *Collected Courses* (1998), 159, 172; G. Buzzini, "La théorie des sources face au droit international général", 106 *Revue générale de droit international public* (2002), 581; this also is what leads R. Kolb to contend that Article 38 does not lay down an entirely formal system of sources. See R. Kolb, *Réflexions de philosophie du droit international. Problèmes fondamentaux du droit international public: Théorie et Philosophie du droit international* (2003), 51.

[48] M. W. Janis, *An Introduction to International Law*, 2nd ed. (1993), 44.

[49] See the discussion in H. Thirlway, *International Customary Law and Codification* (1972), 25–30. See also the remarks by Condorelli, *supra* note 39, 179–211, 186.

[50] G. Abi-Saab has compared the formalization through the two elements to a genealogy of a newborn on his state of health. See G. Abi-Saab, "La Coutume dans tous ses Etats", in *Essays in Honor of Roberto Ago*, Vol. I, (1987), 59. James Crawford understands the emergence of customary rules as a dialogue between international actors over time that include proto-legal and legal steps. See James Crawford, *Chance, Order, Change: The Course of International Law. General Course on Public International Law*, Pocketbooks of the Hague Academy of International Law, (2013), at 82–4.

[51] On the idea that customary international law is a formal source of law, see E. Suy, *Les actes juridiques unilatéraux en droit international public* (1962), 5; see G.M. Danilenko, *Law-Making in the International Community* (1993), 30. It is interesting to note that P. Daillier, M. Forteau and A. Pellet, for their part, argue that customary international law is a formal source of law because it originates in a law-creating process which is governed by international law and is itself formal. See P. Daillier, M. Forteau and A. Pellet, *Droit international public*, 8th ed. (2009), 353 and 355.

refinement of these two custom ascertainment criteria, albeit it may have given some systemic feature to the doctrine,[52] is insufficient to ensure formal-custom-identification[53] and has not transformed custom-ascertainment into a formal process.[54] What is more, in practice, these elements have been deployed and applied in an extremely liberal manner, notably by conflating the constitutive and the constative dimensions of each of them, thereby allowing international lawyers to enjoy an unprecedented argumentative leeway in connection with customary international law.[55] This has not been without exacerbating the limitations

---

[52] J. Crawford, *Chance, Order, Change: The Course of International Law*. General Course on Public International Law, Pocketbooks of the Hague Academy of International Law, (2013), at 84.

[53] One of the most famous objections to this formal conception of customary international law has been offered by R. Ago who has construed custom as "spontaneous law". See R. Ago, "Science juridique et droit international", 90 *Collected Courses* (1956), 2, 851, 936–41; some support for Ago's conception of custom has been expressed by B. Stern, "La Coutume au Coeur du droit international, quelques réflexions", in Bardonnet, *supra* note 41, 479, 84.

[54] In the same vein, see Dupuy, *supra* note 34, 166–7; P.-M. Dupuy, "Théorie des sources et coutume en droit international contemporain", in M. Rama-Montaldo (ed.), *Le Droit international dans un monde en mutation: liber amicorum en hommage au Professeur Eduardo Jimenez de Arechaga* (1994), 51, 61–3; see R. Jennings, "The identification of international law" in B. Cheng (ed.), *International Law: Teaching and Practice* (1982), 3, 9.

[55] It now seems widely accepted that modern sophistications have failed to alleviate the contradictions in the theory of customary international law. What is more a matter of concern, however, is that the new sophistications witnessed today have not really helped mend the contradictions in the theory of customary international law. On the contrary, it could be said that the simplifying moves observed in the current international legal scholarship lend even more support to the compelling criticisms leveled against the theory of customary law. It seems today that, under the guise of a greater argumentative freedom, there is an even stronger denial of the deductive process at stake in customary international law. The above-mentioned emancipatory moves further obfuscate the deductive process of custom-based argumentation, thereby exacerbating the false inductive objectivity on the basis of which customary international law is meant to produce authority. For some observations on this phenomenon, see J. d'Aspremont, *Customary International Law as a Dance Floor: Part I* at http://www.ejiltalk.org/customary-international-law-as-a-dance-floor-part-i/ and J. d'Aspremont, *Customary International Law as a Dance Floor: Part II*, at http://www.ejiltalk.org/customary-international-law-as-a-dance-floor-part-ii/; see also W. Worster, "The inductive and deductive methods in customary international law analysis: traditional and modern approaches", 45 *Georgetown Journal of International Law* (2014), 445; see also S.A.G. Talmon, "Determining customary international law:

inherent in the deformalization of the law-identification criteria found in the doctrine of customary law.

The conclusion that the doctrine of customary international law rests on the deformalization of custom-identification also holds for the ascertainment of written treaties. Indeed, although the ascertainment of written treaties is based on a formal instrument, the identification of "treaty status" ultimately remains dependent on the informal criterion in the mainstream doctrine of the sources of international law.[56] Written treaties' ascertainment is exclusively dependent upon the intent of the authors of these acts. Although the Vienna Convention is silent as to the treaty-ascertainment criterion,[57] the International Law Commission made clear that the legal nature of an act hinges on the intent of the parties,[58] an opinion that is shared by most international legal scholars.[59] The same is true with respect to unilateral written declarations, considered to enshrine an international legal rule where the author's intent to be bound can be evidenced.[60] This means that, although law-ascertainment

---

the ICJ's methodology between induction, deduction and assertion", 25 *European Journal of International Law* (2014)/(forthcoming).

[56] On the regime governing international treaties, see the Vienna Conventions on the Law of Treaties of 1969 and 1986 and the commentary of P. Klein and O. Corten (eds), *Les Conventions de Vienne sur le Droit des Traités. Commentaire article par article* (2006). On the unsuccessful codification of the legal regime of unilateral acts, see the work of the International Law Commission and the comments of J. d'Aspremont, "Les travaux de la commission du droit international relatifs aux actes unilatéraux", 109 *Revue générale de droit international public* (2005), 163–89.

[57] Fitzmaurice had explicitly made a distinction between the law-ascertainment criterion and the consequence of an agreement being ascertained as a treaty. See ILC Report, A/3159 (F) (A/11/9), 1956, chp. III(I), para. 34.

[58] ILC Report A/6309/Rev.1 (F) (A/21/9), 1966, part I (E), paras 11–12, and part II, chp. II, paras 9–38; see however Fitzmaurice who sought to make it an explicit criterion: ILC Report, A/3159 (F) (A/11/9), 1956, chp. III (I), para. 34.

[59] Among others, see A. Aust, *Modern Treaty Law and Practice*, 2nd ed. (2007), 20; R. Jennings and A. Watts (eds), *Oppenheim's International Law*, Vol. I (1992), 1202; J. Klabbers, *The Concept of Treaty in International Law* (1996), 68; M. Fitzmaurice, "The identification and character of treaties and treaty obligations between states in international law", 73 *British Yearbook of International Law* (2003), 141, 145 and 165–6; Orakhelashvili, *International Law*, supra note 34, 59; J.-P. Jacqué, *Elements pour une théorie de l'acte juridique en Droit international public* (1972), 121.

[60] ICJ, *Nuclear Tests* case (Australia v. France), 20 December 1974, para. 43: "When it is the intention of the State making the declaration that it should

remains, on the surface, formal because it hinges on the existence of a written instrument, the legal nature of that instrument is itself determined on the basis of an informal criterion: *intent*.[61] Nothing could be more at odds with formal law-identification than the omission of a linguistic or tangible manifestation of intent as a prerequisite in intent-based law-ascertainment. Indeed such a criterion ultimately bases the identification of international legal acts on a fickle and indiscernible psychological element and inevitably brings about the same difficulties as those encountered in the ascertainment of oral promises and oral treaties. It can thus be said that the identification of a written treaty – and other legal acts – has remained a deeply speculative operation aimed at reconstructing the author(s)' intent.[62]

In the light of the mainstream theories of customary international law and treaties, the argument can be made that deformalization is certainly not unknown in the traditional doctrine of sources. Deformalization has been with us for quite some time. The contention made in this chapter is however that these traditional non-formal law-ascertainment models have now been amplified by new types of deformalization. The following section attempts to describe the latest manifestations of deformalization.

## II. CONTEMPORARY MANIFESTATIONS OF DEFORMALIZATION

Deformalization, be it the rejection of formal law-ascertainment and the embrace of informal law-identification criteria or the utter abandonment of law-ascertainment, has grown more diverse and complex in the international legal scholarship. A comprehensive description of all the forms of deformalization of international law-ascertainment would certainly exceed the scope of this chapter. This chapter is only concerned with the most common expressions of deformalization in the theory of the sources of international law. The chapter will turn upon the remnants of substantive validity theories which bring about a deformalization of law-identification (1) as well as effect-based (2) and process-based (3)

---

become bound according to its terms, that intention confers on the declaration the character of a legal undertaking". See Suy, *supra* note 51, 28.

[61] See e.g. Orakhelashvili, *International Law*, *supra* note 34, 59–60.

[62] In the same vein see Klabbers, *supra* note 59, 11. See also the remarks of Danilenko, *supra* note 51, 57 (who pleads for the necessity of a formal act of acceptance).

conceptions of international law. A few words will also be said about the general acceptance of the notion of soft law (4).

## 1. Contemporary Persistence of Substantive Validity

Despite being the object of compelling objections from international legal scholars, the idea of substantive validity continues to thrive. Substantive validity's persistence is illustrated by the work of those scholars who, faced with the impossibility to resort to formal identification criteria of customary international law, have designed a doctrine of customary international law that is informed by moral or ethical criteria.[63] According to this view, customary international rules ought to be ascertained by virtue of some fundamental ethical principles.[64]

The work of some radical contemporary liberal scholars,[65] especially those who have been labelled as "anti-pluralists",[66] warrants mention. Indeed, the allegedly Kantian foundations of their understanding of international law have led some to revive the classical kinship between

---

[63] See J. Tasioulas, "Customary international law and the quest for global justice", in A. Perreau-Saussine and J.-B., Murphy (eds), *The Nature of Customary Law* (2007), 307; J. Tasioulas, "In defence of relative normativity: communitarian values and the Nicaragua case", 16 *Oxford Journal of Legal Studies* (1996) 1, 85; see also B.D. Lepard, *Customary International Law, A New Theory with Practical Applications* (2010), esp. 77. This echoes some isolated proposals made at the time of the drafting of Article 38. See e.g. the Argentinian amendment to draft Article 38 according to which customary international should be construed as "evidence of a practice founded on principles of humanity and justice, and accepted as law", League of Nations, Documents Concerning the Action Taken by the Council of the League of Nations under Article 14 of the Covenant and the Adoption of the Assembly of the Statute of the Permanent Court (1921), 50. For a criticism of this understanding of custom, see J. Beckett, "Behind relative normativity: rules and process as prerequisite of law", 12 *European Journal of International Law* (2001), 4, 627.

[64] *Id.*, 648

[65] Liberalism in American legal scholarship is often associated with the exodus of the German legal science which enriched the expanding US legal scholarship. In that sense, the Kantian-grounded liberal cosmopolitan views of many of the most important educational institutions of US elites was considerably reinforced by this influx of scholars: S. Oeter, "The German influence on public international law", in Société francaise pour le droit international, *Droit international et diversité des cultures juridiques* (2008), 29, 38.

[66] G. Simpson, "Two liberalisms", 12 *European Journal of International Law* (2001), 3, 537.

morality and international law.[67] It is fair to say that, in doing so, these scholars have embraced a law-identification blueprint based on substantive validity.[68]

International case-law is occasionally informed by naturalist approaches of law-ascertainment as well. A good illustration is provided by the conception of customary international law advocated by the International Tribunal for the Former Yugoslavia. Although its case-law on this point is admittedly inconsistent, the tribunal deemed that the "demands of humanity or the dictates of public conscience" could be conducive to the creation of a new rule of customary international law, even when practice is scant or non-existent.[69]

Although formal criteria are not entirely absent from Brunnée and Toope's articulation, their transposition of Fuller's theory to international law can also be viewed as an expression of a substantive validity theory leading to a deformalization of law-ascertainment.[70] Although modern natural law theory in international law, like most modern natural law theory, has been more concerned with the authority of law than the identification of international legal rules, these two authors have made use of Fuller's eight procedural criteria in a way that leads them to elevate the "fidelity to law" into a law-ascertainment criterion. Indeed, Fuller's eight criteria of legality, in their view, "are not merely signals, but are conditions for the existence of law".[71] They "create legal obligation".[72] Yet, it must be emphasized that, in the eyes of these authors, Fuller's criteria of legality are not themselves the direct law-ascertaining criteria. They are solely "crucial to generating a distinctive legal legitimacy and a sense of commitment ... among those to whom

---

[67] The most famous example is F. Tesón, "The Kantian theory of international law", 92 *Columbia Law Review* (1992), 1, 53. See also F. Tesón, *A Philosophy of International Law* (1998). On Tesón's understanding of international law, see G.J. Simpson, "Imagined consent: democratic liberalism in international legal theory", 15 *Australian Yearbook of International Law* (1994), 103, 116. For a criticism of Tesón from a natural law standpoint, see A. Buchanan, *Justice, Legitimacy and Self-Determination. Moral Foundations for International Law* (2007), 17–18.

[68] For a criticism see P. Capps, "The Kantian project in modern international legal theory", 12 *European Journal of International Law* (2001), 5, 1003.

[69] *Prosecutor v. Kupreskic*, Case No. IT-95-16-T, 14 January 2000, para. 527.

[70] See J. Brunnée and S.J. Toope, *Legitimacy and Legality in International Law. An Interactional Account* (2010).

[71] *Id.*, 41.

[72] *Id.*, 7.

law is addressed".[73] In that sense, it is rather the "adherence to law" that is the central indicator by which international legal rules ought to be identified. Accordingly, Brunnée and Toope's theory comes down to a mix of the substantive validity and effect-based concepts of international law. The deformalization of law-ascertainment conveyed by their theory is thus as much the result of their resort to substantive validity as to a theory of international law whereby law is restricted to what generates a sense of obligation among the addressees of its rules.

The resilience of the idea of substantive validity discussed here contributes to the contemporary deformalization of law-ascertainment, as the ethical or moral law-identification criteria that they employ are made informal law-identification parameters.

## 2. Effect- (or Impact-) based Conceptions of International Law-ascertainment

The most common informal law-ascertainment framework is found in effect- (or impact-) based approaches of international law which have been embraced by a growing number of international legal scholars.[74] For these scholars, what matters is "whether and how the subjects of norms, rules, and standards come to accept those norms, rules and standards ... [and] if they treat them as authoritative, then those norms can be treated as ... law".[75] In their view, any normative effort to influence international actors' behavior, if it materializes in the adoption of an international instrument, should be viewed as part of international law. Such an effect- (or impact-) based conception of international law – which entails a shift from the perspective of the norm-maker to that of the norm-user – has itself taken various forms. For instance, it has led to conceptions whereby

---

[73] *Id.*, 7.

[74] For a few examples see J.E. Alvarez, *International Organizations as Law-makers* (2005); J. Brunnée and S.J. Toope, "International law and constructivism, elements of an international theory of international law", 39 *Columbia Journal of Transnational Law* (2000–2001), 19, 65. These effect-based approaches must be distinguished from the subtle conception defended by Kratochwil based on the *principled rule-application* of a norm which refers to the explicitness and contextual variation in the reasoning process and the application of rules in "like" situations in the future. See Kratochwil, *supra* note 21, 206–8. See also F. Kratochwil, "Legal theory and international law", in D. Armstrong (ed.), *Routledge Handbook of International Law* (2009), 1, 58.

[75] On that approach, see the remarks of J. Klabbers, "Law-making and constitutionalism", in J. Klabbers, A. Peters and G. Ulfstein (eds), *The Constitutionalization of International Law* (2009).

compliance is elevated to the law-ascertaining yardstick.[76] It has also resulted in behaviorist approaches to law where only the "normative ripples" that norms can produce seem to be crucial.[77] Whatever their actual manifestations, effect- (or impact-) based approaches to law-ascertainment have proliferated throughout in contemporary international legal scholarship.

The use of the effect or impact of norms to identify rules has not only been observed in studies about the traditional forms of international law-making. Attention must be paid here to two well-known research projects which, although not directly centered on international law but on the new forms of contemporary norm-making, show how international

---

[76] See e.g. Brunnée and Toope, *supra* note 10, 68: "We should stop looking for the structural distinctions that identify law, and examine instead the processes that constitute a normative continuum bridging from predictable patterns of practice to legally required behavior". The same authors argue: "Once it is recognized that law's existence is best measured by the influence it exerts, and not by formal tests of validity rooted in normative hierarchies, international lawyers can finally eschew the preoccupation with legal pedigree (sources) that has constrained creative thinking within the discipline for generations", Brunnée and Toope, *supra* note 10, 65. As has been argued above, their interactional account of international law is nonetheless based on both substantive validity and the impact of rules on actors. For a more elaborated presentation of their interaction theory, see Brunnée and Toope, *supra* note 70.

[77] Alvarez, *supra* note 74. Alvarez argues: "Although we have turned to such institutions for the making of much of today's international law, the lawyers most familiar with such rules remain in the grip of a positivist preoccupation with an ostensibly sacrosanct doctrine of sources, now codified in article 38 of the Statute of the International Court of Justice, which originated before most modern IOs were established and which, not surprisingly, does not mention them", Alvarez, *supra* note 74, Preface x. He adds, "we continue to pour an increasingly rich normative output into old bottles labeled treaty, custom, or (much more rarely) general principles. Few bother to ask whether these state-centric sources of international law, designed for the use of judges engaged in a particular task, remain a viable or exhaustive description of the types of international obligations that matter to a variety of actors in the age of modern IOs", Alvarez, *supra* note 74, Preface x–xi. He exclusively focuses on the normative impact and "the ripples" of norms, see Alvarez, *supra* note 74, Preface xiii, 63, 122. A similar account can be found in D.J. Bederman, "The souls of international organizations: legal personality and the lighthouse at Cape Spartel", 36 *Virginia Journal of International Law* (1996) 2, 275, 372; N. White, "Separate but connected: inter-governmental organizations and international law", 5 *International Organizations Law Review* (2008), 1, 175, esp. 181–6.

norms are being ascertained by virtue of their effect or impact: the Heidelberg research project on the Exercise of Public Authority by International Institutions and Global Administrative Law project. It is true that, because of the specificities of the normative phenomenon with which these two projects deal, the use of an informal benchmark of norm-identification in their studies is absolutely central. They nevertheless illustrate how, outside the classical realm of international law, effect- (or impact-) based approaches of norm-ascertainment are thriving.

Some very subtle and elaborate effect- (or impact-) based norm-ascertainment models informed by the need to continuously ensure the legitimacy of the exercise of public authority at the international level have, for instance, been defended by Armin von Bogdandy, Philipp Dann and Matthias Goldmann within the framework of the Heidelberg research project on the Exercise of Public Authority by International Institutions. Their model of norm-ascertainment is not strictly based upon the impact of the examined norms but rather the expected impact that these norms create.[78] Drawing on such an expectations-based conception to capture norm-making outside the traditional international law-making blueprint, these scholars have attempted to devise "general principles of international public authority"[79] with a view to fostering both the effectiveness and the legitimacy of international public authority.[80] These endeavors have not gone so far as to claim that any exercise of international public authority should be construed as law. The use of informal criterion – like the impact of norms – is designed to capture expressions of norm-making which do not, strictly speaking, constitute international legal rules and are unidentifiable as such by virtue of formal criteria. However, their "legal conceptualization"[81] reflects a deformalization of norm-identification[82] necessary to ensure the legitimacy of the

---

[78] See also M. Goldmann, "Inside relative normativity: from sources to standards instruments for the exercise of international public authority", 9 *German Law Journal* (2008) 11, 1865 and A. von Bogdandy, P. Dann and M. Goldmann, "Developing the publicness of public international law: towards a legal framework for global governance activities", 9 *German Law Journal* (2008), 11, 1375.

[79] Bogdandy, Dann and Goldmann, *supra* note 78, 1375. With respect to the development of "standard instruments", see A. von Bogdandy, "General principles of international public authority: sketching a research field", 9 *German Law Journal* (2008), 11, 1909. See Goldmann, *supra* note 78, 1865.

[80] Goldmann, *supra* note 78, 1867.

[81] *Id.*, 1865.

[82] Bogdandy, Dann and Goldmann, *supra* note 78, 1376.

exercise of international public authority.[83] Interestingly, the deformalization of law-identification that inevitably accompanies the conceptualization at the heart of this project is only meant to be temporary, since these scholars' ultimate aim is to re-formalize the identification of those "alternative instruments".[84]

Global Administrative Law also warrants mention. Although it is primarily focused on alternative modes of norm-making and not on international law, it captures the normative product of these processes through an effect- (or impact-) based conception of norm-ascertainment. In particular, Global Administrative Law is premised on the idea that, regarding these alternative modes of norm-making, problems of law-ascertainment cannot be fully resolved.[85] This is unsurprising since those norms cannot be ascertained under the classical doctrine of the sources.[86] Global Administrative Law accordingly resorts to informal benchmarks, particularly effect- (or impact-) based criteria, to identify what it considers a normative product.[87] Interestingly the principles that these norms are subject to are themselves identified through substance-based criteria, especially under the principle of publicness.[88] Although some of its leading figures have curiously professed that Global Administrative Law

---

[83] Goldmann, *supra* note 78, 1866–8.

[84] *Id.*, 1867–8.

[85] See B. Kingsbury, N. Krisch and R. Steward, "The emergence of global administrative law", 68 *Law and Contemporary Problems* (2005), 3 and 4, 15–61, 29; C. Harlow, "Global administrative law: the quest for principles and values", 17 *European Journal of International Law* (2006), 1, 187, 197–214. According to Kingsbury, global administrative law rests on an "extended Hartian conception of law" which elevates publicness to a constitutive element of law. According to that view, publicness is a necessary element in the concept of law under modern democratic conditions. By publicness, Kingsbury means the claim made for law that it has been wrought by the whole society, by the public, and the connected claim that law addresses matters of concerns to the society as such. See Kingsbury, "The concept of 'law' in global administrative law", 20 *European Journal of International Law* (2009), 1, 23, 29–31 [Kingsbury, Concept of Law].

[86] Kingsbury, Krisch and Steward, *supra* note 85, 25–6.

[87] "The legal mechanisms, principles and practices, along with supporting social understandings, that promote or otherwise affect the accountability of global administrative bodies, in particular by ensuring that these bodies meet adequate standards of transparency, consultation, participation, rationality and legality and by providing effective review of the rules and decisions these bodies make", Kingsbury, *supra* note 85, 25.

[88] Kingsbury, Krisch and Steward, *supra* note 85, 30–31.

bespeaks a Hartian conception of law,[89] Global Administrative Law can be understood as resting on a subtle use of both effect- (or impact-) and substance-based norm-ascertainment indicators.

I shall return to this and the Heidelberg research project in section V to show that, despite their reliance on some preliminary deformalization to define new forms of normative exercises, these undertakings ultimately seek to develop formal procedures and standards for regulatory decision-making outside traditional domestic and international frameworks in order to promote a formalization of global normative processes.[90] That said, it is noteworthy that they rely on a preliminary two-fold deformalization of norm-ascertainment in order to define their object of study. First, the impact that the normative activities they capture is not subject to formal identification for it necessitates that one looks at the behavior of actors – an approach which Judge Ago had famously criticized in his separate opinion in the *Nicaragua Case*.[91] Second, the actors whose behavior is impacted have also remained free of any formal definition – which is hardly surprising for even the state in mainstream doctrine has proven to be indefinable through formal criteria as was discussed in Chapter 1.

Interestingly, and somewhat paradoxically, all the abovementioned effect- (or impact-) based approaches to law-ascertainment resemble the compliance-based approaches of international law found in theories according to which law only exists to the extent with which it is complied.[92] It is equally noteworthy that the success of these effect- (or impact-) based approaches to law-ascertainment in contemporary legal scholarship has not been without consequence for the general research agenda of international legal scholars, since effect- (or impact-) based

---

[89] *Id.*, 23–57; see also B. Kingsbury and L. Casini, "Global administrative law dimensions of international organizations law", 6 *International Organizations Law Review* (2009), 2, 319.

[90] In the same vein, see S. Chesterman, "Global administrative law" (Working Paper for the S.T. Lee Project on Global Governance) (September 2009) available at http://lsr.nellco.org/nyu_plltwp/152 (last visited 29 August 2011), 3–4.

[91] See *Case Concerning Military and Paramilitary Activities in and against Nicaragua,* Separate Opinion of Judge Ago, ICJ Reports 1984, 514, 527 ("A ce sujet je dois faire ... une reserve expresse quant à l'admissibilité de l'idée même que l'exigence indéniable d'un acte forme l d'acceptation puisse être remplacée ... par une simple conduite de fait").

[92] J.L. Goldsmith and E.A. Posner, *The Limits of International Law* (2005). For a criticism of their conception of law, see the very interesting contribution of A. Somek, "Kelsen lives", 18 *European Journal of International Law* (2007), 3, 409.

conceptions have revived interest in the theory of the fairness of law. Indeed, it is uncontested that the fairness or the justness of a rule encourages compliance by those subject to it[93] – an assertion also at the heart of modern natural law theories. For this reason, effect- (or impact-) based studies have also spurred a need to bolster the legitimacy of international legal rules. The newly-devoted attention to the question of the legitimacy of international law – which was directly shored up by effect- (or impact-) based law-ascertainment theories – has further drawn the attention of international legal scholars away from the problems of effect- (or impact-) based conceptions of law, especially in the context of law-ascertainment.

## 3. Process-based Approaches of International Law-identification and other Manifestations of the Deformalization of International Law-ascertainment

The effect- (or impact-) based approaches of international law are not the exclusive manifestation of the deformalization of law-ascertainment in contemporary legal scholarship. Indeed, the general skepticism against formal law-ascertaining criteria has also led to a revival of process-based law-identification. New Haven School is well-known for its vindication of the deformalization of law-ascertainment.[94] A resuscitation of New Haven has occasionally been expressed in functionalist terms.[95] Whatever its ultimate manifestation, process-based approaches involve a significant

---

[93] See the famous account made by T. Franck, *The Power of Legitimacy Among Nations* (1990), 25.

[94] For a classical example of this type of deformalization, see R. Higgins, *Problems and Process: International Law and How We Use It* (1995), 8–10. For another illustration of the contemporary tendency to identify the law through processes, see P.S. Berman, "A pluralist approach to international law", 32 *The Yale Journal of International Law* (2007), 2, 301. For a hybrid law-ascertainment approach based on both effect and processes, see H.G. Cohen, "Finding international law: rethinking the doctrine of sources", 93 *Iowa Law Review* (2007), 1, 65. The New Haven approach to law-ascertainment has been examined above. It is interesting to note that an author like M. Reisman has however advocated the need for "authority signal" albeit in a way that preserves discretion at all stages of the law-application process. See M.W. Reisman, "International Law-making: A Process of Communication" 75 *ASIL Proceedings* (1981), 101, at 110–11.

[95] See Johnston's hybrid theory which is both outcome- and process-based. See D.M. Johnston, "Functionalism in the theory of international law", 26 *Canadian Yearbook of International Law* (1988), 3, esp. 30–31.

deformalization of law-ascertainment, for it has proved very difficult to formally ascertain the process by which international legal rules are identified.[96]

It will not be surprising that reference must be also made here to the turn to liberal individualism through global institutionalism advocated by the Manhattan Law School in the 1970s and 1980s[97] and notoriously spearheaded by Tom Franck.[98] Indeed, the Manhattan movement has generated deep structural consequences on Anglo-American scholarship and practice not only because it has brought about a move away from conceptual investigation of the self-validating nature of international law[99] but also because of its move away from formalism.[100] By allowing empirical inquiries about why States comply with international law to conveniently converge with definitional inquiries about what international law is,[101] and despite some attachment to mechanisms of symbolic validation,[102] it has made formal law identification through sources less relevant.

---

[96] On the difficulty of formally ascertaining processes, see G. Abi-Saab, "Cours général de droit international public", 207 *Collected Courses of the Hague Academy of International Law* (1987), 7, 9, 39–49; I. Brownlie "International law at the fiftieth anniversary of the United Nations: general course on public international law", 255 *Collected Courses of the Hague Academy of International Law* (1995), 9, 29; Van Hoof, *supra* note 21, 283.

[97] M. Koskenniemi, "Law, Teleology and International Relations: An Essay in Counterdisciplinarity", 26, *International Relations* (2012), 3, 15.

[98] See T. Franck, *Fairness in International Law and Institutions* 6 (1995).

[99] On the Manhattan School of International Law and especially Tom Franck's school, see the symposium in the 13 *Eur J Int Law* (2002), 901. See also D. Kennedy, "Tom Franck and the Manhattan School", 35 *NYU Journal of International Law and Politics* (2003), 397.

[100] See also J. Desautels-Stein, "Chiastic law in the crystal ball: exploring legal formalism and its alternative futures", *Lond. Rev. Int. Law*, (2014), 2 (2): 263–96. doi:10.1093/lril/lru011 – see http://lril.oxfordjournals.org/content/current; and S. Moyn, "The International Law That Is America: Reflections on the Last Chapter of Martti Koskenniemi's Gentle Civilizer of Nations", 27 *Temple International and Comparative Law Journal* (2013), 399, 405.

[101] On this aspect of the turn to legitimacy, see David Bederman, *The Spirit of International Law* (2002), 3.

[102] T. Franck, *The Power of Legitimacy among Nations*, (NY, OUP, 1990), at 92.

There are other, more marginal, expressions of the deformalization of law-ascertainment in contemporary international legal scholarship.[103] For instance, it has sometimes been argued that a rule's purpose should be turned into a law-ascertaining criterion.[104] While these – more isolated – approaches are not discussed here, they warrant mention, as they illustrate the general deformalization of law-ascertainment in contemporary international legal scholarship.

## 4. The Softness of International Law

International legal scholars have also come to acknowledge the existence of a grey zone where distinguishing law from non-law is impossible. More particularly, international law is increasingly viewed as a *continuum* between law and non-law, and formal law-ascertainment is viewed as no longer being capable of defining legal phenomena in the international arena. This occurred hand-in-hand with a conflation between legal acts and "legal facts" *(faits juridiques)*[105] in the theory of the sources of international law,[106] and the embrace of the general softness of legal concepts.[107] Indeed, the theory of the softness of

---

[103] For a more precise and systematic taxonomy of these other approaches, see Klabbers, *supra* note 75.

[104] This is what J. Klabbers has described the "Functionalist turn". For examples, see Klabbers, *supra* note 75, 99.

[105] The term "legal fact" is probably not the most adequate to translate a concept found in other languages. It however seems better than "juridical fact". I have used the former in earlier studies about this distinction. See J. d'Aspremont, "Softness in international law: a self-serving quest for new legal materials", 19 *European Journal of International Law* (2008), 5, 1075.

[106] For an early systematization of the distinction between legal acts and legal facts, see D. Anzilotti, *Cours de droit international, premier volume: introduction – theories générales* (1929). See also G. Morelli, "Cours général de droit international public", 89 *Collected Courses of the Hague Academy of International Law* (1956), 1, 437, 589; J.-P. Jacqué, "Acte et norme en droit international public", 227 *Collected Courses of the Hague Academy of International Law* (1991), 2, 357, 372. See also, M. Virally, *La pensée juridique* (1960), 93; G. Abi-Saab, "Les sources du droit international. Essai de déconstruction", in M. Rama-Montaldo (ed.), *Le Droit international dans un monde en mutation: liber amicorum en hommage au Professeur Eduardo Jimenez de Arechaga* (1994), 29, 40.

[107] I have studied that phenomenon in greater depth elsewhere. See d'Aspremont, *supra* note 105, 1075. For a sophisticated three-pronged account of the softness of international law, see K. Abbott and D. Snidal, "Hard and soft law in international governance", 54 *International Organizations* (2000), 3, 421.

international law has gained acceptance in international legal scholarship. It has been argued that not only has law become soft, but that governance,[108] law-making,[109] international organizations,[110] enforcement,[111] and even – from a critical legal perspective – international legal arguments have too.[112] The general concept of softness – especially the softness of the instrument (*instrumentum*) in which international legal rules can supposedly be contained – originates in the above-mentioned presupposition that law's binary nature is ill-suited to accommodate the growing complexity of contemporary international relations and that international law contains a very large grey zone where there is no need to define law and non-law.[113] Norms enshrined in soft instruments, for example, political declarations, codes of conduct and gentlemen's agreements, are considered as part of this continuum between law and non-law. In the traditional doctrine of the sources of international law, norms enshrined in a non-legal instrument (i.e. those norms with soft *instrumentum*) can still have legal effect.[114] For instance, they can partake in the *internationalization of the subject-matter*,[115] provide guidelines for

---

[108] K.W. Abbott and D. Snidal, "Hard and soft law in international governance", 54 *International Organizations* (2000), 3, 421.

[109] P.-M. Dupuy, "Soft law and the international law of the environment", 12 *Michigan Journal of International Law* (1990–1991), 420, esp. 424.

[110] J. Klabbers, "Institutional ambivalence by design: soft organizations in international law", 70 *Nordic Journal of International Law* (2001), 3, 403.

[111] O. Yoshida, "Soft enforcement of treaties: the Montreal Protocol's non-compliance procedure and the functions of internal international institutions", 95 *Colorado Journal of Environmental Law & Policy* (1999) 1, 95; Boyle, *supra* note 19, esp. 909.

[112] D. Kennedy, "The Sources of International Law", 2 *American University Journal of International Law and Policy (American University International Law Review)* (1987), 1, 1, esp. 20–22.

[113] On this point see particularly L. Blutman, "In the trap of a legal metaphor: international soft law", 59 *International and Comparative Law Quarterly* (2010), 3, 605, 613–14.

[114] For a sophisticated explanatory framework of the effects of soft law, see A. Guzman and T. Meyer, "International soft law", 2 *Journal of Legal Analysis* (2010), 171–225.

[115] On this question, see J. Verhoeven, "Non-intervention: affaires intérieures ou 'vie privée'?", in *Mélanges en hommage à Michel Virally: Le droit international au service de la paix, de la justice et du développement* (1991), 493–500; R. Kolb, "Du domaine réservé – Réflexion sur la théorie de la competence nationale", 110 *Revue Générale de Droit International Public* (2006), 3, 597, 609–10; B. Sloan, "General assembly resolutions revisited (forty years later)", 58 *British Yearbook of International Law* (1987), 39, 124.

the interpretation of other legal acts[116] or pave the way for further subsequent practice that may one day be taken into account for the emergence of a norm of customary international law.[117] Yet, if formal pedigree were to be the only law-ascertainment criterion, such norms would simply be legal facts. Nonetheless, international legal scholarship has witnessed a strong tendency to construe these legal facts as law.[118] The softness inherent in the growingly accepted idea of a grey zone and the elevation of the norms enshrined in non-legal instruments – which are at best legal facts – into international legal rules reinforce the current deformalization of the ascertainment of international legal rules described in the previous section.[119] Softness can thus be seen as constituting an

---

[116] See A. Aust, "The theory and practice of informal international instruments", 35 *International and Comparative Law Quarterly* (1986), 4, 787; R.J. Dupuy, "Declaratory law and programmatory law: from revolutionary custom to 'soft law'", in R.J. Akkerman, P.J. van Krieken and C.O. Pannenborg (eds), *Declarations of Principles. A Quest for Universal Peace* (1977), 247, 255. U. Fastenrath, "Relative normativity in international law", 4 *European Journal of International Law* (1993), 1, 305. See Schachter, *supra* note 19, 296.

[117] This is, for instance, the intention of Article 19 of the ILC Articles on Diplomatic Protection on the "recommended practice" by states, see General Assembly, Report of the International Law Commission, UN Doc. Supplement No. 10 (A/61/10), 1 May–9 June and 3 July–11 August 2006.

[118] A. Boyle and C. Chinkin, *The Making of International Law* (2007), 211–29; V. Lowe, *International Law* (2007), 96–7; A.T. Guzman, "The design of international agreements", 16 *European Journal of International Law* (2005), 4, 579. Pellet has hinted at the idea of a "degrade normatif", A. Pellet, "Le 'bon droit' et l'ivraie – plaidoyer pour l'ivraie" in *Mélanges offerts à Charles Chaumont, Le droit des peuples à disposer d'eux-mêmes. Méthodes d'analyse du droit international* (1984), 465, esp. 488. See also G. Abi-Saab, "Eloge du 'droit assourdi'", in E. Bruylant, *Nouveaux itinéraires en droit: Hommage à François Rigaux* (1998) 59, 62–3; Baxter, *supra* note 19, 549; R. Ida, "Formation des norms internationals dans un monde en mutation. Critique de la notion de Soft Law", in *Mélanges en hommage à Michel Virally: Le droit international au service de la paix, de la justice et du développement* (1991), 333, 336; M. Virally, "La distinction entre texts internationaux de portée juridique et texts internationaux dépourvus de portée juridique, Rapport provisoire à l'Institut de droit international", 60 *Annuaire de l'Institut de Droit International* (1983), 166, 244; O. Elias and C. Lim, "General principles of law, soft law and the identification of international law", 28 *Netherlands Yearbook of International Law* (1997), 3, 45.

[119] C.M. Chinkin, "The challenge to soft law, development and change in international law", 38 *International and Comparative Law Quarterly* (1989), 4, 850, 865.

integral part of the contemporary deformalization of international law-ascertainment.[120]

## III. MULTIPLE AGENDAS OF DEFORMALIZATION

This section seeks to illustrate that the abovementioned manifestations of the deformalization of law-ascertainment are informed by very different agendas.[121] Interestingly, similar conceptions of law-ascertainment sometimes serve contradictory agendas. This is well-illustrated by the use of effect- (or impact-) based approaches by some of the abovementioned scholars and behavioral approaches defended by (neo-) realists who, although resorting to somewhat comparable approaches to law-identification, pursue radically different aims. The following paragraphs do not seek to identify the motive behind the various understandings of law-ascertainment mentioned in this chapter. I only sketch some of the main objectives that scholars may be – sometimes unconsciously – pursuing by deformalizing the ascertainment of international legal rules.

The presentation of the agenda of deformalization attempted in the following paragraphs take an "external" point of view. It does not deal with the motives influencing the behavior of international actors engaged in international norm-making processes and those behind their choices regarding the nature of the norm which they seek to create.[122] Mention is made here of the attempts to programme the future development of

---

[120] I have expounded on the idea of softness of international law elsewhere. See d'Aspremont, *supra* note 105, 1075. See also J. d'Aspremont, "Les dispositions nonnormatives des actes juridiques conventionnels à la lumière de la jurisprudence de la cour international de justice", 36 *Revue Belge de Droit International* (2003), 2, 496.

[121] I have mentioned some of these agendas in previous works, d'Aspremont, *supra* note 105, 1075. See also J. d'Aspremont, "La doctrine du droit international et la tentation d'une juridicisation sans limite", 112 *Revue Générale de Droit International Public* (2008), 4, 849.

[122] On the reasons why international actors prefer soft law to hard law and vice versa, see gen. H. Hillgenberg, "A fresh look at soft law", 10 *European Journal of International Law* (1999), 3, 499, 501–2; see also the insightful three-tiered analysis of K. Raustiala, "Form and substance in international agreements", 99 *American Journal of International Law* (2005), 3, 581, 591–601; D. Carreau, *Droit International*, 8th ed. (2004), 205; G. Shaffer and M. Pollack, "Hard vs. soft law: alternatives, complements and antagonists in international governance", 94 *Minnesota Law Review* (2010), 3, 706, 717–21.

international law (1), expand international law (2), promote accountability mechanisms (3), unearth new legal materials worthy of legal studies (4), devise innovative legal arguments for adjudicative purposes (5), provide an explanatory framework to evaluate legitimacy of global governance (6) as well as promote legal pluralism (7).

### 1. Programming the Future Development of International Law

The most common driving force behind the deformalization of law-ascertainment is probably what could be called the *programmatic* character of the use of informal law-ascertainment criteria.[123] I hereby refer to international lawyers' use of informal criteria for law-identification with the hope of contributing to the subsequent emergence of new rules in the *lex lata*. In mind are the identification of rules which although not strictly speaking legal rules are seen as constituting an experimentation ground for future legal rules whose emergence is deemed desirable.[124] In this case, the resort to non-formal law-ascertainment is meant to be conducive to the subsequent emergence of new rules. This programmatic attitude is widespread in the field of human rights law and environmental law.[125]

### 2. Promoting the Expansion of International Law

Laying the foundation for the construction of formally ascertainable future rules is not the only driving force behind the abovementioned deformalization of law-ascertainment. The latter is also widely informed by the idea that international law is inherently good and should therefore be expanded. International lawyers tend to consider that any international legal rule is better than no rule at all and that the development of

---

[123] This argument has also been made by Blutman, *supra* note 113, 617–18. In the same vein, see M. Reisman, "Soft law and law jobs", 2 *Journal of International Dispute Settlement* (2011), 1, 25, 25–6.

[124] For an avowed programmatic use of soft law and customary international law, see R.-J. Dupuy, "Droit déclaratoire et droit programmatoire de la coutume sauvage à la 'soft law', in Société française pour le droit international" (ed.), *L'élaboration du droit international public, Colloque de Toulouse* (1975) 132; see also Pellet, *supra* note 19, 415; Fastenrath, *supra* note 116, 324; see also F. Sindico, "Soft law and the elusive quest for sustainable global governance", 19 *Leiden Journal of International Law* (2006), 3, 829, 836.

[125] See e.g. A. Pellet, "The Normative Dilemma: Will and Consent in International Law-Making", 12 *Australian Yearbook of International Law* (1988–1989), 22, 47.

international law should be promoted as such.[126] This faith in the added value of international law in comparison to other social norms is often accompanied by the belief that the cost non-compliance necessarily outweighs the benefit thereof. Seen in this light, international law is envisaged as an essential element of any institutionalized form of an international community,[127] and any new legal rule is deemed a step away from the anarchical state of nature towards a greater integration of that community.[128] Accordingly, deformalizing international law-ascertainment is seen as instrumental in expanding the realm of the international community with a view to ensuring what is seen as progress.[129] While the idea that international law is necessarily good and should be preferred to non-legal means of regulation can be seriously questioned, it helps explain how the use of non-formal international law-ascertainment has turned into a tool to expand international law. Using informal law-identification criteria is yet another strategy that complements the existing interpretive instruments developed by international lawyers to expand international law.[130]

### 3. Accountability for the Exercise of Public Authority

As previously stated, most of today's international normative activity unfolds outside the traditional framework of international law, generating norms which, according to the traditional law-ascertainment criteria of mainstream theory of the sources of international law, do not qualify as

---

[126] This was insightfully highlighted by J. Klabbers, "The undesirability of soft law", 67 *Nordic Journal of International Law* (1998), 4, 381, 383.

[127] See e.g. G. Fitzmaurice, "The general principles of international law considered from the standpoint of the rule of law", 92 *Collected Courses of the Hague Academy of International Law* (1957), 2, 1, 38; Abi-Saab, *supra* note 96, 45.

[128] On the various dimensions of this enthusiasm for the international, see D. Kennedy, "A new world order: yesterday, today and tomorrow", 4 *Transnational Legal and Contemporary Problems* (1994), 329, 336; see also S. Marks, *The Riddle of All Constitutions* (2003), 146.

[129] On the idea of progress see T. Skouteris, *The Notion of Progress in International Law Discourse* (LEI Universiteit Leiden 2008), chapter 3, later published as *The Notion of Progress in International Law Discourse* (The Hague: T.M.C. Asser Press, 2010).

[130] On the use of treaty interpretation to expand international law, see L. Lixinski, "Treaty interpretation by the Inter-American Court of Human Rights: expansionism at the service of the unity of international law", 21 *European Journal of International Law* (2010), 3, 585.

international legal rules. International legal scholars have nonetheless been prompt to identify a new phenomenon not to be overlooked within these new forms of norm-making at the international level. It is particularly by virtue of a preoccupation for the accountability deficit generated by the sweeping impact that such norms could bear on international and national actors, that international legal scholars have tried to incorporate these new phenomena into the discipline of international legal studies. Encapsulating these new normative phenomena has required the use of informal law-ascertainment. Some of them have even been exclusively focused on this pluralization of norm-making at the international level with a view to designing instruments addressing this accountability deficit. While American liberal scholars and their interest in governmental networks may have been the first to seriously engage in such an endeavor,[131] they were quickly followed by others, such as NYU's Global Administrative Law[132] and the Max Planck Institute's study of the "International Exercise of International Public Authority".[133] While, strictly speaking, the latter do not concentrate on traditional international legal rules, they rely on informal law-ascertainment criteria as part of an endeavor to address accountability deficit.

## 4. A Self-serving Quest for New Legal Materials

Deformalization of law-ascertainment also stems from international scholars' – conscious or unconscious – quest to *stretch the frontiers of their own discipline*. In that sense, deformalization of law-identification could be a means to alleviate the unease that has followed the sweeping changes in international legal scholarship. Indeed, there is no doubt today that international law has acquired an unprecedented importance in legal discourse and has proven to be an indispensable component of legal studies. Hence, universities and research institutes have significantly increased the number of staff charged with teaching and research in the field of international law. At the same time, many people have "discovered" their calling for international law. International law is now studied to an unprecedented extent. As a result, the international legal scholarship

---

[131] See e.g. Slaughter, *supra* note 7. See also A.-M. Slaughter, "Global Government Networks, Global Information Agencies, and Disaggregated Democracy", 24 *Michigan Journal of International Law* (2003), 4, 1041.

[132] See Kingsbury, Krisch and Steward, *supra* note 85, 29; Harlow, *supra* note 85, 197–214; Kinsgbury, *supra* note 85, 23–57.

[133] See also Goldmann, *supra* note 78, 1865; and von Bogdandy, Dann and Goldmann, *supra* note 78, 1375.

has mushroomed, and the number of research projects and publications on international law has soared. We presently face a proliferation of international legal thinking.[134] Although this may be viewed as an encouraging development that should be celebrated,[135] it has not come about without problems. Because of an abundance of scholars, it is much harder for each to find his or her *niche* in order to distinguish him- or herself. As a result, there are fewer unexplored fields and less room for original findings that are sometimes demanded by incongruous institutional constraints.[136] Consequently, it is now much more difficult to make a significant contribution to the field than at the infancy of international legal thinking. The greater hurdle in finding a niche has placed scholars into more aggressive competition with each other, and ignited a feeling of constriction as if their field of study is too small to accommodate all of them. This battle within the profession has simultaneously been fostered by a battle among professions and, particularly the growing interest of non-legal disciplines for subjects traditionally reserved to legal scholarship.[137] Against that backdrop, many scholars have chosen to advocate for classical international law's expansion by "legalizing" phenomena outside of international law by virtue of informal law-ascertainment criteria. The use of informal law-ascertainment criteria, in this context, has helped scholars find new subject materials and open new avenues for legal research.[138]

---

[134] This is what I have expounded on in J. d'Aspremont, "Softness in international law: a rejoinder to Tony D'Amato", 20 *European Journal of International Law* (2009), 3, 911. See also d'Aspremont, *supra* note 120. See also Raustiala, *supra* note 122, 582 (he contends that "pledges are smuggled into the international lawyer's repertoire by dubbing them soft law").

[135] The variety and richness of scholarly opinions is often seen as one positive consequence of the unforeseen development of legal scholarship. See the remarks of B. Stephens on the occasion of the panel on "Scholars in the construction and critique of international law" held on the occasion of the 2000 ASIL meeting, 94 *ASIL Proceedings* (2000), 317, 318.

[136] See contra Kennedy, *supra* note 128, 370.

[137] On the battle for controlling the production of discourse, see gen. M. Foucault, "The order of discourse", in R. Young (ed.), *Untying the Text: A Post-Structuralist Reader* (1981), 48, 52.

[138] For an illustration of that phenomenon, see e.g. D. Johnston, "Theory, consent and the law of treaties: a cross-disciplinary perpective", 12 *Australian Yearbook of International Law* (1988–1989), 109.

## 5. Creative Argumentation (especially before Adjudicative Bodies)

Eventually, reference is made to the abiding and inextricable inclinations of advocates and counsels in international judicial proceedings to take some liberty with the doctrine of the sources of international law.[139] To them, formal law-ascertainment frustrates creativity.[140] Deformalizing law-ascertainment conversely grants them leeway to stretch the limits of international law and unearth rules that support the position of the actor which they represent.[141] The use of informal law-ascertainment criteria thus offers more freedom for creative argumentation before adjudicative bodies – and even beyond.[142] This tendency – which bears resemblance to the aforementioned inclination to nurture the development of international law or to promote the expansion thereof – does not appear to conflict with the profession's standards of conduct.[143] It usually manifests itself in cases where applicable rules are scarce.[144] It commonly materializes in the invocation of soft legal rules or the use of a very liberal ascertainment of custom and general principles of law.

---

[139] See gen. S. Rosenne, "International Court of Justice: practice direction on agents, counsel and advocates", in S. Rosenne (ed.), *Essays on International Law and Practice* (2007), 97; J.-P. Cot, "Appearing 'for' or 'on behalf of' a state: the role of private counsel before international tribunals", in N. Ando, E. McWhinney, R. Wolfrum et al. (eds), *Liber Amicorum Judge Shigeru Oda*, Vol. 2 (2002), 835; J.P.W. Temminck Tuinstra, *Defence Counsel in International Criminal Law* (2009); U. Draetta, "The role of in-house counsel in international arbitration", 75 *Arbitration* (2009), 470–80.

[140] Interestingly, the same argument has been made as far as legal scholars are concerned. See Brunnée and Toope, *supra* note 10, 65.

[141] I owe this argument to an interesting discussion with Alan Boyle.

[142] This seems to be one of the reasons informing the deformalization advocated by the New Haven Law School. See M.W. Reisman, "International law-making: a process of communication", 75 *ASIL Proceedings* (1981), 101, at 113.

[143] The Study Group of the International Law Association on the Practice and Procedure of International Courts and Tribunals, *The Hague Principles on Ethical Standards for Counsel Appearing before International Courts and Tribunals* (27 September 2010) available at http://www.ucl.ac.uk/laws/cict/docs/Hague_Sept2010.pdf (last visited 29 August 2011); see also J. Paulsson, "Standards of conduct for counsel in international arbitration", 3 *American Review of International Arbitration* (1992), 214–22.

[144] For a recent example, see e.g. *Pulp Mills on the River Uruguay (Argentina v. Uruguay)*, 132–42.

## 6. Evaluating Legitimacy

Deformalization, and especially the embrace of a sliding scale, has been promoted because it provides a better tool to evaluate and identify legitimate exercises of authority. According to this position, the supposedly formal doctrine of sources does not allow to measure the legitimacy of exercise of public authority and does not permit the distinction between legitimate and less legitimate exercise of public authority.[145] Deformalization is here commended, because it provides an evaluative framework for the outcome of the exercise of power that is absent under the doctrine of sources.

## 7. The Promotion of Legal Pluralism

If legal pluralism is understood as eschewing a legal uniformity and common framework of identification,[146] the preservation of formal indicators for international law-ascertainment purposes appears to be at odds with legal pluralism.[147] In that sense, deformalization is meant to enable the development of a more pluralistic discipline that better reflects with the pluralistic international society.[148] Thus, the promotion of legal pluralism is one of the driving forces behind the contemporary deformalization.

---

[145] See M. Goldmann, "We need to cut off the head of the king: past, present, and future approaches to international soft law", 25 *Leiden Journal of International Law* (2012), pp. 33568. This is also a concern informing Global Administrative Law and the Heidelberg Project on the Exercise of International Public Authority discussed above.

[146] On the multiple meanings of legal pluralism, see N. Krisch, *Beyond Constitutionalism – The Pluralist Structure of Postnational Law* (2010), 71–8.

[147] See, however, on the possibility of withholding a rule of recognition and safeguarding pluralism, S. Besson, "Theorizing the sources of international law", in S. Besson and J. Tasioulas (eds), *The Philosophy of International Law* (2010), 163, 184; W. Twining, "Implications of 'globalisation' for law as a discipline", in A. Halpin and V. Roeben (eds), *Theorising the Global Legal Order* (2009), 44–5. On the specific question whether Hart's theory can sustain legal pluralism, see J. Waldron, "Legal pluralism and the contrast between Hart's Jurisprudence and Fuller's", in P. Cane (ed.), *The Hart–Fuller Debate in the Twenty-First Century* (2010), 135–55 and M. Davies, "The politics of defining law", in P. Cane (ed.), *The Hart–Fuller Debate in the Twenty-First Century* (2010), 157–67.

[148] For example, Krisch, *supra* note 146, 11–12 and 69–105.

## IV. THE COST OF DEFORMALIZATION

The foregoing has shown that international lawyers have found a formidable instrument in deformalization, allowing them to steer the future development of international law, expand international law, promote accountability mechanisms, devise innovative legal arguments for adjudicative purposes, or ensure greater pluralism. Yet, deformalization does not come without costs, some of which are well known in studies on customary international law and treaty law. The following paragraphs briefly sketch out the main perils associated with deformalization and, in particular, its cost for the normative character and authority of international law (1), the significance of scholarly debate (2), the feasibility of a critique (3) and the international rule of law (4). Other possible ramifications are also mentioned (5).

### 1. Eroding the Normative Character and Authority of International Law

Deformalization of law-ascertainment first comes with a high price in terms of the normative character of international law. It is widely accepted that some elementary formal law-ascertainment in international law is *a necessary condition to preserve the normative character of international law*, and thus the greater difficulty of identifying international legal rules that accompanies the forsaking of formal law-ascertainment prevents such rules from providing meaningful commands.[149] In the absence of these elementary formal standards of identification – a result of deformalization – actors are less able to anticipate, and thus adapt to, the consequences (or lack thereof) of the rule in question.[150] Likewise, short of any formal law-ascertainment

---

[149] In the same vein, see H.L.A. Hart, *The Concept of Law*, 2nd ed. (1997), 124. Hart borrows from J.L. Austin the speech-act theory and the claims of the latter regarding the performative function of language, a notion that can be understood in Hart's view by recognizing that "given a background of rules or conventions which provide that if a person says certain words then certain other rules shall be brought into operation, this determines the function, or in a broad sense, the meaning of the words in question". See H.L.A. Hart, "Jhering's heaven of concepts and modern analytical jurisprudence", in *Hart's Collected Essays in Jurisprudence and Philosophy* (1983), 265, 274–6.

[150] It is interesting to note that some authors of the New Haven School, despite advocating a deformalization and a move away from sources, recognize the need of preserving "authority signal" without which the authority of law

criteria, law-applying authorities will be at pains to evidence the applicable law in cases before them, which will further reduce the ability of actors to anticipate the consequences (or lack thereof) of the relevant rules. As a result, the rule that cannot be clearly ascertained will fall short of altering the behavior of its addresses.[151] This is why it is argued here that deformalization and its accompanying heightened difficulty in distinguishing law from non-law can debilitate the normative character of international legal rules. Normativity's preservation is not only doctrinally important[152] as it fundamentally bears upon the ability of international law to fulfill most of the functions assigned to it.[153] Indeed, many of the functions that can be assigned to international law[154] – and I do not want to prejudge any of them here – presuppose that international

---

would be imperilled. See M.W. Reisman, "International law-making: a process of communication", 75 *ASIL Proceedings* (1981), 101, at 110–11.

[151] J. Hathaway, "American Defender of Democratic Legitimacy" 11 *European Journal of International Law* (2000), 1, 121, 128–9. Although he embraces a relative normativity, M. Goldmann also pleads for some formalization in the identification of alternative instruments of law with a view to preserving its normative character. See Goldmann, *supra* note 78, 1865, 1879 ("The operator with an internal perspective cannot wait until the instrument causes certain effects, is being complied with or not, before he or she makes a judgment about its legal quality that will allow him or her to determine the conditions for its validity and legality ... Only by way of formal criteria the operator within a legal system may anticipate the legal quality of the instrument he or she intends to adopt and apply the legal regime provided by international institutional law for instruments of this kind. Formal criteria would enable the identification and classification of an instrument before its 'normative ripples'").

[152] For an account of the necessity of preserving law-ascertainment for reasons pertaining to the preservation of international law as a proper field of study, see Kratochwil, *supra* note 21, 205.

[153] D. Lefkowitz, "The sources of international law: some philosophical reflections", in S. Besson and J. Tasioulas (eds), *The Philosophy of International Law* (2010) 187, 195. For a review of some of the most important functions that international law can play, see D.M. Johnston, "Functionalism in the theory of international law", 26 *Canadian Yearbook of International Law* (1988), 3, 25.

[154] In that sense my argument also departs from that of Prosper Weil (see P. Weil, "Towards relative normativity in international law", 77 *American Journal of International Law* (1983), 413, 420–21) and bears some limited resemblance with that of M. Koskenniemi (M. Koskenniemi, "What is international law for?", in M. Evans (ed.), *International Law*, 2nd ed. (2006), 57. For a rebuttal of the idea that Koskenniemi expresses a total disinterest for the question of the functions of international law, see J. Beckett, "Countering uncertainty and ending up/down arguments: prolegomena to a response to NAIL", 16 *European Journal of International Law* (2005), 2, 213.

law retains sufficient meaning to be capable of guiding the actors subject to it. Second, normativity ought to be supported if international law is to retain some *authority*.[155]

## 2. International Legal Scholars Talking Past Each Other

The current embrace of deformalization in international legal scholarship is not foreign to the growing cacophony in contemporary scholarly debates in the field of international law. Indeed, nowadays, international legal scholars often talk past each other.[156] It is as if the international legal scholarship had turned into a cluster of different scholarly communities, each of them using different criteria for the ascertainment of international legal rules. The use of formal standards to ascertain international legal rules, which does not do away with the rules' inevitable indeterminacy, helps preserve the significance of scholarly debates about international law and prevent them from becoming a henhouse or a tower of Babel. Deformalization, to the contrary, hinders the existence of a common language among scholars, thereby making it difficult for scholars to debate about the exact same object.

## 3. Frustrating the Possibility of a Critique of International Legal Rules

Because deformalization makes the distinction between law and non-law very elusive, it frustrates the possibility of a critique of international law.

---

[155] In the same sense, Danilenko, *supra* note 51, 21. Although he phrased it in terms of effectiveness, A. Orakhelashvili seems to be of the same opinion. See Orakhelashvili, *International Law, supra* note 34, 51. S. Besson is more reserved as to the impact of sources of international law on the authority of international legal rules – a debate she phrases in terms of "normativity". She however recognizes that validity – a debate she phrases in terms of "legality" – is an important part of the legitimacy of international law. See S. Besson, *supra* note 123, 174 and 180. Although contending that formal law-identification is insufficient to ensure the authority of international law, J. Brunnée and S.J. Toope argue that the distinction between law and non-law is fundamental to preserve it. See J. Brunnée and S.J. Toope, *Legitimacy and Legality in International Law: An Interactional Account* (2010), 46.

[156] I already made this point in J. d'Aspremont, "Softness in international law: a self-serving quest for new legal materials: a rejoinder to Tony D'Amato", 20 *European Journal of International Law* (2009), 3, 911–17. See also J. d'Aspremont, "La doctrine du droit international face à la tentation d'une juridicisation sans limites", 112 *Revue Générale de Droit International Public* (2008), 849–66.

Indeed, any critique of law – whether moral, economic, political, etc. – presupposes that international rules are already ascertained. In that sense, formal law-ascertainment of international legal rules is also a prerequisite of a critique. Even though formalism in law-ascertainment does little to determine the whole phenomenon of law – and especially the content of legal rules – and only applies to the identification of legal rules, it enables the possibility of a critique of law in the first place. Short of any ascertainment – and, in my view, only formal law ascertainment provides a satisfactory ascertainment tool – less critique is possible due to the greater ambiguity shrouding the object of the critique itself.[157] It should nonetheless be made clear that, while being a prerequisite to the critique of law, formal law-ascertainment does not, however, provide a yardstick model or standard of evaluation for that critique. The standard of evaluation is entirely relative, for it stems from the critique itself and not from law-ascertainment criteria.

## 4. Impairing the International Rule of Law

Deformalization does not come without impairing the sustainability of the rule of law in the legal system concerned.[158] Deformalization arguably does away with one of the indispensable conditions for ensuring that international law reflects the rule of law.[159] Indeed, for law to be a substitute to unbridled arbitrary power, clear law-ascertaining criteria are

---

[157] W. Twining, *General Jurisprudence: Understanding Law from a Global Perspective* (2009), 27; J.S. Boyle, "Positivism, natural law and disestablishment: some questions raised by MacCormick's moralistic amoralism", 20 *Valaparaiso University Law Review* (1985–1986), 55; A. Buchanan, *Justice, Legitimacy and Self-Determination. Moral Foundations for International Law* (2007), 21.

[158] On the rule of law in international law, see gen. Société française pour le droit international, *L'Etat de droit en droit international: Colloque de Bruxelles* (2007). On the various meanings of the rule of law in the context of international law, see A. Nollkaemper, "The internationalized rule of law", 1 *Hague Journal on the Rule of Law* (2009), 1, 74–8.

[159] This point is irrespective of who is entitled to the rule of law. See the argument of J. Waldron according to whom states are not entitled to the rule of law. J. Waldron, "Are sovereigns entitled to the benefit of the international rule of law?", *NYU Public Law and Legal Theory Research Paper No. 90-01* (5 January 2009) available at http://papers.ssrn.com/sol3/papers.cfm?abstract_id=1323383 (last visited 10 August 2011), 2. See the reaction of A. Somek, "Defective Law", 5, *University of Iowa Legal Studies Research Paper No. 10-33* (16 September 2010) available at http://papers.ssrn.com/sol3/papers.cfm?abstract_id=1678156 (last visited 29 August 2011).

needed.[160] By the same token, the inability to ascertain legal rules with sufficient certainty – the consequence of the deformalization described above – permits a high degree of subjectivity in the identification of the applicable law,[161] thereby allowing "addresses" to more easily manipulate the rules.[162] This argument is echoed by constitutionalist legal scholars.[163] International legal constitutionalist approaches presuppose the existence of some elementary formal standards to ascertain the law. According to that view, without formal law-ascertaining standards, no system can sustain the rule of law. Without necessarily espousing here a constitutionalist understanding of international law,[164] it seems indisputable that the rule of law cannot be realized without some elementary law-ascertaining standards. The ascertainment-avoidance strategies that some states deliberately engage to preserve their freedom of action[165] – which allows some glaring manipulations of international legal rules – are blatantly obvious in the case of customary international law which, as has been discussed in section I, is identified by virtue of informal criteria.

## 5. Other Potential Hazards of Deformalization

The question of legal systems' viability has always been a central concern of legal theory. For instance, it has been contended that a legal

---

[160] N. Onuf, "The constitution of international society", 5 *European Journal of International Law* (1995), 1, 1, 13; F. Schauer, "Formalism", 97 *Yale Law Journal* (1998), 509; A.L. Paulus, "International law after postmodernism", 14 *Leiden Journal of International Law* (2001), 748; B. Cheng, "On the nature and sources of international law", in B. Cheng (ed.), *International Law: Teaching and Practice* (1982), 203, 206; Lefkowitz, *supra* note 153, 187, 195; see also the introductory remarks of H. Charlesworth, "Human rights and the rule of law after conflict", in P. Cane (ed.), *The Hart–Fuller Debate Fifty Years On* (2010), 43, 44.
[161] See gen. J. Raz, "The Rule of Law and its Virtue", in J. Raz (ed.), *The Authority of Law – Essays on Law and Morality* (1979), 210, 215–16.
[162] In the same vein, see Danilenko, *supra* note 51, 16–17. See also Hathaway, *supra* note 151, 121, 128–9.
[163] See e.g. C. Tomuschat, "General course on public international law", 26–9. On this aspect of constitutionalism, see the remarks of J. Klabbers, "Constitutionalism and the making of international law: Fuller's procedural natural law", 5 *No Foundations: Journal of Extreme Legal Positivism* (2008), 84, 85 and 103.
[164] I have elsewhere taken dispute with the constitutionalist understanding of international law. See d'Aspremont, *supra* note 11, 261–97.
[165] See the account made by C. Lipson of the practice of deformalization and the benefits thereof. C. Lipson, "Why are some international agreements informal", 45 *International Organization* (1991), 4, 495, 501.

system whose rules are systematically left unenforced would probably grow nonviable.[166] This issue has also been discussed in connection with immoral rules,[167] especially since Hart's famous reference to the minimum content of natural law, which – in my view – was the object of much misunderstanding.[168] Likewise, the argument has been made in the literature that, short of any elementary law-ascertainment yardstick, a legal system would prove nonviable. Indeed, formal law-ascertainment arguably contributes to the viability of the international legal system.[169] This position is certainly not unreasonable, for it cannot be ruled out that a legal system without any clear law-identification standards, in addition to failing to generate meaningful guidance to those subject to it, could be beset by insufficiencies affecting its viability. In that sense, deformalization, beyond a certain threshold, could put the viability of the legal system concerned at risk.

Deformalization could also been seen as frustrating the achievement of a formal unity of international law.[170] This concept of unity of international law has been subject to various and divergent theories.[171] It is true that, if international legal rules are identified on the basis of a unified

---

[166] A. D'Amato, "What 'Counts' as Law?", in N.G. Onuf (ed.), *Law-Making in the Global Community* (1982), 83, 85–6. See B. Tamanaha's assumption that a legal system may exist despite the fact that an overwhelming majority of those subjected to the rules live in general disregard of the vast bulk of them. B. Tamanaha, *A General Jurisprudence of Law and Society* (2001), 142–8. According to Tamanaha, the requirement of general obedience does not correspond to social reality.

[167] In the same sense, see D'Amato, *supra* note 34, 83, 84.

[168] See Hart, *supra* note 147, 193–200 and H.L.A. Hart, "Positivism and the separation of law and morals", 71 *Harvard Law Review* (1958), 4, 593, 622–3. The reference to the minimum concept of natural law has often been the object of misunderstanding. It has, for instance, been conflated with a criterion of law-ascertainment. For an illustration of a misuse of Hart's minimum content of natural law as requiring some morality in law to be obligatory, see K.E. Himma, "Hart and Austin together again for the first time: coercive enforcement and theory of legal obligation" (21 May 2006) available at http://ssrn.com/abstract=727465 (last visited 29 August 2011).

[169] This argument has been made by C. Tomuschat, "International law: ensuring the survival of mankind on the eve of a new century: general course on public international law", 281 *Collected Courses* (1999), 9, 26–9; Abi-Saab, *supra* note 96, 35. See also Jennings, *supra* note 54, 3.

[170] See gen. Dupuy, *supra* note 34, 9–489.

[171] For a survey of the various conceptions of the formal unity of international law, see M. Prost, *Unitas multiplex – Les unités du droit international et la politique de la fragmentation* (2008), 149.

standardized pedigree, they can be seen as belonging to a single set of rules. Such a set of rules can be construed as an order or a system, the distinction between the two – more common in the French and German scholarships – depends on whether international law is not a "random collection of such norms" and whether there are "meaningful relationships between them".[172] There seems to be little doubt that formal law-ascertainment is conducive to systemic unity of international law and that, in that sense, deformalization comes at the expense of that unity.

## V. THE ENDURANCE OF FORMALISM

While we witness a deformalization at the level of law-ascertainment as described in section 2, it is noteworthy that we simultaneously see formalism's resilience. In other words, the deformalization described above is accompanied by a consequent survival of formalism, albeit in various – and sometimes divergent – ways which are all too remarkable when one knows the fundamental challenge in upholding formalism.[173]

Needless to say that bemoaning the deformalization of law-identification – that is the primary function of the doctrine of sources – and warning against its possible hazards is itself informed by a certain agenda. This should certainly not be concealed or denied here. Formalism is valued by some scholars in relation to its cartographic and border-drawing virtues[174] as well as its ability to protect against interdisciplinary, managerialism, or arbitrary identification of law.[175] In that sense,

---

[172] See the conclusion of the Report of the ILC Study Group of the International Law Commission, Fragmentation of International Law: Difficulties Arising From the Diversification and Expansion of International Law, UN Doc A/CN.4/L.702, 18 July 2006, 7, para. 14 (1). See also the seminal article of J. Combacau, "Le droit international: bric-à-brac ou système?", 31 *Archives de philosophie du droit* (1986), 85.

[173] See S. Fish, *Doing What Comes Naturally*, Duke University Press, (1989), at 43 ("don't think formalism is a simple position").

[174] On the various mechanisms deployed by international lawyers to define boundaries, see F. Johns, *Non-Legality in International Law – Unruly Law* (CUP, 2013).

[175] Singh, S., "Appendix 2: International Law as a Technical Discipline: Critical Perspectives on the Narrative Structure of a Theory" (May 26, 2013). Appendix 2 in J. d'Aspremont, *Formalism and the Sources of International Law* (Oxford: OUP, 2013), pp. 236–61; University of Cambridge Faculty of Law Research Paper No. 22/2013. Available at SSRN: http://ssrn.com/abstract= 2270415.

formalism is as much politically loaded as the deformalization process outlined in the previous sections.[176]

It is with the agenda of formalism in mind that four examples of formalism's endurance are discussed here. Each pertains to a different type of formalism and, except for one example, is not restricted to the context of formalism in law-ascertainment. These four different illustrations suffice to show that, for some scholars, the deformalization of law-ascertainment described above is often a preliminary, provisional methodological step to expand the net with which they capture their object of study. Attention will be paid here to Global Administrative Law (1), the Heidelberg project on the Exercise of International Public Authority (2), and Martti Koskenniemi's culture of formalism (3). Each of them promotes a unique incarnation of formalism not restricted to the identification of legal rules. Attention is eventually paid to a new emerging stream of international legal positivism which, while accepting descriptive models informed by informal tools, strongly advocates for the preservation of some elementary formalism in law-ascertainment and is the most direct counterpoint to the abovementioned deformalization (4).

## 1. The Return to Formalism in Global Administrative Law

Global Administrative Law, briefly examined above, embodies an expression of the current deformalization of law-making. Global Administrative Law has grown very diverse and extremely heterogeneous. It is difficult to define it accurately, for it has deliberately been left undefined. It is however not unreasonable to claim that, as has been explained above, Global Administrative Law, despite still resting, among others, on "formal sources" including classical sources of public international law,[177] espouses deformalization in the form of substantive validity (publicness)[178] or effect-based ascertainment of rules.[179] However, Global Administrative Law simultaneously remains focused on the development of institutional procedures, principles and remedies which encompass

---

[176] For some criticism of the agenda of formal law-ascertainment, see I. Venzke, "Multidisciplinary reflections on the relationship between professionals and the(ir) international law", (December 4, 2013). *ESIL* (2013). 5th Research Forum: International Law as a Profession, Conference Paper No. 4/2013, p. 16.
[177] Kingsbury, Krisch and Stewart, *supra* note 85, 29–30.
[178] Kingsbury, *supra* note 85, 30 ("Only rules and institutions meeting these publicness requirements immanent in public law ... can be regarded as law").
[179] Kingsbury, *supra* note 85, 25; see also *supra* C.I.

formal mechanisms.[180] The emerging rules it refers to encapsulate formal procedures and standards for regulatory decision-making outside traditional domestic and international frameworks,[181] promoting a formalization of global processes.[182] While capturing the phenomenon at the origin of Global Administrative Law involves deformalization, its objective remains the development of formal rules and procedures.

## 2. Formalism in the Heidelberg Project on the Exercise of Public Authority

As mentioned above, the Heidelberg project on the Exercise of Public Authority rests on some very subtle and elaborate forms of expectations-based norm-ascertainment models with the goal of capturing normative production outside the traditional international law-making framework.[183] Yet, these scholars' ambition remains the elaboration of formal "principles of international public authority"[184] to foster both the effectiveness and the legitimacy of international public authority.[185] Their use of informal criteria has been designed to capture norms which are not international legal rules and are otherwise unidentifiable by formal criteria. Their ultimate aim remains a "legal conceptualization"[186] to the extent necessary to ensure that the exercise of international public authority retains its legitimacy.[187] In that sense, the deformalization of law-identification inherent in their attempt to capture new forms of exercises of public authority is accompanied by a reformalization of those "alternative instruments" and, in the same vein as Global Administrative Law, an attempt to devise formal principles of public authority.[188]

---

[180] Kingsbury, Krisch and Stewart, *supra* note 85, 27.

[181] S. Chesterman, "Global administrative law (Working Paper for the S.T. Lee Project on Global Governance)" (9 January 2009) available at http://lsr.nellco.org/nyu_plltwp/ 152, 4 (last visited 29 August 2011).

[182] In the same vein, see *id.*, 3–4.

[183] See also M. Goldmann, *supra* note 78, 1865 and Bogdandy, Dann and Goldmann, *supra* note 78, 1375.

[184] Bogdandy, Dann and Goldmann, *supra* note 78, 1375–400. With respect to the development of "standard instruments", see A. von Bogdandy, "General principles of international public authority: sketching a research field", 9 *German Law Journal* (2008), 11, 1909–39. See Goldmann, *supra* note 78, 1865–1908.

[185] *Id.*, 1865, 1867.

[186] *Id.*, 1865.

[187] *Id.*, 1867–8.

[188] *Id.*

## 3. The "Culture of Formalism"

The critique of formalism formulated by scholars affiliated with critical legal studies and deconstructivism has primarily been directed at formalism in legal argumentation[189] – rather than formal law-ascertainment itself. These scholars' work has nonetheless simultaneously – and sometimes inadvertently – delivered a fundamental critique of formal law-ascertainment models. In particular, when applied to law-ascertainment, this critique of formalism equates formal law-ascertainment criteria to a problem-solving tactic purported to avoid theoretical controversies and indeterminacy,[190] an attempt that has similarly failed.[191] As problem-solving tactics, formal law-ascertainment criteria, like formal legal argumentation, remain inextricably apologetic or utopian.[192] Yet, at the same time, some of these scholars have proved strong advocates of formalism. The best example is Martti Koskenniemi's "culture of formalism".

Martti Koskenniemi's plea for a "culture of formalism" is well known.[193] This part of his work – which is not devoid of irony – has

---

[189] See generally, Koskenniemi, *Apology to Utopia*, *supra* note 29. See also the remarks of Koskenniemi, *supra* note 30, 57, 69.

[190] M. Koskenniemi, "Letter to the editors of the symposium", 93 *American Journal of International Law* (1999), 2, 351, 354.

[191] Skouteris, *supra* note 29. According to Skouteris, "the success of the doctrine of sources cannot be attributed to its (alleged) claim of bringing closure to the perennial questions of law making and law-ascertainment. Sources talk, however, manage to capture the fantasy of an entire profession as a means of moving forward with the discipline. The idea was that, if only one was able to devise a set of finite, universally applicable formal categories of legal norms, one would be able to end the problems of indeterminacy", Skouteris, *supra* note 29, 81.

[192] M. Koskenniemi, "The politics of international law", 1 *European Journal of International Law* (1990), 4, 20–27; D. Kennedy, "A new stream of international legal scholarship", 7 *Wisconsin International Law Journal* (1988–1989), 1, 30. On the differences between Koskenniemi's and Kennedy's denunciations of the contradictions in a formal understanding of law, see D. Kennedy, "When renewal repeats: thinking against the box", 32 *New York University Journal of International Law and Politics* (1999–2000), 2, 335, 407. Kennedy emphasized that Koskenniemi's account, while echoing Kennedy's earlier work, has the advantage of dynamism, for one moves repeatedly from apology to utopia.

[193] See the famous plea of M. Koskenniemi for a culture of formalism. See Koskenniemi, *Gentle Civilizer*, *supra* note 29, 502–9. M. Koskenniemi, "What is international law for?", in M. Evans (ed.), *International Law*, 2nd. ed. (2006), 57, 69–70. See also M. Koskenniemi, "Carl Schmitt, Hans Morgenthau and the image of law in international relations", in M. Byers (ed.) *The Role of Law in*

singled him out among critical legal studies and deconstructivism because his plea is perceived as an endeavor to soften some of deconstruction's effects.[194]

From Koskenniemi's own work and the interpretations thereof,[195] this culture of formalism can be understood as a "culture of resistance to power, a social practice of accountability, openness and equality whose status cannot be reduced to the political positions of any one of the parties whose claims are treated within it".[196] It is primarily influenced by a Kantian approach to law and the world.[197] In particular, this culture of formalism, while still premised on the idea of an impossibility of "the universal", represents the possibility of universal legal argumentation as it avoids the dangers of imperialism by remaining empty while preserving the opportunity for alterative voices to be heard and raise claims about the deficiencies of the law. In that sense, it is opposed to the Kantian formalism in legal argumentation and must be construed as a "regulative ideal"[198] or an unattainable "horizon".[199] According to Koskenniemi, this culture of formalism necessarily accompanies the

---

*International Politics: Essays in International Relations and International Law* (2000), 17, 32–3.

[194] He has been categorized as a mild "crit" for attempting to domesticate deconstruction. On the distinctive aspects of the critical legal project of Martti Koskenniemi, see e.g. J.A. Beckett, "Rebel without a cause? Martti Koskenniemi and the Critical Legal Project", 7 *German Law Journal* (2006), 12, 1045, 1065. Such attempts to domesticate deconstruction have long been the object of criticisms in general legal theory. See e.g. P. Schlag, "Le hors de texte, c'est moi – the politics of form and the domestication of deconstruction", 11 *Cardozo Law Review* (1990), 5–6, 1631.

[195] Among others, see E. Jouannet, "Présentation critique", in M. Koskenniemi, *La Politique du Droit International* (2007), 32–3. See also I. de la Rasilladel Moral, "Martti Koskenniemi and the spirit of the beehive in international law", 10 *Global Jurist* (2010); J. von Bernstorff, "Sisyphus was an international lawyer. On Martti Koskenniemi's 'From apology to utopia' and the place of law in international politics", 7 *German Law Journal* (2006), 12, 1015, 1029–31; Beckett, *supra* note 194, 1045; see also the book review of N. Tsagourias "Martti Koskenniemi: the gentle civilizer of nations: the rise and fall of international law 1870–1960", 16 *Leiden Journal of International Law* (2003), 2, 397, 398–9.

[196] Koskenniemi, *The Gentle Civilizer*, *supra* note 29, 500.

[197] M. Koskenniemi, "Miserable Comforters: International Relations as New Nature Law", 15 *European Journal of International Relations* (2009), 395–422, at 416.

[198] Koskenniemi, *supra* note 30, 70.

[199] Koskenniemi, *supra* note 196, 508.

"critique" of law, for it protects the critique from being hijacked by those who previously instrumentalized the law to conceal their political goals while preserving the possibility of a universal debate. This is why the culture of formalism is a cornerstone of Koskenniemi's project, as it invites international lawyers, once they have laid bare the subjectivity of their claim, to focus on the universality of all legal claims.

Koskenniemi's culture of formalism – like the formalism discussed – is not a tool dictating the outcome of legal reasoning or providing ready-made solutions for political questions to which the law is applied. It is rather a practice or a communicative culture which aspires to the universality of legal arguments for equality and openness's sake. The culture of formalism is thus an "interpretative safeguard".[200]

While the work of Martti Koskenniemi is aimed at spurring the critique of formal legal argumentation, it is interesting, for the sake of this chapter, to note that scholars affiliated with critical legal studies and deconstructivism have themselves been advocating the preservation of some elementary forms of formalism. Whether the culture of formalism encompasses formal law-ascertainment is another question that does not need to be addressed here.

## 4. Reductionist Legal Positivism

Eventually, a few remarks must be made about a contemporary attempt to confront the deformalization described above head-on while accepting the descriptive virtues of deformalization. Indeed, there have been recent attempts to reanimate international legal positivism[201] – often in a reductionist manner.[202] These scholarly enterprises cannot be lumped together with uncritical "orthodox" positivist approaches, for they have included a move away from consensualism, the latter being seen as nothing more than another form of natural law. These attempts have simultaneously recognized the arbitrary character of their scholarly approach and have come to terms with the idea that positivism was only one of many ways to cognize international law. Some of their views are

---

[200] Beckett, *supra* note 194, 1070.
[201] See J. d'Aspremont and J. Kammerhofer (eds), *International Legal Positivism in a Postmodern World* (2014); J. Kammerhofer, *Uncertainty in International Law. A Kelsenian Perspective,* (2010); J. d'Aspremont, *supra* note 43. See also O. Corten, *Pour un positivisme critique* (2008).
[202] J. d'Aspremont, "Reductionist Legal Positivism in International Law, Proceedings of the 106th Annual Meeting of the American Society of International Law", 2012.

fundamentally value-relativist with regard to methodology and the possible content of positive regulation.[203] Another characteristic that they sought to address is the illusion of formalism which shrouds the mainstream theory of the sources of international law.[204] Some of these scholars have also recognized the benefits of the insights of TWAIL and feminist critiques as well as the studies on the dialogue between law-applying authorities, especially since these works can be used to contribute to the clarification of ascertainment's mechanisms of international rules.

Of particular interest for the argument made is that this new generation of international legal scholars has come to accept the relevance of a few deformalized models of cognition for the sake of describing some of the processes of law. To them, static formalism in itself does not provide any satisfactory descriptive framework to capture these new forms of exercise of public authority and comes with poor descriptive and evaluative frameworks.[205] They accordingly accept that deformalization may be a necessary step to make sense of a reality unable to be fully captured with formal categories.[206] In their opinion, law can also be considered a process, and law-making processes can be diverse and include different actors.[207] Yet, in their attempt to cognize the rules of the international legal system, some of these scholars have attempted to propose a counterpoint to the deformalization described in this chapter. Indeed, they suggest that the international legal order is identified through formal criteria enshrined in the rules on law-making (the "sources of law"), albeit in a different way than the current model offered by the mainstream doctrine of sources.[208] They have maintained the doctrine of sources at the centre of their modes of cognition of law, thereby claiming that the rules of the international legal system ought to be ascertained via the formal pedigree defined by a doctrine of sources. In that sense, they have distanced themselves from the project on Global Administrative

---

[203] D'Aspremont, *supra* note 11, 261–97.
[204] This has partly been the ambition of section 1 of this chapter. For an in-depth analysis of the illusions of formalism permeating the traditional doctrine of sources, see d'Aspremont, *supra* note 43, especially chapter 7.
[205] This point no longer seems contested. See H. Charlesworth, "Law-making and sources", in J. Crawford and M. Koskenniemi, *Cambridge Companion to International Law* (CUP, 2012), 187.
[206] For an example, see d'Aspremont, *supra* note 20, 1.
[207] See gen. J. d'Aspremont (ed.), *Participants in the International Legal System: Multiple Perspectives on Non-State Actors in International Law* (2011).
[208] See d'Aspremont, *supra* note 43.

Law and the International Exercise of Public Authority where the formal ascertainment found in the doctrine of sources is preliminarily discarded in order to capture the greatest possible number of new forms of the exercise of public authority. It is noteworthy that, by elevating the doctrine of sources into the cornerstone of the cognition of law, many, but not all,[209] of these authors have embraced a social approach to law well-known in British analytical jurisprudence[210] according to which the meaning of formal pedigree indicators is found in the practice of law-applying authorities broadly defined, and not exclusively restricted to judicial bodies.[211] The conclusions drawn from their theory are applicable to new forms of exercises of public authority at the international level, for the pluralization of international norm-making, including the deformalization of norm-making processes themselves, need not accompany a deformalization of norm-ascertainment.

It is probably not the place for further elaboration on the emergence of such a refreshed form of international legal positivism. The latter is still too disparate to constitute a new coherent and identifiable stream.

## VI. CONCLUDING REMARKS: THE CHOICE FOR DEFORMALIZATION

The international law's construction and disambiguation fundamentally boils down to a political decision, based on the political stakes associated

---

[209] This posture has not been espoused by all of them. See e.g. J. Kammerhofer, *Uncertainty in International Law. A Kelsenian Perspective* (2010), 226 (who argues that the social thesis presupposes the same type of absolute and external standard as natural law does).

[210] See d'Aspremont, *supra* note 45, especially chapter 7; see also Besson, *supra* note 147, 180–81.

[211] Although contesting such a social and restrictive form of positivism, B. Kingsbury and M. Donaldson have pointed out that: "the orientation of positivism towards law as a social practice makes it at least a valuable point of departure for further efforts to build a useful concept of (international) law for the current era of increasingly dense global regulatory governance, if only because it grounds a concept of law capable of regeneration from within, in accordance with changing practices that themselves will be driven not only by material interest, but also by moral and political contestations" (B. Kingsbury and M. Donaldson, "From bilateralism to publicness in international law", in U. Fastenrath, R. Geiger, D.-E. Khan, A. Paulus, S. von Schorlemer and C. Vedder (eds), *From Bilateralism to Community Interest – Essays in Honour of Bruno Simma* (OUP, 2011), 79–89, at 89.)

with each mode of disambiguation,[212] especially when no authority can decisively clinch an issue for practical purposes.[213] Accordingly, maintaining or rejecting formalism at the level of law-ascertainment is only one of several political options available to international lawyers. It has not been the intent of this chapter to advocate for or to reject deformalization.[214] Its sole objective has been to show that deformalization, for the reasons mentioned above, is prevalent in the contemporary international legal scholarship. This chapter has simultaneously sought to show that this deformalization is not unqualified and that various forms of formalism have endured. The strong deformalization discussed in this chapter thus continues to coexist with multiple forms of formalism.

The existence of such variations seems to confirm that, like formalism in legal argumentation – which, insightfully described by David Kennedy,[215] weathers periods of disuse before being revived – all forms of formalism undergo such fluctuations in international legal scholarship. This seems to be true with formal law-ascertainment as well. In that sense, it is entirely possible that the current deformalization of the identification of international legal rules may someday be survived by a more resilient formal law-ascertainment. At the same time this does not foreclose the possibility of the exact opposite. In fact, because of the growing pluralization of international law-making and the new exercises of public authority at the international level, it is equally possible that deformalization will continue unabated. It is probably hard (and useless

---

[212] L. Murphy, "Better to see law this way", 83 *New York University Law Review* (2008) 4, 1104; L. Murphy, "The political question of the concept of law", in J. Coleman (ed.), *Hart's Postscript: Essays on the Postscript to "The Concept of Law"* (2001), 371; see also L. Murphy, "Concepts of law", 30 *Australian Journal of Legal Philosophy* (2005), 1. See U. Scarpelli, *Qu'est-ce que le positivism juridique* (1996), 57; F. Schauer, "Postivism as pariah", in R.P. George (ed.), *The Autonomy of Law: Essays of Legal Positivism* (1996), 31, 34; J. Waldron, "Normative (or ethical) positivism", in J. Coleman (ed.), *Hart's Postscript: Essays on the Postscript to the Concept of Law* (2001), 410, 411–33; J. Beckett, "Behind relative normativity: rules and process as prerequisites of law", 12 *European Journal of International Law* (2001), 4, 627, 648; Beckett, *supra* note 154, 214–19.

[213] Kingsbury, *supra* note 85, 23, 26.

[214] This is something I have attempted elsewhere. See d'Aspremont, *supra* note 43.

[215] Kennedy, *supra* note 194, 335. It is interesting to note that such a finding had already been made by Hart. See Hart, *supra* note 147, 130.

to try) to predict the directions of such future trends. What matters now is that the movements of this pendulum are ultimately determined by international legal scholars' own conceptual and normative choices.

# 3. Law-making

## I. INTRODUCTION

The doctrines of subjects and sources have always proved insufficient to explain and apprehend international law-making processes. This is not surprising as their main goal is to provide a static account of the international legal order and hence they have very limited descriptive and explanatory values. It is to offset such descriptive and explanatory deficiency that international lawyers have put a lot of effort into the design of doctrine(s) of international law-making. The doctrine(s) of law-making, like those of sources and subjects, provides interesting insights on the social arrangements sought by international lawyers. This is the object of this chapter.

It has long been claimed that international norm-making has grown pluralized in the sense that it has allegedly moved away from the traditional "Westphalian" and state-centric model of law-making.[1] New processes outside traditional diplomatic channels and involving non-state actors are said to qualify as law-making, and the products thereof have come to be ascertainable as genuine legal rules.[2] Such an assertion of a pluralization of international law-making is now common, and those studies that fail to give it sufficient emphasis are demoted to obsolete scholarship.[3]

This uncontested prejudice in favor of pluralistic representations of law-making processes[4] calls for a preliminary remark that will inform the

---

[1] See gen. P.M. Stirk, "The Westphalian model and sovereign equality", 38 *Review of International Studies*, (2012), 641–60; for some critical remarks, see S. Beaulac, "The Westphalian legal orthodoxy: myth or reality?", 2 *Journal of the History of International Law*, (2000), 148–77.

[2] For a few examples, see J. Brunnée and S. Toope, "International law and constructivism: elements of an international theory of international law", 39 *Columbia Journal of Transnational Law*, (2000), 19–74.

[3] A. Boyle and C. Chinkin, *The Making of International Law* (OUP, 2007) at 97.

[4] Section 2 will offer a brief overview of the state of the literature in this respect. For some critical remarks, see J. d'Aspremont, "The doctrinal illusion of

argument subsequently made in this chapter. Although uncontested in mainstream international legal scholarship,[5] the mere finding that international law-making is now more heterogeneous, accommodates new forms of law-generating processes and gives a say to new types of actors presupposes that international law-making was, in the past, monolithic and state-centric. In that sense, the claim of the pluralization of international law rests on a strong prejudice about the state of the pre-pluralized era of law-making.[6] The empirical finding of a pluralization of international law-making, albeit being almost unanimously shared among observers and scholars, manifests a consensus on some preconceived data, that is the pre-existence of something like the Westphalian order. Needless to say that such preconceived data is itself the expression of a construction.[7]

This being said, it is not the aim of these introductory considerations to shed a radical, skeptical veil on all attempts to make sense of international law-making. While acknowledging the prejudices informing the conceptualizations of law-making in the literature, the foregoing only means to recall the uncontroversial relativity of any basic empirical or conceptual finding about law. Indeed, one cannot seriously engage with the theories of law-making – as this chapter is supposed to do – without bringing to mind such an elementary observation. Currently, it seems beyond dispute that the way in which lawyers construct not only law, but also the fact – practices of creation or application of rules – is contingent on the cognitive lens with which one has – consciously or unconsciously – chosen to look at international law.[8]

If one applies the abovementioned elementary epistemological remarks to the question of international law-making under discussion here, the

---

the heterogeneity of international law-making processes", in H. Ruiz Fabri, R. Wolfrum and J. Gogolin (eds), *Select Proceedings of the European Society of International Law*, (2010), vol. 2., Oxford, Hart Publishing, pp. 297–312.

[5] For some critical remarks, see J. d'Aspremont, "The doctrinal illusion of the heterogeneity of international law-making processes", in H. Ruiz Fabri, R. Wolfrum and J. Gogolin (eds), *Select Proceedings of the European Society of International Law*, (2010), vol. 2, Oxford, Hart Publishing, pp. 297–312

[6] S. Charnovitz, "Two centuries of participation: NGOs and international governance," 18 *Michigan Journal of International Law*, (1997), 183.

[7] See gen. A. MacIntyre, *Whose Justice? Which Rationality?* (London: Duckworth, 1988), 333 ("There are no preconceptual or even pretheoretical data").

[8] The relativity of cognitive tools is one of the paradigms of the inquiry carried out in J. d'Aspremont (ed.), *Participants in the International Legal System* (Routledge, 2011).

story would go as follows. When one wants – as most international legal scholars do – to make sense of and systematize the international law-making process, one needs to choose a paradigm through which to cognize norm-generating processes in international law. A few dominant paradigms seem to have emerged in the literature about law-making processes. They ought to be briefly sketched out at this introductory stage before they are further examined in the paragraphs that follow.

When it comes to cognizing international law-making, one of the most dominant paradigms found in the literature has been the subjecthood paradigm. Indeed, subjecthood has been used to cognize all the practices of international norm-generating processes in international law. Processes that could not be captured by virtue of the concept of subjecthood would not qualify as international law-making.[9] Subjecthood is a static model for the apprehension of international law-making processes. International legal scholarship on law-making has also given rise to another static conceptualization of law-making, one grounded in the "pedigree" of the norm produced. According to this paradigm, law-making would be any process that leads to the creation of a norm that can be ascertained as a legal rule by virtue of its pedigree.[10]

As is well known, the paradigm of subjecthood and that of formal pedigree came under the fire of the "New Haven School", whose disciples contended that subjecthood or the pedigree must be abandoned, because their inherent staticism was said not to allow one to comprehend international law-making processes.[11] International norm-generating processes should not be cognized on the basis of a static and arbitrary concept like subjecthood. Rather, a more dynamic concept, like that of participation, offers better cognitive tools to comprehend (the dynamics of) international law-making processes and their actors.[12] This old schism between staticism – associated with subjecthood – and dynamism – associated with participation – has continued uninterrupted for the last several decades, fueling immense controversy and generating reams of repetitive scholarship.[13]

Against the backdrop of a seemingly irreconcilable tension between staticism and dynamism in scholarly models of international law-making, as well as the cognitive limitations of approaches exclusively based on participation, scholars have endeavored to develop other perspectives on

---

[9] For an overview of such an approach, see below 3.1.
[10] For an overview of such an approach, see below 3.2.
[11] For criticisms of static approaches, see below 3.3.
[12] For an overview of such an approach, see below 3.3.
[13] See below 3.3.

international law-making. In particular, and as will be discussed below, new conceptualizations have attempted to understand law-making from the standpoint of the impact of its input.[14] This is the cognitive twist found in approaches informed by Global Administrative Law or the Heidelberg Project on the Exercise of Public Authority, which have already been mentioned in Chapter 2. Others, coming to terms with the abiding divide between the abovementioned static and dynamic approaches, have attempted to overcome the debate between subjecthood, pedigree, and participation by advocating a neostatic and neoformalistic pedigree-based approach to law-making. The main difference with the classic static approach originates in the pedigree being itself in constant evolution and flux, constantly allowing new norm-generating processes to be elevated to law-making status.

As demonstrated by this introductory overview, the international legal scholarship, in its quest for a paradigm able to apprehend international norm generating processes qualifying as law-making, has been oscillating between static approaches and dynamic approaches. The former are based on the author of the norm (subjecthood) or its formal origin (pedigree) while the latter (e.g., participation) try to capture and explain the intricate and multidimensional fluxes between the authors of the norms and the norms themselves (impact or dynamic pedigree). International legal scholars have thus been resorting to various and diverging paradigms to make sense of international law-making. All these approaches will be described in further detail below.

This chapter endeavors to shed some light on the reasons guiding scholars to choose one of these paradigms. After a brief outline of the mainstream empirical construction of current norm-generating processes in international law (II) and a further detailed description of the main cognitive choices found in international legal scholarship (III), this chapter elaborates on the driving forces behind each of the main paradigms permeating contemporary literature on international law-making (IV). In doing so, this chapter draws attention to the politics of empiricism and cognition with the aim of providing some reflection on how international legal scholars and practitioners have been making sense of international law-making.

---

[14] For an overview of such approaches, see below 3.4.

## II. EMPIRICAL CONCORD: THE PLURALIZATION OF INTERNATIONAL LAW-MAKING

This section recalls the main traits of the contemporary pluralization of international law-making as it is empirically depicted in mainstream scholarship. While there seems to be a consensus on the principal characteristics of the move away from the Westphalian, state-centric law-making blueprint (1), some disagreement persists regarding the extent of the resilience of states as the principal legal actors (2). All in all, however, the phenomenon of pluralization has not been disputed. As the subsequent section (3) will demonstrate, the major source of disagreement among experts has not been their empirical model to understand the practice but rather the analytical tool that they have used to reconstruct that practice and its significance for international law as a whole.

### 1. Manifestations of Pluralization in the Practice of International Law-making

The mainstream view is that, in practice, the making of modern international law has witnessed a growing pluralization *ratione personae*, for states have incrementally been joined by other actors in the law-making processes.[15] As the story goes, states have ceased to be (perceived as) the only actors in charge of international law-making. While not being an utterly new phenomenon,[16] this pluralization *ratione personae* of international law-making has, over the last few decades, reached an unprecedented degree.[17] As a result, it has become uncontested nowadays that law-making processes at the international level involve a myriad of actors, regardless of who may ultimately, formally hold the rights and obligations created thereby.[18] Consequently, normative authority is seen

---

[15] S. Charnovitz, "Two centuries of participation: NGOs and international governance," 18 *Michigan Journal of International Law*, (1997), 183. See also the brief outline of A. Boyle and C. Chinkin, *The Making of International Law*, Oxford: Oxford University Press, (2007), pp. 42–3.

[16] S. Charnovitz, "Two centuries of participation: NGOs and international governance," 18 *Michigan Journal of International Law*, (1997), 183. See also the brief outline of A. Boyle and C. Chinkin, *The Making of International Law*, Oxford: Oxford University Press, (2007), pp. 42–3.

[17] A. Boyle and C. Chinkin, *The Making of International Law*, Oxford: Oxford University Press, (2007), at 97.

[18] Ibid.

as no longer being exercised by a closed circle of high-ranking officials acting on behalf of states, but has instead turned into an aggregation of complex procedures involving non-state actors.[19] In that sense, public authority is now exercised at the international level in a growing number of informal ways that are estranged from the classical international law-making processes.[20]

Compelling empirical evidence is usually produced to underpin these conclusions.[21] On the basis thereof, it is said that, over the last two decades, non-state actors have been expanding their say in international law-making processes and they also wield some influence in the review[22] and amendments[23] procedures of conventional instruments. It is nonetheless acknowledged in the literature that, while the extent of their influence is probably unprecedented, the involvement of non-state actors is not entirely unheard of. Indeed, in a famous article, Steve Charnovitz demonstrated that NGOs have been involved in international law-making for more than 200 years.[24] Despite recognizing that the role of non-state actors in international law-making processes is not entirely new, most scholars agree that the extent of their contribution to law-making has undergone a noteworthy increase.[25]

---

[19] This has sometimes been called "verticalization". See J. Klabbers, "Setting the scene", in J. Klabbers, A. Peters and G. Ulfstein (eds), *The Constitutionalization of International Law*, (2009), Oxford: Oxford University Press, p. 14.

[20] See M. Goldmann, "Inside relative normativity: from sources to standard instruments for the exercise of international public authority", 9 *German Law Journal*, (2008), 1865–908; and A. von Bogdandy, P. Dann and M. Goldmann, "Developing the publicness of public international law: towards a legal framework for global governance activities", 9 *German Law Journal*, (2008), 1375–400.

[21] See gen. the significant amount of empirical materials provided by A. Boyle and C. Chinkin throughout their study, *The Making of International Law*, (2007), Oxford: Oxford University Press.

[22] See Article 12 of the Convention on the Prohibition of the Use, Stockpiling, Production and Transfer of Anti-Personnel Mines and on Their Destruction (adopted 18 September 1997, entered into force 1 March 1999) 36 ILM 1507 and the Dublin Convention on Cluster Munitions (adopted 30 May 2008, not yet in force) CCM/77.

[23] See Convention on the Prohibition of the Use, Stockpiling, Production and Transfer of Anti-Personnel Mines and on Their Destruction, Article 13.

[24] S. Charnovitz, "Two centuries of participation: NGOs and international governance," 18 *Michigan Journal of International Law*, (1997), 183.

[25] See gen. Gaëlle Breton-Le Goff, "NGO's perspectives on non-state actors" in J. d'Aspremont (ed.), *Participants in the International Legal System*

Besides the abovementioned pluralization *ratione personae* of law-making at the international level, other types of pluralization are mentioned in the literature. For instance, international law-making processes are said to have undergone a diversification of the types of instruments through which norms are produced at the international level, a diversification that has been perceived as either the reflection of a healthy pluralism or a daunting fragmentation.[26] The present chapter does not fully develop these contentions. It only argues that there seems to have been an overall consensus on the existence of the pluralization of law-making.

## 2. Persisting State Dominance?

While there seems to have been a consensus among authors and experts about the empirical manifestations of the pluralization of international law-making, some of them have argued that the abovementioned types of pluralization of norm making at the international level – and especially the growing participation of non-state actors – should certainly not obfuscate the fact that states have retained a strong grip over global law-making processes.[27] These scholars have argued that, in at least some contexts, states have conversely preserved their clout.[28] Such a preservation of state dominance, according to that view, may take various forms. First, it may be the result of continuous intensive law-making activity

---

(Routledge, 2011), 248–66; T.G. Weiss and L. Gordenker, (eds) *NGOs, the UN, & Global Governance* (Providence: Brown University Press, 1996).

[26] On the discourses about the pluralization of the substance of law see M. Koskenniemi, "The fate of public international law: between technique and politics" 70 *Modern Law Review*, (2007), 1–30.

[27] A. Clapham, *Human Rights Obligations of Non-State Actors*. Oxford and New York: Oxford University Press, 2006, pp. 5–6; see also d'Aspremont (2010), *supra* note 24. This is also acknowledged by A. Peters, T. Förster and L. Koechlin, "Towards non-state actors as effective, legitimate, and accountable standard setters" in A. Peters, L. Koechlin, T. Förster, G. Fenner Zinkernagel (eds), *Non-State Actors as Standard Setters*, Cambridge: Cambridge University Press, (2009), pp. 496–7; J. d'Aspremont (ed.), *Participants in the International Legal System* (Routledge, 2011).

[28] This is also an argument made by A. Boyle and C. Chinkin, "The making of international law", at 97.

through the classical state-centric convention-making system.[29] This is also manifest in the steady resort to existing institutional law-making mechanisms within international organizations – which are discussed in Chapter 4 – where states still wield sweeping influence. The best example thereof is the more frequent use by states of the UN Security Council to create wide-ranging and binding rules,[30] including rules regulating activities of non-state actors themselves.[31]

The idea of resilience of the state amidst pluralization of international law-making is said not to be limited to a greater use of the classical channels of law-making.[32] The emergence of new forms of law-making, outside the normal above-mentioned blueprints, has arguably also contributed to reinforcing the dominance of states.[33] For example, individual government agencies and actors nowadays negotiate directly with their foreign counterparts, and these intercourses are the source of new transnational regulatory networks (TRNs).[34] TRNs illustrate how the

---

[29] See for instance the area of international economic law (e.g. the overhaul of the international economic order through the Final Act of the 1986–1994 Uruguay Round of trade negotiations or the United Nations Framework Convention on Climate Change (adopted 9 May 1992, entered into force 21 March 1994) 1771 UNTS 107.

[30] See e.g., UNSC Res 1373 (28 September 2001) UN Doc S/RES/1373. On this issue, see generally S. Talmon, "The Security Council as world legislature", 99 *American Journal of International Law*, (2005), 175.

[31] See Resolution 942 (1994) – Bosnian Serb; or UNITA in Angola (Resolution 864 (1993)). On this practice of the Security Council and its ability to create obligations for non-state actors, see ICJ, Advisory Opinion, "Accordance with international law of the unilateral declaration of independence in respect of Kosovo" (Request for Advisory Opinion), 22 July 2010, ICJ Rep., (2010), paras 116–17.

[32] J. d'Aspremont, "Inclusive law-making and law enforcement processes for an exclusive international legal system", in *Participants in the International Legal System*, (Routledge, 2011), 425–39, esp. 430–31.

[33] Ibid.

[34] See e.g. A.-M. Slaughter, *A New World Order*, Princeton: Princeton University Press, (2004). A.-M. Slaughter, "Global government networks, global information agencies, and disaggregated democracy", 24 *Michigan Journal of International Law*, (2002–2003), 1041–75; see also K. Raustalia, "The architecture of international cooperation: transgovernmental networks and the future of international law", 43 *Virginia Journal of International Law* (2002), 1. For some recent critical reappraisal, see P.-H. Verdier, "Transnational regulatory networks and their limits," 34 *The Yale Journal of International Law*, (2009), 113; see also G. Shaffer, "Transnational legal process and state change: opportunities and constraints", IILJ Working Paper 2010/4, available at www.iijl.org.

power of states has been thriving outside traditional law-making frameworks.[35] This traces back, the story goes, to a deliberate attempt by states to design norms or standards outside the classical law-making processes[36] with a view to escaping the rigidity and accountability constraints – although they are limited – that accompany formal rules of international law.[37] According to that view, states remain present and influential, even in areas traditionally adverse to them, without being subject to accountability mechanisms.[38] Those recognizing the resilience of state dominance have simultaneously submitted that these developments do not necessarily contradict the unprecedented involvement of non-state actors in law-making processes.[39] These two simultaneous phenomena may simply reflect an unprecedented complexity.[40]

The idea of resilient state dominance remains controversial. Yet, such limited controversies on the remaining clout of states do not suffice to obfuscate the overall consensus according to which, from an empirical perspective, international law-making processes have undergone dramatic pluralization. This consensus at the empirical level is however where the

---

[35] Ibid.

[36] In the same sense, see E. Benvenisti, "Coalitions of the willing and the evolution of informal international law", in C. Calliess, C. Nolte and G. Stoll (eds), *Coalitions of the Willing – Avantgarde or Threat?* Göttinger Studien zum Völker- und Europarecht, Bd. 8, (2008), p. 2. See also P.-H. Verdier, "Transnational regulatory networks and their limits", 34 *The Yale Journal of International Law*, (2009), 113, pp. 171–2.

[37] Compensating for the lack of accountability of these new forms of law-making is precisely the aim of projects like Global Administrative Law (GAL) or the project on Informal International Public Policy Making (IIPPM). On Global Administrative Law, see gen. B. Kingsbury, N. Krisch and R. Steward, "The emergence of global administrative law" 68 *Law and Contemporary Problems*, (2005), 15–61, p. 29; C. Harlow, "Global administrative law: the quest for principles and values" 17 *EJIL*, (2006) 197–214. On Informal International Public Policy Making, see J. Pauwelyn, "Mapping the action and testing concepts of accountability and effectiveness", Project Framing Paper, 31 May 2010, available at http://www.hiil.org/assets/902/Publication_Transnational Constitutionality_IIPPM_Framing_Paper_Pauwelyn_draft_31_May_2010.pdf.

[38] J. d'Aspremont, "Non-state actors in international law: oscillating between concepts and dynamics" in J. d'Aspremont (ed.), *Participants in the International Legal System: Multiple Perspectives on Non-state Actors in International Law*, (Routledge 2011), pp. 1–21.

[39] J. d'Aspremont, "Inclusive law-making and law enforcement processes for an exclusive international legal system", in *Participants in the International Legal System* (Routledge, 2011), 425–39, esp. 430–31

[40] J. d'Aspremont, *supra* note 39.

scholarly concord ends. Indeed, at the conceptual level, when it comes to make sense of international law-making as a whole, the international legal scholarship is riven by deep conceptual disagreements. It is the object of the following paragraphs to spell out some of these paradigmatic divides.

## III. CONCEPTUAL DISCORD: THE PARADIGMATIC DIVIDES IN THE COGNITION OF INTERNATIONAL LAW-MAKING

The previous section (2) argued that, notwithstanding the limited debates as to the actual extent of the resilience of state dominance, the finding that international law-making is undergoing a sweeping pluralization has mustered a wide consensus among observers, experts, scholars and practitioners. How they make sense of it, however, shows great divergences among them. Indeed, despite concurring on their empirical finding, observers, experts, scholars and practitioners disagree on the treatment thereof and in particular on the way they cognize the multiplicity of actors whose participation has been empirically apprehended. This section seeks to outline some of the main cognitive discrepancies found in the literature.

As was mentioned in the introductory observations of this chapter, five main approaches to law-making seem to permeate the literature: a static approach grounded in the concept of subjecthood, another static understanding informed by the concept of pedigree, a dynamic conception of law-making based on participation, a dynamic conception based on the exercise of public authority and, eventually, a perspective which, while primarily static, aims at bridging a pedigree-based conception of lawmaking with social processes. These approaches will be introduced here in the chronological order of their emergence in international legal scholarship. Being the traditional cognitive take on norm-generating processes, subjecthood and pedigree are the first forms of cognition of international law-making that ought to be mentioned (1 and 2). Because the conceptions based on participation arose in reaction to static approaches, they are subsequently examined (3). Because they tried to offset the cognitive limitations of participation-based conceptions of law-making while trying to accommodate greater dynamism, outputbased perspectives (4) and neo-formalist pedigree-based approaches (5) ought to be mentioned last.

## 1. Subject-based Approaches to Law-making

The subject-based approach to law-making seems to have been ingrained in the very early systematization of international law.[41] Indeed, the appellation *international law* directly refers to its main "fabricants", for as is well-known, it is this reference to nation-states as the makers of international law that prodded Bentham's *An Introduction to the Principles of Morals and Legislation* to coin the expression *international law*.[42]

According to this approach, the makers of international law were deemed – originally the sole – subjects of international law in that they enjoyed legal personality. A correlation was thus established between states as the makers of international law and subjecthood.[43] In this sense, "International Law is conceived of as horizontal law, in which the subjects of the law are also the makers of the law".[44] The kinship so established between prominence in law-making and subjecthood constituted a prejudice that permeated the legal scholarship for more than a century. As a result, law-making processes had always been perceived – despite being a common object of study in political science and international relations[45] – as falling outside the scope of legal scholarly

---

[41] For a historical account of the concept of subject, see the fascinating work of J. Nijman, *The Concept of International Legal Personality – An Inquiry into the History and Theory of International Law*, (CUP, 2004).

[42] J. Bentham, *An Introduction to the Principles of Morals and Legislation*, London, (2005), first published 1781, at 326.

[43] See Permanent Court of Arbitration, *Russian Indemnity Case* (1912), 2 R.I.A.A., 829, p. 870; T.J. Lawrence, *The Principles of International Law*, London: Macmillan, (7th ed.), 1923, pp. 1–14; L. Oppenheim, *International Law*, London: R.F. Roxburgh, (3rd ed.), 1920 & 1921, p. 1. See J.L. Brierly in H. Waldock (ed.) *The Law of Nations*, Oxford: Clarendon Press, (6th ed.) 1963, first published in 1930, pp. 1 and 41 et seq.; C. Rousseau, *Principes généraux du droit international public*, Paris: Pedone, Vol. 1, 1944, p. 1. Rousseau subsequently qualifies the affirmation that international law only regulates relations between states: see p. 3. See, however, Kelsen for whom international law has no inherent "domaine de validité matériel". See H. Kelsen, "Théorie générale du droit international public", *Recueil des Cours*, Vol. 42, 1932–IV, pp. 182–3.

[44] Ph. Allott, "The True Function of Law in the International Community" 5 *Global Legal Studies Journal*, (1998), 391, at 404.

[45] R. Keohane and J. Nye (eds), *Transnational Relations and World Politics*, Cambridge, MA: Harvard University Press, 1972; J. Nye and J. Donahue (eds), *Governance in a Globalizing World*, Washington: Brookings Institution Press, 2000; J. Rosenau and E.-O. Czempiel (eds), *Governance without Government: Order and Change in World Politics*, Cambridge: Cambridge University Press,

inquiries.[46] Law-making was seen as a matter for subjects of international law. An entity not qualifying as a subject could not claim to be participating in law-making. Interestingly, it is this very prejudice between the prominent law-making role of states and subjecthood that long barred the recognition of an international legal personality for international organizations.[47] Indeed, for several decades, scholars and judges resisted the claim that international organizations could enjoy subjecthood for reasons pertaining to the abovementioned law-making prejudice.[48] It is in this sense that, in the opinion of the author, the 1949 International Court of Justice (ICJ) advisory opinion on the *Reparation for Injuries Suffered in the Service of the United Nations* (hereinafter *Reparations*) produced a liberating effect.[49] As will also be discussed in Chapter 4, this opinion formed a "constitutionalizing"[50] breaking point because law-making and subjecthood came to be severed from one another. Indeed, in the case of international organizations, subjecthood was accordingly no longer derived from their law-making role but rather, as is well-known, from their functions (the objective school) or the will of their creators (the subjective school).[51] The severance between law-making and subjecthood performed in the mid-twentieth century bore two main consequences that ought to be highlighted here.

---

1992; J. Rosenau, *The Study of World Politics: Globalization and Governance*, London: Routledge, 2006.

[46] See J. d'Aspremont, "Non-state actors from the perspective of legal positivism: the communitarian semantics for the secondary rules of international law" in J. d'Aspremont (ed.), *Participants in the International Legal System: Multiple Perspectives on Non-State Actors in International Law*, (Routledge 2011), pp. 23–40.

[47] David J. Bederman, "The Souls of International Organizations: Legal Personality and the Lighthouse at Cape Spartel", 36 *Virginia Journal of International Law*, (1996), 275.

[48] R. Collins, "Classical positivism in international law revisited" in J. d'Aspremont and J. Kammerhofer (eds), *International Legal Positivism in a Post-Modern World*, (CUP, 2014), 23–49.

[49] ICJ, "Reparations of Injuries Suffered in the Service of the United Nations, Advisory Opinion", ICJ Reports, (1949), p. 174.

[50] D.J. Bederman, "The souls of international organizations: legal personality and the lighthouse at Cape Spartel", 36 *Virginia Journal of International Law*, (1996), 275

[51] For some critical remarks, see R. Collins, "Non-state actors in international institutional law. Non-state, inter-state or supra-state? The peculiar identity of the intergovernmental organization", in J. d'Aspremont (ed.), *Participants in the International Legal System*, (Routledge, 2011), pp. 311–25.

First, as a result of the disconnection of legal personality from law-making, the question of subjecthood came to arise with respect to all kinds of other actors who did not directly participate in law-making. In addition to internationally personified international organizations, some other non-state actors came to be recognized as international legal persons, although this has been less construed as the outcome of a direct conferral of international legal personality upon non-state actors than an indirect consequence stemming from them having rights and duties.[52] This has thus not put into question the state-centricism of the pre-*Reparations* era. Indeed, it was not contested that the rights and duties that non-state actors may now hold have arguably remained the result of a state-centric law-making process.[53] Above all, it was continuously said that these actors may well now have a formal international legal personality derived from their rights and duties, but that has not endowed them with any formal and actual law-making powers.[54] Thus, the severance between legal personality and law-making allowed the recognition of a legal personality to actors deprived of any major law-making powers.

The second consequence of the mid-twentieth century dissociation between law-making and subjecthood is that law-making roles were recognized for a new range of actors not necessarily endowed with legal personality. In the post-*Reparations* era, participation in law-making does not turn the actor concerned into a new legal subject.[55]

It must be acknowledged here that, while the severance between law-making and subjecthood quickly gained widespread acceptance, some reactionaries continued to deduct legal status from participation in law-making, not in the form of subjecthood, but rather in the form of a formal lawmaker status. This "light subjecthood thesis" is at the heart of the work of the legal scholars who infer a formal status of lawmaker

---

[52] This has led scholars to deem that the question of international legal personality was described as "circular", "sterile" and boiling down to an "intellectual prison". See Reinisch 2005, Clapham 2006: 60.

[53] J. d'Aspremont, "The doctrinal illusion of the heterogeneity of international law-making processes", in H. Ruiz Fabri, R. Wolfrum and J. Gogolin (eds), *Select Proceedings of the European Society of International Law*, vol. 2., Oxford, Hart Publishing, 2010, pp. 297–312.

[54] See e.g. G. Abi-Saab, "Cours general de droit international public", *Recueil des Cours*, Vol. 207, 1987-VIII, p. 39.

[55] On this point, J. d'Aspremont, "The doctrinal illusion of the heterogeneity of international law-making processes", in H. Ruiz Fabri, R. Wolfrum and J. Gogolin (eds), *Select Proceedings of the European Society of International Law*, vol. 2., Oxford, Hart Publishing, 2010, pp. 297–312.

from developments of a new international law-making framework described in section 2.[56] In the same vein, a significant group of scholars, while acknowledging that contemporary law-making processes are still fundamentally state-centric, have come to the conclusion that granting a law-making status to non-state actors should at least be advocated and promoted.[57] Many international legal scholars thus prove, in one way or another, amenable to the idea of a law-making role for non-state actors.[58] This continuous scholarly appeal of the junction between law-making and personality has, however, remained too isolated and marginal. This is why it is not further explored here.

The main outcome of such a perspective is that the pluralization mentioned in section 2 can be cognized short of legal personality. Said differently, the subject-based model, once severed from law-making, has allowed its proponents to more easily recognize the pluralization of international law-making processes.

Yet, even severed from legal personality, such a subject-based approach remained burdened with cognitive deficiencies which explains its limited success in the literature. Indeed, it is argued here that it is not only that such an approach fails to capture norm-generative activities between subjects that are not legal persons. It is also that, even with respect to these norm-generating processes between legal persons, the cognitive value of subjecthood is limited. Indeed, it has always been close to impossible to formally certify the existence of subjects of international law, for their identification has inextricably remained immune from any formal capture, which is as much the cause as the consequence of the

---

[56] G. Teubner, "Global bukowina, legal pluralism in the world society", in G. Teubner (ed.), *Global Law Without a State*, (Aldershot: Dartmouth, 1997), pp. 3–28; M. Reisman, "Unilateral action and the transformation of the world constitutive process, the special problem of humanitarian intervention", 11, *European Journal of International Law*, 3–18; M.T. Kamminga, "The evolving status of NGOs under international law, a threat to the inter-state system?" in P. Alston (ed.), *Non-State Actors and Human Rights*, (Oxford and New York: Oxford University Press, 2005), p. 93–111.

[57] See gen. C. Arend, *Legal Rules and International Society*, (Oxford, Oxford University Press, 1999); R. Falk and A. Strauss, "On the creation of a global peoples' assembly, legitimacy and the power of popular sovereignty" 36, *Stanford Journal of International Law*, (2000) 191–220.

[58] It is also particularly well illustrated by the fact that we have witnessed the creation of a special law journal devoted to the question (*Non-State Actors and International Law* – published by Brill until 2005) or that of a book series initiated by M. Noortmann (*Non-State Actors in International Law, Politics and Governance*) and published by Ashgate.

utterly political nature of subject-identification processes on the international plane. For instance, as far as the identification of states is concerned, international law continues to be largely dependent on recognition. As was discussed in Chapter 1, international legal scholars – who classically resent such political contingencies – have nonetheless long tried to convince themselves that the determination of the subjects of international law are, to some extent, governed by international law.[59] This has been the illusion at the heart of the scholarly construction of the three- or four-element theories of statehood.[60] Although it is true that some international legal rules, like those pertaining to self-determination, human rights, and democracy, may occasionally impinge on the formation of new subjects and the gender of the newborn,[61] this illusion – which I call the *Montevideo mirage*[62] – has not sufficed to formalize the identification of the subjects of international law and rein in the politics of subject-certification.[63] As far as non-state actors are concerned, their identification may prove even more elusive. It is not difficult to understand that this impossibility to formally certify the existence of subjects of international law, aggravated by the overarching determinative role of recognition and the illusion of formalism behind the theories of statehood, have reinforced the move away from the subject-based approach to

---

[59] See e.g. J. Crawford, *The Creation of States in International Law*, Oxford: Oxford University Press, 2006, at 40 et seq.

[60] For a critical presentation, T. Grant, "Defining statehood: the Montevideo Convention and its discontents", 37 *Columbia Journal of Transnational Law*, 403–57 (1999).

[61] J. d'Aspremont, "Regulating statehood: the Kosovo status settlement", 20 *Leiden Journal of International Law*, (2007), 649–68; J. d'Aspremont, "Post-conflict administrations as democracy-building instruments", 9, *Chicago Journal of International Law*, (2008,) 1–16; J. d'Aspremont, "Legitimacy of governments in the age of democracy", 38, *N.Y.U. Journal of International Law & Politics*, 2006, 877–918.

[62] By reference to the famous 1933 Montevideo Convention on the Rights and Duties of States, which, for the sake of the Convention, elaborates on the criteria an entity should satisfy to be considered a state. See J. d'Aspremont, "Non-state actors in international law: oscillating between concepts and dynamics" in J. d'Aspremont (ed.), *Participants in the International Legal System: Multiple Perspectives on Non-State Actors in International Law*, (Routledge 2011), p. 2.

[63] J. d'Aspremont, "Non-state actors in international law: oscillating between concepts and dynamics", in J. d'Aspremont (ed.), *Participants in the International Legal System: Multiple Perspectives on Non-State Actors in International Law*, (Routledge 2011), pp. 1–3.

law-making and paved the way for other approaches to law-making. Such alternative approaches are now examined.

## 2. Static Pedigree-based Approaches to Law-making

Either from the very beginning or as a result of the abovementioned severance of law-making power and subjecthood, many international legal scholars have long shied away from approaching international law-making from the vantage point of the legal personality. Rather, they argue that it is only as soon as the normative product of a process is identified as law that this process can properly be considered a law-making process. In that sense, qualification as a law-making process hinges on the normative product thereof. Only when the latter is identified by virtue of its pedigree as law can a norm-generating process be considered law-making. This approach to law-making, albeit not the initial one, is possibly the most dominant.[64]

This view came to prevail in twentieth-century international legal scholarship. Scholars of the twentieth century having resolutely retreated from the dualism of natural law and endorsed a rule-based approach or source-based approach of law-identification.[65] In their great majority, these twentieth century scholars did not shed the idea of their predecessors that international law rests on the consent of the primary lawmakers. Subject to a few exceptions,[66] they agreed that natural law does not constitute a source of law per se, although the content of rules may

---

[64] For an overview of that approach in the contemporary legal scholarship, see J. d'Aspremont, *Formalism and the Sources of International Law*, (OUP, 2011), chapter 3.

[65] T.J. Lawrence, *The Principles of International Law* (Macmillan, London, 7th ed., 1923) pp. 1–14; L. Oppenheim, "The science of international law: its task and method", 2 *AJIL* 313 (1908) and L. Oppenheim, *International Law: A Treatise* (1st ed. 1905 & 1906), especially at p. 92; G. Schwarzenberger, *International Law*, (3d ed. 1957); P. Guggenheim, "What is positive international law?", in G. Lipsky, *Law and Politics in the World Community, Essays on Hans Kelsen's Pure Theory and Related Problems of International Law*, (Berkeley, University of California Press, 1953), pp. 15–30.

[66] See e.g. L. Le Fur, "La théorie du droit naturel depuis le XVIIème siècle et la doctrine moderne" 18 *Collected Courses*, (1927–III), 259–442. For an understanding of natural law as a formal source of law, see G. Fitzmaurice, "Some problems regarding the formal sources of international law", in *Symbolae Verzijl* (Martinus Nijhoff, The Hague, 1958) pp. 161–8.

reflect some principles of morality.[67] The consensus on the idea that the will of the state is the most obvious *material source* of law[68] remained unchallenged.[69] The main difference between nineteenth-century and twentieth-century international legal scholars lies in the fact that the latter tried to devise formal law-ascertaining criteria with which to capture state consent.[70] This is precisely how twentieth-century scholars ended up grounding the identification of international legal rules in a doctrine of allegedly formal sources[71] – a construction which continues to enjoy strong support among twenty-first-century scholars and which was already discussed in Chapter 2.[72] In their view, international legal rules stem from the will of states expressed through one of the formal sources of international law. The systemic character of the doctrine of the sources which they elaborated proved instrumental in their vision of international law as constituting a system.[73] It simultaneously allowed international law-making to be captured through prisms alien to legal personality, for

---

[67] J. Basdevant, "Règles générales du droit de la paix", 58 *Collected Courses*, (1936–IV), pp. 477–8. This came to be reflected in the case-law as well. See the statement of the ICJ in the *Southwest Africa Case*: "a court of law can take account of moral principles only in so far as these are given sufficient expression in legal form" Second Phase, 1966, ICJ Report, para. 49 (18 July 1966).

[68] On the distinction between material and formal sources, see gen. L. Oppenheim, *International Law*, vol. 1, 8th ed., London, 1955, p. 24. See the remarks of P.E. Corbett, "The consent of states and the sources of the law of nations", 5 *BYIL* (1925), 20–30; C. Rousseau, *Principes généraux du droit international public*, Vol. 1, Paris, Pedone, (1944), at 106–8; G. Fitzmaurice, "Some problems regarding the formal sources of international law", in *Symbolae Verzijl*, Martinus Nijhoff, The Hague, (1958), at 153 et seq.

[69] For a more recent manifestation of the voluntary nature of international law, see P. Weil, "Towards normative relativity in international law?", 77 *AJIL*, (1983), pp. 413–42. For a judicial expression of that idea, see PCIJ, *Lotus*, PCIJ Publications, Series A, No. 10, at 18.

[70] See the refinement of the theory of consent by Elias and Lim, *The Paradox of Consensualism in International Law*, (Kluwer, 1998).

[71] See gen. A. Pellet, "Cours général: le droit international entre souveraineté et communauté internationale", *Anuário Brasileiro de Direito Internacional*, vol. II, (2007), pp. 12–74, esp. at 15, 19 and 31.

[72] See e.g. A. Orakhelashvili, *The Interpretation of Acts and Rules in Public International Law*, Oxford, Oxford University Press, (2008), at 51–60.

[73] Likewise, it cannot be excluded that the practice of law-applying authorities will itself yield contradictions. That does not bar that practice from providing a meaning to law-ascertainment criteria. See a.o. A.-C. Martineau, "The rhetoric of fragmentation: fear and faith in international law", 22 *Leiden Journal of International Law*, (2009), 1–28, at 7–8

only the formal source of law – and the relevant pedigree associated with each source – is relevant for the apprehension of international law-making.

It is true that, among those scholars who abide by such a source-based approach to law-making, there has not been a consensus on the exact sources – the pedigree inherent in each of them – that ought to be recognized as the main cognitive tool to capture international law-making. Although being a mere list of the applicable law of a given judicial body,[74] the endless debate about the ambit, meaning, and authority of the list of admitted sources of Article 38 of the Statute of the Permanent Court of International Justice and later of the International Court of Justice (ICJ)[75] has been very symptomatic of these remaining disagreements. Certainly, here is not the place to revisit these controversies.

More important is to emphasize the consequences of such a dominant pedigree-based approach to the cognition of international law-making. It is argued here that, like the subjecthood perspective, the pedigree-based is very exclusionary. As long as the norm produced is not formally ascertainable as "law", the process of its creation will not be recognized as a formal law-making process – and its epistemic interest will be deemed very limited.

Likewise, it is worth realizing that such an approach to law-making rests on an ex post facto reconstruction. Indeed, it is only once a given rule is recognized as a rule of law that the process leading thereto will be endowed with the status of the law-making process. For instance, if an agreement is recognized as a treaty, the negotiations and the – formal or informal – process preceding that agreement will be elevated into a treaty-making process.

It is not difficult to understand that, as a result of these cognitive effects of the pedigree-based approach to international law-making, the explanatory virtue of such a static approach to law-making, irrespective of its other merits – for instance, in terms of rule-ascertainment[76] – remain limited. As is well-known, it is these explanatory and descriptive

---

[74] In the same vein, see A. Pellet, "Article 38", A. Zimmermann et al. (eds), *The Statute of the International Court of Justice – A Commentary*, Oxford: Oxford University Press, (2006), 693–735.

[75] On the controversies during the drafting process of Article 38, see T. Skouteris, *The Notion of Progress in International Law Discourse*, (The Hague: T.M.C. Asser Press, 2010).

[76] On the question of law-ascertainment, see gen. J. d'Aspremont, *Formalism and the Sources of International Law*, (OUP 2011), esp. chapters 1 and 2.

deficiencies that led to the emergence of more dynamic approaches to law-making.

## 3. Dynamic Participation-based Approaches to Law-making

The explanatory and descriptive handicaps of the static approach to law-making, whether based on subjecthood or pedigree, have led, in the second half of the twentieth century, to a move away from any formal category to describe law-making. This turn – sometimes described as the instrumentalist turn[77] – came to be embodied by the famous scholars of the Yale Law School (on New Haven) which was already mentioned in Chapter 2. The New Haven approach is premised on the inability of formal concepts – whether subjecthood or pedigree – to describe the multiple facets of law-making and capture the great variety of legal actors involved therein. Scholars affiliated with New Haven invite us to back away from any quest for a determination of the subjects of international law (and the correlative concept of legal personality) and, rather, to embrace the far more complex idea that what should be looked at are the *participants* in the process of international law-making. They argue that the static concepts of subject as well as that of pedigree are too restrictive to encapsulate the multiple dimensions of that process and that a more dynamic concept like that of participation is needed to unravel the various fluxes in which law originates. It is well-known that the invitation to look at participants rather than subjects or pedigree made by these scholars did not come out of the blue. It was inherent in their presupposition that law is primarily a comprehensive process of decision-making rather than a defined set of rules and obligations.[78] According to Myles S. McDougal, international law is:

> a comprehensive process of authoritative decision in which rules are continuously made and remade; that the function of the rules of international law is

---

[77] M. Koskenniemi, "What is international law for?", in Malcolm D. Evans, *International Law*, (Oxford University Press, 2003), 89–114 (2nd ed. 2006), 57–81.

[78] See M.S. McDougal, "International law, power and policy", 83 *HR*, (1952), p. 133; M.S. McDougal, H. Lasswell and W.M. Reisman, "Theories about international law: prologue to a configurative jurisprudence", 8 *Virginia Journal of International Law*, (1968), p. 188; M.S. McDougal, "International law and the future", 50 *Mississippi Law Journal*, (1979), p. 259; H. Lasswell and M.S. McDougal, *Jurisprudence for a Free Society*, New Haven: New Haven Press, 1992; M.S. McDougal and W.M. Reisman, *International Law in Contemporary Perspective*, New Haven: New Haven Press, 1980, p. 5.

to communicate the perspectives (demands, identifications and expectations) of the peoples of the world about this comprehensive process of decision; and that the national application of these rules in particular instances requires their interpretation, like that of any other communication, in terms of who is using them, with respect to whom, for what purposes (major and minor), and in what context.[79]

Worded differently, international law is "a flow of decision in which community prescriptions are formulated, invalidated and in fact applied."[80] In the same vein, Rosalyn Higgins sees international law as "the whole process of competent persons making authoritative decisions in response to claims which various parties are pressing upon them, in respect of various views and interests."[81] In sum, international law is accordingly regarded as a comprehensive process of decision-making rather than as a defined set of rules and obligations.[82] In the context of this chapter, it will not come as a surprise that, if law is envisaged as a process, scholars are brought to observe a more complex field of inquiry that requires a different type of sophistication and more dynamic concepts.[83]

As is well-known, while it successfully prompted a new wave of interest in process-based approaches and the cross-disciplinary perspectives that it involves, the New Haven School quickly became the object of criticisms. Some of these objections may explain why the policy-oriented approach could be said to have failed to significantly overturn the adherence to formal law-ascertainment found in mainstream international

---

[79] M.S. McDougal, "A footnote", 57 *AJIL*, 1963, p. 383.

[80] M.S. McDougal, "International law, power, and policy: a contemporary conception" 82 *Collected Courses* 1953-I, 133–259, p. 181.

[81] R. Higgins, "Policy considerations and the international judicial process", 17 ICLQ 58 (1968) at 59.

[82] See M.S. McDougal, "International law, power and policy", 83 HR (1952) p. 133; M.S. McDougal, H. Lasswell and W.M. Reisman, "Theories about international law: prologue to a configurative jurisprudence", 8 *Virginia Journal of International Law*, 1968, p. 188; M.S. McDougal, "International law and the future", 50 *Mississippi Law Journal*, 1979, p. 259; H. Lasswell and M.S. McDougal, *Jurisprudence for a Free Society: Studies in Law, Science and Policy*, (New Haven, New Haven Press/Martinus Nijhoff Publishers, 1992); M.S. McDougal and W.M. Reisman, *International Law in Contemporary Perspective* (New Haven, 1980) p. 5.

[83] On the idea of participation, see gen. see J. d'Aspremont, "Non-state actors in international law: oscillating between concepts and dynamics", in J. d'Aspremont (ed.), *Participants in the International Legal System: Multiple Perspectives on Non-State Actors in International Law*, (Routledge 2011), 1–21.

legal scholarship, at least until recently.[84] Most of the criticisms leveled against the process-based approach of New Haven is based on the suspicion that it was in collusion with the American foreign policy decision-makers. According to that view, the New Haven School placed a veil of legitimacy over ideological American foreign policy.[85] In that sense, the New Haven School proves vulnerable to the same criticisms as naturalism.[86] It has also been claimed that the New Haven approach does not provide enough guidance as to whether a behavior is wrongful or not.[87] Because the policy-oriented schools like New Haven construe the "authoritative" character of the process so broadly, international law ends up indiscriminately encompassing any decision made by any international decision-maker,[88] thereby fuelling a lot of uncertainty. Such uncertainty strips international law of the "certainty required for meaningful accountability".[89] The resulting arbitrariness cannot be avoided without returning to a rule-based approach.[90]

Whatever the actual success of New Haven, its legacy, when it comes to cognizing law-making, is dramatic. Indeed, the sweeping move observed in contemporary scholarship towards the study of law-making as a set of processes rather than through the lens of formal subjects or lawmakers is a move that partly traces back to the influence exerted by

---

[84] See the remarks by R.A. Falk according to whom New Haven cannot survive the vision of its founders. See R.A. Falk, "Casting the spell: The New Haven School of International Law", 104 *Yale LJ* (1995), 1991 at 1997.

[85] This has been famously explained by J. Hathaway, "America, defender of democratic legitimacy", 11 *EJIL*, (2000), 121–34. See also J. Hathaway, *Rights of Refugees under International Law* (Cambridge University Press, 2005) p. 20. In the same sense, see R.A. Falk, "Casting the spell: The New Haven School of International Law", 104 *Yale LJ* (1995) p. 1997; see also C. Tomuschat, "General course on public international law" 281 *Collected Courses* 9–438, (1999), 26–9.

[86] N. Purvis, "Critical legal studies in public international law", 32 *Harvard JIL* 81 (1991) at 86; see also J. Hathaway, "America, defender of democratic legitimacy", 11 *EJIL* (2000) 121–34 at 129 or J. Hathaway, *Rights of Refugees under International Law*, (Cambridge University Press, 2005) p. 21.

[87] J. Hathaway, *Rights of Refugees under International Law* (Cambridge University Press, 2005) p. 22. See the tentative rebuttal of that type of criticism by R. Higgins, *Problems and Process: International Law and How We Use It*, (OUP, Oxford, 1995), p. 8.

[88] A. D'Amato, "Is international law really law?", 79 *Northwestern University Law Review*, 1293 (1984–1985), p. 1302.

[89] J. Hathaway, *Rights of Refugees under International Law*, (Cambridge University Press, 2005), p. 18.

[90] M. Koskenniemi, "International law in a post-realist era", 16 *Australian Yearbook of International Law*, 1 (1995).

schools of thought like New Haven.[91] Indeed, subject to the specific difficulties of treaty-making processes and law-making by international organizations and other limited exceptions, law-making processes, according to the static approaches described above, had always been perceived – despite being a common object of study in political science and international relations[92] – as falling outside the scope of legal scholarly inquiries.[93]

The consequences of such a new cognitive approach have been wide-ranging. Indeed, once scholars elevated law-making processes – or standard setting[94] – into a noble topic worthy of scholarly inquiry,[95] their attention became automatically drawn to the participation of actors which do not qualify as formal legal subjects. This is why, in only a few decades, international legal scholars massively delved into the study of the question of law-making and non-state actors. Certainly, this came at the price of a deformalization of international law-ascertainment

---

[91] A. Chayes, T. Ehrlich and A.F. Lowenfeld, *International Legal Process*, Boston: Little Brown & Co., 1968. See M.E. O'Connell, "New International Legal Process", 93 *American Journal of International Law*, (1999), 334. See also H.H. Koh, "Why do nations obey international law?", 106 *Yale Journal of International Law*, (1999), 2599 and H.H. Koh, "Bringing international law home", 35 *Houston L. Rev.*, (1998), 623.

[92] R. Keohane and J. Nye (eds), *Transnational Relations and World Politics*, Cambridge, MA: Harvard University Press, (1972); J. Nye and J. Donahue (eds), *Governance in a Globalizing World*, Washington: Brookings Institution Press, (2000); J. Rosenau and E.-O. Czempiel (eds), *Governance without Government: Order and Change in World Politics*, Cambridge: Cambridge University Press, (1992); J. Rosenau, *The Study of World Politics: Globalization and Governance*, London: Routledge, (2006).

[93] See J. d'Aspremont, "Non-state actors from the perspective of legal positivism: the communitarian semantics for the secondary rules of international law" in J. d'Aspremont (ed.), *Participants in the International Legal System: Multiple Perspectives on Non-State Actors in International Law*, (Routledge 2011), pp. 23–40.

[94] A. Peters, L. Koechlin, T. Förster, and G. Fenner Zinkernagel, (eds), *Non-State Actors as Standard Setters*, (Cambridge: Cambridge University Press, 2009).

[95] For some classical studies on international law-making processes, see, R. Wolfrum and V. Röben (eds), *Developments of International Law in Treaty Making*, (Berlin: Springer, 2005), or A. Boyle and C. Chinkin, *The Making of International Law*, Oxford: Oxford University Press, 2007.

criteria,[96] which was discussed in Chapter 2. Yet, whatever its consequences, it is this move away from a scholarship strictly centered on static concepts that has allowed the international legal scholarship to focus its attention on this whole range of new participants in international law-making processes.[97]

## 4. Dynamic Output-based Approaches to Law-making

Against the backdrop of the cognitive limitations of the approaches to international law-making based on subject, pedigree, or participation, new models of cognition of international law-making have emerged in the literature focusing on the output of norm-generating processes.[98] Although not directly centered on international law but on the new forms of contemporary norm making, this is also the understanding found in the Heidelberg research project on the Exercise of Public Authority by International Institutions[99] and Global Administrative Law[100] which cognize norm-generating processes by virtue of the impact of the norm and which have already been discussed in Chapter 2.

---

[96] See e.g. A. Peters, T. Förster and L. Koechlin, "Towards non-state actors as effective, legitimate, and accountable standard setters" in A. Peters, L. Koechlin, T. Förster and G. Fenner Zinkernagel (eds) *Non-State Actors as Standard Setters* (Cambridge: Cambridge University Press, 2009), pp. 550–51.

[97] M. Noortmann and C. Ryngaert (eds), *Non-State Actor Dynamics in International Law: From Law-Takers to Law-Makers* (Aldershot, Ashgate, 2010); A. Peters, L. Koechlin, T. Förster, and G. Fenner Zinkernagel, (eds), *Non-State Actors as Standard Setters* (Cambridge: Cambridge University Press, 2009); A. Bianchi (ed.), *Non State Actors and International Law*, Aldershot: Ashgate Publishing, 2009.

[98] For a few examples see, J.E. Alvarez, *International Organizations as Law-Makers* (2005); J. Brunnée and S.J. Toope, "International law and constructivism, elements of an international theory of international law", 39 *Columbia Journal of Transnational Law*, (2000–2001), 19, 65. These effect-based approaches must be distinguished from the subtle conception defended by F. Kratochwil based on the *principled rule-application* of a norm which refers to the explicitness and contextual variation in the reasoning process and the application of rules in "like" situations in the future. See F. Kratochwil, *Rules Norms and Decisions: On the Conditions of Practical and Legal Reasoning in International Relations and Domestic Affairs*, (Cambridge, 1989), 206–8. See also F. Kratochwil, "Legal theory and international law", in D. Armstrong (ed.), *Routledge Handbook of International Law*, (2009) 1, 58.

[99] See also M. Goldmann, "Inside Relative Normativity: From Sources to Standards Instruments for the Exercise of International Public Authority", 9 *German Law Journal*, (2008) 11, 1865 and A. von Bogdandy, P. Dann and M.

From such an output-based perspective, what matters is "whether and how the subjects of norms, rules, and standards come to accept those norms, rules and standards ... [and] if they treat them as authoritative, then those norms can be treated as ... law."[101] In such a view, any normative effort to influence international actors' behavior, if it materializes in the adoption of an international instrument, should be viewed as part of international law. It is argued here that such an effect-based (or impact-based) conception of international law entails a shift from the perspective of the norm maker to that of the norm user. According to that understanding, international law-making is accordingly identified by the use of the norm by its addressee.

It is submitted here that output-based approaches resemble pedigree-based cognition in the sense that law-making processes are retroactively reconstructed. It is once the product of a norm-generating process has impacted its addressees' behaviors that such a process is turned into a law-making process. Output-based perspectives nonetheless differ from pedigree-based ones in that it is not the normative product that comes to elevate the process in law-making, but its impact. Looking at law-making from the vantage point of its output thus comes with a behaviorist dimension which makes it more dynamic than pedigree-based approaches to law-making. Indeed, the motion of law-making evolves together with the impact of norms.

These approaches to international law-making have proved rather popular among international legal scholars as a result of their cognitive

---

Goldmann, "Developing the Publicness of Public International Law: Towards a Legal Framework for Global Governance Activities", 9 *German Law Journal*, (2008) 11, 1375.

[100] See B. Kingsbury, N. Krisch and R. Steward, "The emergence of global administrative law", 68 *Law and Contemporary Problems*, (2005) 3 & 4, 15–61, 29; C. Harlow, "Global administrative law: the quest for principles and values", 17 *European Journal of International Law*, (2006) 1, 187, 197–214. According to Kingsbury, global administrative law rests on an "extended Hartian conception of law" which elevates publicness to a constitutive element of law. According to that view, publicness is a necessary element in the concept of law under modern democratic conditions. By publicness, Kingsbury means the claim made for law that it has been wrought by the whole society, by the public, and the connected claim that law addresses matters of concerns to the society as such. See Kingsbury, "The concept of 'Law' in global administrative law", 20 *European Journal of International Law*, (2009) 1, 23, 29–31.

[101] On that approach, see the remarks of J. Klabbers, "Law-making and constitutionalism", in J. Klabbers, A. Peters and G. Ulfstein (eds), *The Constitutionalization of International Law*, (2009), 81–124.

advantages. Indeed, like participation-based approaches, they allow the capture of dimensions of international law-making which subject-based and pedigree-based perspectives would leave aside. Likewise, their dynamism permits a constant rejuvenation and allows them to accommodate new forms of exercise of public authority at the international level. It must nonetheless be stressed that they are not without problems, especially in terms of the – albeit sometimes temporary – deformalization of law which they bring about.[102] This is a conceptual drawback, which a fifth and last take on international law-making has tried to contain while also trying to preserve dynamism.

## 5. Dynamic Pedigree-based Approaches to Law-making

Looking at international law from the vantage point of participation is not inherently linked to New Haven. Arguing that law is exclusively a process is not necessarily incompatible with a pedigree-based approach. Indeed, a last category of scholars needs to be mentioned as they have ventured to embrace a more formal pedigree-based conception of law-making without rejecting any exploration of law-making from the vantage point of participation.

Certainly, attempts to reconcile the process-based approach of the New Haven School and the more static conceptions of international law are not new.[103] It is not certain that this reconciliation has always been successful.[104] The author has himself tried to reconcile static pedigree-based approaches to law (and law-making) with more dynamic social

---

[102] This is an aspect that was discussed in depth in Chapter 2.

[103] See e.g. G. Abi-Saab, "Cours general de droit international public" *Recueil des Cours*, Vol. 207, 1987–VIII, p. 39. According to M. Koskenniemi, this also was the ambition of Virally in his general course *Recueil des Cours*, (1983 V) and Schachter in his general course, *Recueil des Cours*, vol. 178 (1982 V): M. Koskenniemi, *From Apology to Utopia,* New York: Cambridge University Press, 2005, p. 159. See also, O. Schachter, "Towards a Theory of International Obligation", 8 *VA J IL*, (1967–1968), 300. See also the earlier attempts by C.W. Jenks, *The Common Law of Mankind*, London: Stevens, 1958 or G.J.H. Van Hoof, *Rethinking the Sources of International Law*, Deventer: Kluwer Publishing, 1983, p. 44.

[104] According to R. Higgins, it is highly questionable that these authors have attempted to float a conciliatory understanding of international law. See R. Higgins, *Problems and Process: International Law and How We Use It*, Oxford: Oxford University Press, 1995, p. 8.

processes in the law.[105] While acknowledging that approaching international law from the standpoint of its sources corresponds to a formal conception of law focused on law as a product, the author of this volume has argued elsewhere that such a pedigree-based approach does not need to be completely static.[106] Pedigree-based approaches to international law ought not necessarily be condemned to be static. According to that argument, doctrines of sources, if grounded in the social practice of law-applying authorities can change – and can be changed. This is the so-called social thesis – borrowed from English analytical jurisprudence[107] – which provides dynamism for an otherwise entirely static product-centered conception of law. In the specific context of international law, such a conceptualization makes it possible to argue that the social practices of law-applying authorities have long ceased to reflect the practices that the ancestral Article 38 of the ICJ Statute was meant to reflect. This is why, according to this thesis, approaching the sources of international law-making from the standpoint of Article 38 no longer makes much sense because it does not reflect the current consensus among law-applying authorities. Instead, such a doctrine of sources ought to radically depart from the static pedigree-determining blueprints found in the mainstream literature and be shaped as a dynamic model of rule ascertainment grounded in an ever-evolving social practice. On top of advocating a move away from Article 38 – and especially the abandonment of the law-ascertaining role of state intent for the identification of treaties and unilateral promises identification – or associated doctrines – like those conveying illusions of formalism in the delimitation of customary international law – this thesis calls for a more pluralistic conception of law-applying authorities which ought not be restricted to domestic and international courts and tribunals. New actors have come to produce social practice determinative of the ascertainment indicators contained in the doctrine of sources of international law.[108] The virtues of

---

[105] This is the ambition of the book *Formalism and the Sources of International Law*, (OUP, 2011), esp. chapter 8.

[106] This is the thesis I have defended in J. d'Aspremont, *Formalism and the Sources of International Law* (OUP, 2011), chapter 8.

[107] J. d'Aspremont, "Herbert Hart in today's international legal scholarship", in J. d'Aspremont and J. Kammerhofer (eds), *International Legal Positivism in a Post-Modern World*, (Cambridge: Cambridge University Press 2014), 114–50.

[108] For some examples, see J. d'Aspremont, "Non-state actors from the perspective of legal positivism: the communitarian semantics for the secondary rules of international law", in J. d'Aspremont, *Participants, in the International Legal System*, (Routledge, 2011), 23–40.

such a dynamic pedigree-based approach also rest in the abstract possibility to apprehend the international normative activity, which nowadays takes place outside the ambit of traditional international law, which a strictly static approach would fall short of capturing. Indeed, if the social practices that give rise to the criterion of apprehension allow their capture as law-making, nothing precludes their elevation into law-making.

## IV. EPISTEMIC PLURALISM AND EPISTEMOLOGICAL SELF-INTEREST

Making sense of international law-making has long been an ambition of international legal scholars.[109] In that endeavor, they have been resorting to a wide variety of cognitive tools: subject, pedigree, participant and actor, public authority, or a blend of several of them. Each of these approaches has generated a different picture of international law-making. According to the approach chosen, international law-making appears as a more or less formal, systematized, inclusive, and state-centric process.

It is undoubtedly not the aim of these concluding remarks to vindicate one of these cognitive choices. There is probably not one cognitive choice trumping the others. They all rest on a paradigm that has its own merits. Coming to terms with the variety of paradigms found in the literature pertaining to international law-making should certainly not be construed as a call for radical pluralism. In the author's view, merely accepting the plurality of cognitive choices – and the conceptualizations of law-making inherent in each of them – would boil down to nothing more than skeptical relativism. Yet, it seems of great importance, when one grapples with issues of law-making, that one consciously assumes one's cognitive choices. Assuming such choices, however, presupposes awareness, not only of the underlying cognitive choice behind any study of international law-making, but also of the parameters informing it. Indeed, cognitive choices, like those pertaining to the understanding of international law-making, are not neutral.[110] They are informed by an

---

[109] For a critical stocktaking of scholarly attempts to make sense of international law-making, see C. Brölmann and Y. Radi (eds), *Research Handbook on the Theory and Practices of International Law-Making*, (Cheltenham: Edward Elgar 2013).

[110] See M. Greenberg, "How Facts Make Law", 10 *Legal Theory*, (2004), pp. 157–98, 2004; UCLA School of Law Research Paper No. 05-22. Available at SSRN: http://ssrn.com/abstract=797125.

array of different parameters. When it comes to foundational topics like international law-making, one of these parameters is certainly the observer's concept of law. The concept of law of the observer will to a large degree determine the cognitive tool to which one resorts to make sense of international law-making. Another parameter – probably very pregnant in choices determining approaches to international law-making – rests in one's research interest. In the author's view, it can hardly be denied that one necessarily embraces an approach or a method that fits with the type of research that one is interested in. The choice for one of the cognitive tools (and paradigm) mentioned above can thus also be read as an expression of preference for a given dimension of international law-making – and for a given dimension of international law. For instance, those solely interested in the formal sources of international law might favor a pedigree-based approach to international law-making, which will lead them to focus on a very narrow dimension of that process. Because of their extremely narrow cognitive scope, pedigree-based approaches to international law-making could even be seen as the manifestation of a general lack of interest for international law-making processes. On the contrary, participant- and actor-based understandings of international law-making reflect the observer's interest in norm-generating processes.

It is argued that awareness of such epistemological self-interest allows greater mutual coexistence between the various approaches to international law-making that have been outlined in this chapter. But awareness of the influence of our epistemological self-interest on our cognitive choices in studies of international law-making also calls for some relativism. Epistemological interest in one dimension of international law-making necessarily reflects a given epoch – the epoch in which the observers situate themselves. The various cognitive choices behind studies of international law-making inevitably have an epochal dimension. Such an epochal anchorage of scholarly approaches to international law-making is what ineluctably condemns the scholarship on international law-making to a Sisyphean repetition.

# 4. Institutions

This chapter looks at some of the paradigmatic contradictions in the doctrines forming the so-called law of international organizations as well as the underlying social arrangements informing such tensions. Before looking at these paradigmatic tensions, a preliminary question must be raised. It pertains to the coexistence of tensions with the very idea of a law of international organizations. Can one build a "law of international organizations" – and thus the techniques, methods, and narratives that go with it – on dichotomous grounds?

The answer to the above-mentioned question is affirmative as long as the professionals, claiming some membership to it, excel in the art of reconciliation. The law of international organizations epitomizes such a possibility. After submitting that most scholarly and practical debates about the law of international organizations can be construed as a battle between arguments based on the idea of contract and those based on the idea of constitution, this chapter discusses international legal scholars' attempt to translate this tension into a dynamic and dialectic framework. As the argument developed in the following paragraphs goes, international legal scholars, and especially legal academics, while unanimously acknowledging the existence of paradigmatic tensions, are often tempted to iron them out through the promotion of a series of dialectical concepts or moves. This chapter is thus an exercise of discourse analysis which will seek to shed light on such dialectical tactics, with an emphasis on international legal scholarship. In doing so, it will show that the art of reconciliation practiced by international legal scholars involved in the study of the law of international organizations is not without paradox, especially given the extent to which paradigmatic tensions have themselves always been constitutive of the field as well as the identity of the whole discipline.

It goes without saying that acknowledging paradigmatic tensions in the law of international organizations is, in itself, far from being groundbreaking. On the contrary, it could be said that revealing (the consequences of) such an antinomy and the complexity that it brings about, is a conventional move found in any serious piece of scholarship in the field. In that sense, speaking in antinomic terms of the law of international organizations even constitutes the mainstream style with which this subject is discussed and debated.[1] What is more, some professionals in this area even take pride in claiming to be confronted with the tangles that come with the foundational tensions at the heart of the subject and which they relish to (try to) unknot in their scholarship or professional literature. Because confronting paradigmatic tensions is a common practice in the scholarship on the law of international organizations, it would make no sense to embark on a penultimate inquiry into their manifestations in the scholarly discourses about the law of international organizations. These tensions – which, as will be explained below, are understood here as amounting to a more general dichotomy between contractualist and constitutionalist approaches – are too well-known and will only be briefly recalled (I). Moreover, Table 4.1 appended to section I supplements these introductory remarks to help capture the manifestations of those tensions that are deemed to be most fundamental. After these brief reminders, the central part of this chapter will make the argument that international legal scholarship centred on the law of international organizations has been caught in a continuous attempt to reconcile these tensions between contractualism and constitutionalism with a view to flattening the paradigmatic framework within which arguments about the law of international organizations are made. In doing so, this chapter will seek to shed light on some of the reconciliatory moves observed in the practice and the scholarship and their attempt to turn the fundamental dichotomy between contractualism and constitutionalism into a dialectical and dynamic construction (II). The chapter goes on by arguing that many international legal scholars have yet to come to terms with the constitutive character of this dichotomy between contractualism and constitutionalism and accept that it constitutes the defining mould of the techniques, methods, and narratives that are deployed under the banner of a law of international organizations (III).

---

[1] The focus on paradigmatic tensions sometimes comes at the expense of any attention for the actual practice; one could make the same finding as the one F. Kratochwil and J. Ruggie made in relation to *IR literature*. According to them, the field of international organizations has ceased to be a field of practice and doctors have stopped seeing patients. See F. Kratochwil and J. Ruggie, "International organization: a state of the art on an art of the state", 40 *International Organization* (1986) at 754.

## I. AN ABIDING AND ALL-EMBRACING DICHOTOMY: CONTRACTUALISM VS. CONSTITUTIONALISM

Despite the field being dominated by a descriptivist and analytical mindset,[2] it would be incorrect to portray it as lacking any critical self-reflection. There is, indeed, much self-awareness, at least among legal academics, about the paucity of theoretical reflection on the law of international organizations.[3] It is true that theoretical studies of the (foundations of) the law of international organizations are scarce.[4] Yet, it does not take much theoretical grounding to realize the paradigmatic incongruence at play in the (practice of the) law of international organizations. In fact, international legal scholars engaged in the study of this field, however un-theoretical their approach may be, unanimously recognize the existence – and the complexity – of paradigmatic tensions around which the whole law of international organizations articulates itself.[5]

---

[2] For some examples of extremely refined and detailed work in this respect, see H. Schermers and N. Blokker, *International Institutional Law* (2011), 5th edition, Martinus Nijhoff Publishers. See also P. Sands and P. Klein, *Bowett's Law of International Institutions* (2009), 6th edition, Sweet & Maxwell.

[3] H. Schermers and N. Blokker, *International Institutional Law* (2011), 5th edition, para. 13A: "It is true that theoretical reflection in the field of international organizations has been limited"; see also J. Klabbers, *Introduction to International Institutional Law* (2009), 2nd edition, Cambridge University Press at p. 3: he argues that the law of international organizations is "immature" and that we lack a convincing theoretical framework regarding international organizations. See also N. White, *The Law of International Organizations* (2006) 2nd edition, Manchester University Press, 14–23.

[4] D. Bederman, "The souls of international organizations: legal personality and the lighthouse at Cape Spartel", 36 *Virginia Journal of International Law* 275 (1995–1996); D. Kennedy, "The move to institutions", 8 *Cardozo Law Review* (1987), 841. Reprinted in *International Organization*, J. Klabbers, (ed.), Ashgate Publishing Limited (2006); A. Rapisardi-Mirabelli, *Théorie Générale des Unions Internationales*, 341–94 (1925-II0) 7 Recueil des Cours, Académie de Droit International de La Haye; J. Alvarez, *International Organizations as Law-Makers* (2005), Oxford University Press, 17–63; F. Kratochwil and J. Gerard Ruggie, "International organization: a state of the art on an art of the state", *International Organization*, 40, 4 (1986), pp. 753–75 (with an emphasis on IR literature).

[5] V. Engstrom, "Powers of organizations and the many faces of autonomy", in R. Collins and N.D. White (eds), *International Organizations and the Idea of Autonomy: Institutional Independence in the International Legal Order* (Abingdon: Routledge, 2011) p. 224; C. Brölmann, *The Institutional Veil in Public*

It is noteworthy, however, that irrespective of this unanimous acknowledgement, the definition of these foundational tensions infusing the law of international organizations varies greatly as they remain apprehended and cognized through a multitude of dichotomies.[6] These dichotomies are defined in relation to the organization itself, its structure, its identity, its relations with other subjects, its powers, its embedding in the international legal order and all the other traditional objects of studies of the discipline. It suffices here to provide a few examples of how tensions in the law of international organizations are presented and described by experts in the field.

For instance, these tensions are often understood in terms of the diverging capacities, in which states act in their relation with the organization, that is either as creator state or as member state.[7] The same tension is captured by contrasting between the internal role and the external role of member states.[8] This discordance is also sometimes captured in architectural terms by opposing the openness of organizations to their transparency,[9] or in terms of control by contrasting functionalism

---

*International Law: International Organisations and the Law of Treaties* (Hart Publishing, 2007), at 30; N. Blokker, "International organizations and their members" (2004), *International Organizations Law Review* 1(1): 139–61; for more dated recognition of that tension, see M. Virally, "La notion de fonction dans la théorie de l'organization internationales", in *Mélanges Offerts à Charles Rousseau: La Communauté Internationale*, Paris, Pedone (1974), pp. 277–300; see also A. McNair, "Functions and differing legal character of treaties" (1930), 11 *Brit. Y.B. Int'l L.* 100 (1930), at 112; M. Rama-Montaldo, "International legal personality and implied powers of international organizations" (1970), *The British Yearbook of International Law*, 44, pp. 111–55.

[6] J. Klabbers claims that most legal issues in the law of international organizations are examined from three main perspectives: the relations between the organization and its member states, the relations between the various organs inter se and the organization's internal functioning, and the relations between the organization and the world around it. See J. Klabbers, *Theorizing International Organizations* (on file with the author).

[7] N. Blokker, "International organizations and their members" (2004), *International Organizations Law Review* 1(1): 139–61; R. Collins and N.D. White (eds), *International Organizations and the Idea of Autonomy: Institutional Independence in the International Legal Order* (Abingdon: Routledge, 2011).

[8] H. Schermers and N. Blokker, *International Institutional Law* (2011), 5th edition, para. 66; see also N. Blokker, "International organizations and their members" (2004), *International Organizations Law Review* 1(1): 139–161.

[9] C. Brölmann, *The Institutional Veil in Public International Law: International Organizations and the Law of Treaties* (Hart Publishing 2007), p. 32.

and constitutionalism, the former being then construed as freedom and the latter as control.[10] These paradigmatic tensions sometimes manifest themselves in the discussion of the ambiguous nature of the constituent instrument of the organizations.[11] Similar tensions are said to permeate the distinction between the external law and the internal law of the organizations.[12] In the same manner, the different faces of autonomy have also been seen as an expression of the paradigmatic dissonances at the

---

[10] J. Klabbers, "Two contending approaches to the law of international organizations", in J. Klabbers and Å. Wallendahl (eds), *Research Handbook on International Organizations Law: Between Functionalism and Constitutionalism* (Cheltenham: Edward Elgar, 2010), 3–30; see also J. Klabbers, "Two concepts of international organization", 2 *International Organizations Law Review* (2005) 277–93. For an attempt to explain how this tension works in practice, see A. Guzman, "International organizations and the Frankenstein problem", 24 *European Journal of International Law*, 24 (2013), 4, 999–1025. For a previous use of the Frankenstein analogy, see gen. J. Alvarez, *International Organizations as Law-Makers* (2005), Oxford University Press.

[11] C. Ahlborn, "The rules of international organizations and the law of international responsibility", 8 *International Organizations Law Review*, (2011), 397–482. See also A. McNair, "The functions of differing legal character of treaties", 11 *British Yearbook of International Law* (1930), 100 at 112. On this debate, see also C. Brölmann, *The Institutional Veil in Public International Law: International Organizations and the Law of Treaties* (Hart Publishing 2007), p. 144; N. White, *The Law of International Organizations* (Manchester University Press, 2005) at 14; or A. Peters, "L'acte constitutif de l'organization internationale", in E. Lagrange and J.M. Sorel (eds), *Traité de droit des organizations internationales* (LGDJ 2013), 201–45, esp. p. 206.

[12] For a recent and refined study of the question, see C. Alhborn, "The rules of international organizations and the law of international responsibility", 8 *International Organizations Law Review*, (2011), 397–482. For an older study of this debate, see R. Monaco, "Le caractère constitutionnel des actes institutifs d'organizations internationales" in *Mélanges offerts à Charles Rousseau* (1994), Paris: Pedone; see also the tree-tier construction of Finn Seyersted according to which all international organizations possess their own internal law governing their relations with the organs, the officials and the member states in their capacity as members while being subject to international law in their relations with states and other international organizations. They also enter into relations of a private nature with both public and private entities. See gen. F. Seyersted, *Common Law of International Organizations* (Martinus Nijhoff, 2008), esp. 21–4. See also H. Schermers and N. Blokker, *International Institutional Law* (2011), 4th edition pp. 1142–8 (according to whom, the separation between the organization's internal law and general international law has never been settled).

heart of the law of international organizations.[13] Other binary dichotomies are occasionally put forward to express the tensions at the heart of the law of international organizations. It suffices to mention the use of flexibility vs. stability,[14] functionality vs. centralization,[15] politics vs. management,[16] anarchy vs. legalism.[17] Eventually, it could be argued that the paradigmatic tensions of the subject resurface in the various denominations given to the field. On the one hand, a "law of international organizations" often refers to the idea of autonomous subjects which, albeit sharing those common architectural traits that are the object of the discipline, constitute independent sub-orders. On the other hand, the notion of "international institutional law", more often than not, manifests the idea of a set of regulatory structures within which international organizations are somehow diluted.

The foregoing shows the unanimous recognition among professionals in the field of paradigmatic dichotomies in the law of international organizations and their multitude of manifestations. It is interesting to note that, united in their acknowledgement of such antinomies but divided in the modes of expression thereof, international legal scholars systematically resort to the same modernist narrative to justify each of

---

[13] See J. d'Aspremont, "The multifaceted concept of autonomy of international organizations and international legal discourse" in R. Collins and N.D. White, (eds), *International Organizations and the Idea of Autonomy*, (Routledge, 2011). According to that view, autonomy as political independence from member states manifests an idea of international organizations as contractualist creatures whereas autonomy as institutional independence from international legal order as well as member states has great constitutionalist overtones and expresses the idea that international organizations are an autonomous creature with their own political project.

[14] J. Klabbers, *Introduction to International Institutional Law*, 2nd ed., (2009), Cambridge University Press, at 230.

[15] C. Brölmann, *The Institutional Veil in Public International Law: International Organisations and the Law of Treaties* (Hart Publishing 2007), at 30 (for her, functionality corresponds to the sovereignty of states while centralization reflects the independence of the organization).

[16] J. Klabbers, "International Institutions", in J. Crawford and M. Koskenniemi, *Cambridge Companion to International Law*, (2002), Cambridge University Press, 228; D. Kennedy, "The Move to Institutions", 8 *Cardozo Law Review*, 841 (1987). Reprinted in *International Organization*, J. Klabbers, ed., Ashgate Publishing Limited (2006), 833.

[17] M. Koskenniemi, *From Apology to Utopia: The Structure of International Legal Argument (Reissue with new Epilogue)* (Cambridge: Cambridge University Press, 2005) 481, n. 25.

the opposites.[18] Indeed, functionalism, and thus the idea that international organizations are geared towards the performance of some predefined functions (most of the time pertaining to the management of practical problems like peace and security and order),[19] simultaneously underpins the opposite facets of the above-mentioned tensions.[20] Whether one seeks to sustain the autonomous existence of the organizations (and the expansions of its powers) or to subject it to its member states and the international legal order, one always relies on functionalist arguments. In that sense, it is not surprising that one of the main foundational texts of the discipline, that is, the famous 1949 Advisory Opinion of the International Court of Justice on the *Reparations of Injuries*[21] and its

---

[18] For some critical remarks on the functionalist discourse, see J. Alvarez, *International Organizations as Law-Makers*, (2005), pp. 17–28. See also J. Klabbers, "International institutions", in J. Crawford and M. Koskenniemi, *Cambridge Companion to International Law*, Cambridge University Press (2012), 228ff, esp. at 232.

[19] On the idea of functionalism and that according to which international institutions derive their "raison d'être" from the promise of autonomous action, see J. Klabbers, "Autonomy, constitutionalism and virtue in international institutional law" (2011) in *International Organizations and the Idea of Autonomy: institutional independence in the international legal order*, N. White and R. Collins (eds), Routledge, p. 120–40, 21. See also G. Cahin, "La variété des fonctions imparties aux organizations internationales", in E. Lagrange and J.-M. Sorel (eds), *Traité de droit des organizations internationales*, LGDJ, 2013, 671–704. For an early application of this notion, see PCIJ in *Advisory Opinion, Jurisdiction of the European Commission of the Danube Between Galatz and Braila* (1927).

[20] V. Engstrom, "Powers of organizations and the many faces of autonomy" in *International Organizations and the Idea of Autonomy: institutional independence in the international legal order*, N. White and R. Collins (eds), Routledge p. 222; J. Klabbers, "International institutions", in J. Crawford and M. Koskenniemi, *Cambridge Companion to International Law*, Cambridge University Press (2012), p. 232; J. Klabbers, "Autonomy, constitutionalism and virtue in international institutional law" (2011) in *International Organizations and the Idea of Autonomy: institutional independence in the international legal order*, N. White and R. Collins (eds), Routledge, pp. 122–4.

[21] ICJ Rep 1979 174. On the revolution that allegedly brought about the reparations opinion from the standpoint of international law as a whole, see D. Bederman, "The souls of international organizations: legal personality and the lighthouse at Cape Spartel", 36 *Virginia Journal of International Law* 275 (1995–1996) at 279: the opinion "marks the triumph of a revolutionary idea in our discipline. It signaled the final days of the 'law of nations' and ushered in the era of 'international law'".

functionalist narrative are interpreted as buttressing each of these very opposite dimensions of (the law of) international organizations.[22]

For the sake of this chapter, it is probably not necessary to dwell any further on the above mentioned unanimously recognized dichotomies and their various modes of expressions. Rather, this introductory section makes the argument that the above-mentioned tensions can be apprehended through a single and more all-embracing descriptive and conceptual framework, namely, a framework that pits contractualism against constitutionalism.[23] It is more specifically argued here that the dichotomy between contractualism and constitutionalism is one that captures with accuracy most of the above-mentioned tensions found at the heart of the law of international organizations[24] and does so at various levels.[25] This all-embracing descriptive and conceptual framework can certainly not claim any conceptual superiority.[26] The choice for such a descriptive framework is primarily informed by some didactic preferences, for such a framework allows one to apprehend all the dissonances in the law of international organizations through one single lens.

---

[22] D. Bederman, "The souls of international organizations: legal personality and the lighthouse at Cape Spartel", 36 *Virginial Journal of International Law* 275 (1995–1996), at 369; R. Collins, "Non-State Actors in International Institutional Law", in J. d'Aspremont (ed.) *Participants in the International Legal System – Multiple Perspectives on Non-State Actors in International Law* (2011) Routledge, esp. 314–15.

[23] The constitutional view is sometimes called the "organic" approach. See J.H. Barton, "Two Ideas of International Organization" 82 *Michigan Law Review*, (1984), 1520.

[24] In the same vein, see N. White, *The Law of International Organizations* (2006) 2nd ed., Manchester University Press, 14–23.

[25] The dichotomy between contractualism and constitutionalism operates at all the three main levels of analysis identified by J. Klabbers, namely, the relations between the organization and its member states, the relations between the various organs inter se and the organization's internal functioning, and the relations between the organization and the world around it. See J. Klabbers, *Theorizing International Organization* (on file with the author).

[26] This distinction probably echoes the current distinction made between globalist and sovereignist approaches to the state. For some critical remarks on this distinction, see J. Alvarez, "State Sovereignty Is Not Withering Away: A Few Lessons for the Future", in A. Cassese (ed.), *Realizing Utopia* (Oxford University Press, 2012), 26–37. See also M. Koskenniemi, "The Wonderful Artificiality of States", 88 *ASIL Proceedings of the 88th Annual Meeting*, (1994), 22.

According to this all-capturing dichotomy and the way it is understood here, the idea of contract refers to dependence,[27] that is *dependence* on both the contracting parties and on the international legal order. The constitution, on the other hand, expresses the notion of *autonomy* that is the autonomy from both the contracting parties and the international legal order.[28] Said differently, a contractualist approach to the law of international organizations posits that international organizations are conventional products of international law on which states keep a grip while the constitutionalist approach advocates an understanding of international organizations as autonomous normative orders which can pursue their own political project independently. It is argued here that most scholarly and practical debates about the law of international organizations can be construed as a battle between arguments based on the idea of contract

---

[27] For the discussion of this question in connection with the EU, see R.A. Wessel and S. Blockmans, "Between Autonomy and Dependence: The EU Legal Order Under the Influence of International Organizations – An Introduction", in R.A. Wessel and S. Blockmans (eds), *Between Autonomy and Dependence: The EU Legal Order Under the Influence of International Organizations* (2013), The Hague: T.M.C. Asser Press/Springer, 1–9; R.A. Wessel, "Between the Authority of International Law and the Autonomy of EU Law", in J. Díez-Hochleitner, C. Martínez Capdevila, I. Blázquez Navarro, and J. Frutos Miranda (eds), *Últimas tendencias en la jurisprudencia del Tribunal de Justicia de la Unión Europea (Recent trends in the case law of the Court of Justice of the European Union)* (2012), Madrid: La Ley–Grupo Wolters Kluwer, pp. 759–65.

[28] For a similar understanding of constitutionalism see C. Brölmann, "International organizations and treaties: contractual freedom and institutional constraint", in J. Klabbers and Å. Wallendahl (eds), *Research Handbook on International Organizations Law: Between Functionalism and Constitutionalism* (Cheltenham: Edward Elgar, 2010), at 304. J. Klabbers uses the term in a different way and equates it with control; see also J. Klabbers, "Two concepts of international organization", *International Organizations Law Review* (2005), pp. 278–89. While focusing on the former, J. Klabbers nonetheless acknowledges the two possible meanings of constitutionalism: international constitutionalism and organization constitutionalism ("Two contending approaches to the law of international organizations", in J. Klabbers and Å. Wallendahl (eds), *Research Handbook on International Organizations Law: Between Functionalism and Constitutionalism* (Cheltenham: Edward Elgar, 2010), p. 13). For a similar distinction, see F. Dopagne and J. d'Aspremont, "Two constitutionalisms in Europe: pursuing an articulation of the European and international legal orders", *Heidelberg Journal of International Law* (2008), which distinguishes between substantive European constitutionalism (value, HR, democracy, Rule of Law) and systemic European constitutionalism (direct effect, supremacy, no countermeasures and no external dispute settlement).

and those based on the idea of constitution, that is between a contractualist project and constitutionalist project. These two paradigmatic conflicting standpoints are the primary poles from which the law of international organizations is constructed, cognized, denied, interpreted, criticized, evaluated, or legitimized by international legal scholars. They also generate most of the tensions observed in the theory and practice of the law of international organizations.

It is certainly not the place to discuss more specifically how this central dichotomy between the contractualist and constitutionalist approaches to international organizations develops in theory and practice. It suffices to briefly comment on Table 4.1 that is appended to this section, and which illustrates how this dichotomy operates in connection with a wide variety of legal issues. These legal issues are presented around the three main stages in the life of an international organization, namely its creation, its operation and its termination. For each of them, a series of legal issues are identified. Table 4.1 shows that for each of them, contractualist and constitutionalist approaches lead to radically opposed solutions. The table resorts to a series of examples to demonstrate more fundamentally that any legal argument grounded in contractualism will always be counterpointed by an equally valid argument grounded in constitutionalism (and vice-versa).[29] For instance, one can argue that, *from a contractualist standpoint*, an international organization is composed of contracting parties. Its constituent instrument boils down to an interstate treaty, its normative activities generate secondary treaty law, its legal order is a legal order of an international nature permeable to international law, the international legal personality of the organization depends on the will of the contracting parties, the competences are attributed, the organization cannot create new subjects of international law either primary or secondary, the constituent treaty is subject to traditional rules of interpretation, the organization can only be terminated by the contracting parties when they terminate the treaty, and questions of succession ought to be regarded as questions of successions of treaties, etc.

On the contrary, *from a constitutionalist standpoint*, an international organization is rather understood as composed of member states (*membrum*).[30] Its constituent instrument boils down to an act of a

---

[29] For a similar finding but from a more restrictive angle, see J. Klabbers, *An Introduction to International Institutional Law*, 2nd ed. (2005), p. 1.

[30] See gen. N. Blokkers, "Organizations and their members", 1 *International Organizations Law Review* (2004), pp. 139–61.

constitutional nature which cannot be reduced to an inter-state treaty, its normative activities generate rules which have the nature of internal law, its legal order is a separate and autonomous legal order impermeable to international law, the international legal personality of the organization hinges on the fulfilment of some criteria pre-defined by the international legal order itself, the competencies can be extended through the doctrine of implied powers and such expansion is inherent in the constitutional subjecthood of the organization. In the same vein, the organization can create new subjects of international law including primary subjects, the constituent treaty – being of a different nature – is subject to special rules of interpretation, the organization possesses an inherent power to terminate itself, and questions of succession ought to be approached as a question of succession of subjects, etc.

Most of these opposite arguments are well known and have been amply discussed in the literature.[31] They have also been widely echoed in the practice of domestic and international courts.[32] They do not need to be examined any further, for the foregoing sufficiently illustrates the foundational character of the dichotomy between contractualism and constitutionalism. This is why the attention now turns to the way in which international legal scholars, however they apprehend this paradigmatic antinomy, have tried to iron it out through reconciliatory tactics. This is the object of the next section.

---

[31] For an overview of some of these issues, see C. Brölmann, "A flat earth? International organizations in the system of international law", 70 *Nordic Journal of International Law* (2009) 319, at 320–21 (focusing on these areas where the dichotomy produces different results and especially personality, nature of the instrument, legal personality; some examples are also discussed in J. Alvarez, "Constitutional Interpretation in International Organizations," in J.-M. Coicaud and V. Heiskanen (eds), *The Legitimacy of International Organizations* (United Nations University Press, 2001), 104–54; see also M. Rama-Montaldo, "International legal personality and implied powers of international organizations" (1970) *The British Yearbook of International Law*, 44, pp. 111–55

[32] For a useful compendium of the most important judicial decisions, see I.F. Dekker, et al. (eds), *Case Law on International Organizations: Text and Commentary*, Oxford: Oxford University Press, (2015), (forthcoming).

*Table 4.1*

|  |  | Contractualism | Constitutionalism |
|---|---|---|---|
| **Birth** | 1. *Components* | Contracting parties | Member States (*membrum*: part of) |
|  | 2. *Nature of constituent instrument* | Inter-state treaty | Constitution |
|  | 3. *Nature of normative activities (rules of the organizations)* | Secondary treaty law | Internal law |
|  | 4. *Nature of legal order* | A legal order of international law (permeability) | Separate and autonomous legal order (impermeability) |
|  | 5. *Relation with constituent treaty* | Not bound by its constituent instrument | Bound by its constituent instrument |
|  | 6. *Determination of personality* | Voluntarist theory | Objective theory (ex-post) |
|  | 7. *Nature of personality* | Inter-subjective | Objective |
|  | 8. *Capacities* | Determined by constituent instrument | Inherent in personality and determined by the international legal order |
|  | 9. *Competences/powers* | Principle of attributed competences (an expression of consent) | Principle of implied powers (inherent in subjecthood) |
|  | 10. *Reproduction capacity* | None | Power to create new primary and secondary subjects |
|  | 11. *Legitimacy* | Legitimacy of origin | Legitimacy of exercise |
|  | 12. *Privileges and Immunities* | Absolute protection from States | Inherent and limited protection of acts *de iure imperii* |

|   |   | Contractualism | Constitutionalism |
|---|---|---|---|
| **Life** | 13. *Interpretation of the constituent instrument* | Traditional rules of interpretation of treaties | Special rules of interpretation |
|  | 14. *Decision-making (will)* | Corporate will | *"Volonté distincte"* |
|  | 15. *Autonomy* | Political independence (from States) | Institutional independence (vis-à-vis the international legal order) |
|  | 16. *Practice of the organization* | Subsequent practice as an interpretive yardstick | Established practice as a source of normativity |
|  | 17. *Relation to other treaties concluded by Member States* | Automatic succession | Third party |
|  | 18. *Nature of special rules and practices* | Inter-state special rules (*lex specialis*) | *Lex specialis* is inapplicable |
|  | 19. *Ultra vires activities* | External invalidity | Internal invalidity and external wrongfulness |
|  | 20. *Responsibility* | Primary responsibility of States | Primary responsibility of the organization |
|  | 21. *Contribution to the (definition of) general interest* | Only States contribute to the formation/determination of peremptory norms and faculty to take countermeasures as statute-dependent | Contribute to the formation/determination of *ius cogens* and faculty to take counter-measures in the general interest |
| **Death** | 22. *Termination and dissolution* | Power of the States as contractual parties | Inherent power of the organization |
|  | 23. *Succession* | Succession of treaties | Succession of subjects |

## II. THE QUEST FOR RECONCILIATION BETWEEN CONTRACTUALISM AND CONSTITUTIONALISM AND THE TURN TO DIALECTICS

While the previous section sought to outline the unanimity with which international legal scholars recognize the existence of a tension between contractualist and constitutionalist visions – which are at the heart of the law of international organizations – this section makes the argument that, rather than accepting such a tension, international legal scholars have been seeking to reconcile contractualism and constitutionalism through dynamic concepts. More specifically, it is argued here that international legal scholars have been creating reconciliatory moves to create dialectics whereby the whole subject (theory, practice and discourses) is maintained in a state of flux, that is in an oscillation between opposite poles that ends up neutralizing the dichotomy.[33] In making such an argument, the following observations – while recognizing that dialectic approaches constitute analytical tools in their own right – understand the recourse to dialectical reconstruction as a way to stifle paradigmatic dichotomies and water them down in a continuum. In that sense, the remarks made here look at the flattening-out effect of the dialectical and dynamic moves made by those legal scholars confronted with the dichotomies mentioned in the previous one.

This section accordingly reviews some of these dichotomy-avoidance techniques. It is important to note that this account will not be exhaustive.[34] It will start by some general observations on the general proclivity of international legal scholars to seek to reconcile contractualism and constitutionalism and their incapacity to accept that what is there is – in the view of this author – an irreconcilable incongruence (1). It then elaborates on more specific strategies, like the mundane use of the idea of *dédoublement fonctionnel*[35] and some of its variants (2). Mention is also made of the escape sought in grand reconceptualization of the law of international organizations when dialectical moves fail to deliver their ironing-out effect (3).

---

[33] As is well known, this is a finding made by M. Koskenniemi in connection to the international legal discourse as a whole: see M. Koskenniemi, *From Apology to Utopia: The Structure of International Legal Argument (Reissue with new Epilogue)* (Cambridge University Press, 2005).

[34] For instance, it has also sometimes been claimed that these tensions could be overcome through "good governance". This is not an aspect that is discussed here. On this debate, see gen. D. Sarooshi, *International Organizations and their Exercise of Sovereign Power* (2005), Oxford University Press. Estranging concepts from one another has also sometimes been observed. See e.g. M. Rama-Montaldo, "International legal personality and implied powers of international organizations", in *The British Yearbook of International Law* (1970), 44, pp. 111–55 (seeking to estrange personality from powers).

[35] G. Scelle, *Précis, du droit du gens (Vol. I)* (1932), Dalloz, at 298.

## 1. Reconciliatory Proclivity: Ironing Out the Dichotomy between Contractualism and Constitutionalism

It has been recalled above that most international legal scholars acknowledge the existence of tensions in the law of international organizations. Yet, many of them, this section argues, are seeking to suppress or obfuscate such antinomies. Indeed, a great deal of the scholarship in the field – when not devoted to a comprehensive presentation of the rules, principles, and practices of international organizations – is geared towards the creation of images, narratives or concepts which allow a reconciliation between contractualism and constitutionalism. In other words, the discipline puts some unparalleled argumentative engineering and conceptual creativity at the service of the overall paradigmatic coherence of the field. In the eyes of international legal scholars, the world of international organizations, albeit of inevitable diversity, must seemingly be a flat one,[36] that is one that is paradigmatically coherent.

It is noteworthy that the coherence that is sought by international legal scholars in this specific case is not a formal one. It is not the absence of conflict between the sub-regimes of international organizations themselves or with other, domestic, regional or international orders. Rather, the paradigmatic coherence that is sought here is of a systemic nature, for the objective is to smother the dichotomies with a view to ensuring that "the multitudinous rules of [their] developed legal system 'make sense' when taken together".[37]

It is against the backdrop of this quest for a flat and paradigmatically coherent field, that international legal scholars have sought to solve the tension between contractualism and constitutionalism dialectically. Allowing the techniques, methods, and narratives to constantly remain in flux between contractualist and constitutionalist poles has been the mainstream remedy found by international legal scholars to ease their aversion to the paradigmatic incoherence of the field. It will not come as a surprise that this dominant reconciliatory mindset has not translated itself homogeneously. The art of reconciliation has manifested itself in a great variety of theories, concepts or narratives. Despite this diversity, it is submitted here that most of the strategies designed by international legal scholars to flatten the field and ensure paradigmatic coherence

---

[36] The expression is from C. Brölmann, "A flat earth? International organizations in the system of international law", 70 *Nordic Journal of International Law* (2009), 319.

[37] N. MacCormick, "Coherence in Legal Justification" in *Theory of Legal Science* (1984), p. 238.

manifest the seeking of refuge in a dialectical continuum. Indeed, those theories, concepts and narratives that are being relied on to ensure a reconciliation between opposite paradigms, leave the capacity of actors, the nature of the rules and constituent instruments, the relations between them – to name but a few examples – in a constant move between the contractualist and the constitutionalist paradigms, without ever stabilizing on one side or the other. Said differently, according to such reconciliatory moves of international legal scholars, the whole subject is left in a constant move, thereby turning the contraction into a seemingly coherent continuum. Providing a few examples is the object of the next section.

## 2. Some Illustrations of the Turn to Dialectics

The most common of these flattening moves is probably the use of the dialectical notion of *"dédoublement fonctionnel"*.[38] Indeed, in the context of the law of international organizations, the resort to this notion of role splitting is meant to overcome the inextricable antinomy mentioned above by contending the existing of a permanent role-shifting (rather than role-splitting) by states and international organizations. Once imported in the theory of international organizations, the concept of "dédoublement fonctionnel" allows actors to act in several capacities. Paradigmatic anomalies can, in turn, always be bypassed by shifting to the capacity that has the greatest explanatory and justificatory force. As it is employed in the international legal scholarship, the idea of "dédoublement fonctionnel" thus brings about a dynamic image of the law of international organizations, whereby capacities never need to be fixed and are left oscillating between opposite poles.

While the merits of this conceptual twist – especially the possibility of a law of international organizations that can live and thrive in denial of the core fundamental dissonance on which it rests – are incontestable, one can hardly negate that such a resort to the idea of "dédoublement fonctionnel" is a travesty of its original meaning, at least as it was conceived by Georges Scelle. Indeed, it is well known that "dédoublement fonctionnel" (role splitting) as it was originally envisaged by Scelle was the very means by which the objective law (*droit objectif*) was to be

---

[38] See H. Schermers and N. Blokker, *International Institutional Law* (2011), 5th ed., Martinus Nijhoff Publishers, para. 200, p. 151; para. 919, p. 606; para. 1886, p. 1211; see N. Blokkers, "Organizations and their members", *International Organizations Law Review* (2004), p. 139–61; see C. Brölmann, *The Institutional Veil in Public International Law: International Organizations and the Law of Treaties* (Hart Publishing, 2007), p. 32.

translated into positive law (*droit positif*).[39] In that sense, such a "dédoublement fonctionnel" was an expression of solidarity between the components of an overarching and all-embracing order (and of the political project associated with it).[40] It is far from certain the role-splitting function that is nowadays ascribed to the notion of "dédoublement fonctionnel" – as it is construed in the law of international organizations – corresponds to the monist understanding (and the political project) that informed Scelle's original notion. It should be made clear that distorting the original notion of "dédoublement fonctionnelle" is not, in itself, problematic. Concepts have a life of their own, travel in time and across disciplines, evolve and are subject to different interpretations and uses. The point here is thus not that international lawyers have misused the concept but more simply that they have used it in a way that allows them to play down the fundamental tensions of the law of international organizations.

It will not come as a surprise that some authors have been very much aware of the limits of the dialectical notion of "dédoublement fonctionnel", and of those of its transposition to the field of international organizations. This is why much refined and subtle – but equally dialectical – alternative notions have been put forward. The most refined of them is probably the concept of the "institutional veil" that has famously been proposed by Catherine Brölmann.[41] According to this idea, international organizations are neither open nor closed but transparent.[42] They constitute "open structures that are vehicles for states and,

---

[39] See G. Scelle, *Précis, du droit du gens (Vol. I)* (1932), Dalloz, at 298.

[40] H. Thierry writes: "The law-making function, which in the international legal system is accomplished by means of a "dédoublement fonctionnel", does not imply the settlement of conflicting or discordant interests in the international community, but is the expression of solidarity requirements within the international society". See H. Thierry, "The European tradition of international law: G. Scelle" 1 *European Journal of International Law* (1990), 193, at 199–200.

[41] See gen. C. Brölmann, *The Institutional Veil in Public International Law: International Organizations and the Law of Treaties* (Hart Publishing 2007), p. 32.

[42] C. Brölmann, *The Institutional Veil in Public International Law: International Organizations and the Law of Treaties* (Hart Publishing, 2007), p. 32. Transparency is meant to be "an endemic condition of intergovernmental organizations in general international law, partly due to the other two features counteracting: it indicates that organizations are neither entirely closed-off to international law in the way of states, nor entirely open, as instances of non-institutionalized inter-state cooperation would be" (p. 11). This transparency is also multi-layered (p. 33).

at the same time, closed structures that are independent legal actors".[43] It ensues, according to this construction, that there exists a dynamic relation between the entity and member states whereby member states continue to shine through the institutional veil of the organizations,[44] such veil being occasionally pierced to reveal the states behind it.[45]

Another expression of such a resort to dichotomy-avoidance dialectics is found in discussions pertaining to the relation between the legal order of international organizations and the international legal order as a whole. According to that view, the legal order of the international organizations is said to be an autonomous sub-legal order which nonetheless remains permeable to international law and its rules, especially those deemed of a peremptory character.[46] In that sense, the sub-legal order of the organization is said to be oscillating between some autonomy necessary for the realization of the political project of the organization and some limited overture to the most important rules of the international legal order. Such a dialectical position came to be defended, for instance, by a majority of scholars on the occasion of the (in)famous controversy surrounding the review by European courts of the legality of sanctions taken against *Kadi* as a result of the Security Council's anti-terrorist measures.[47] This also constitutes a dialectical move that plays down the paradigmatic tensions at the heart of the law of international organizations.

---

[43] C. Brölmann, *The Institutional Veil in Public International Law: International Organizations and the Law of Treaties* (Hart Publishing 2007), p. 1.

[44] C. Brölmann, "A flat earth? International organizations in the system of international law", 70 *Nordic Journal of International Law* (2009), 319, at 320.

[45] In doing so, C. Brölmann seeks to nuance P. Weil's emphasis on the nudity of states behind the immaterial veil of organizations. See P. Weil, "Le droit international en quête de son identité: cours général de droit international public", *Recueil des Cours*, 237 (1992), at 104. On this point, see C. Brölmann, *The Institutional Veil in Public International Law: International Organizations and the Law of Treaties* (Hart Publishing, 2007), p. 30.

[46] C. Brölmann, *The Institutional Veil in Public International Law: International Organizations and the Law of Treaties* (Hart Publishing, 2007), p. 60; P. Klein and P. Sands, *Bowett's Law of International Institutions* (2009) Sweet & Maxwell, p. 16.

[47] On this question, see the special issue of *International Organizations Law Review* (2008). For a different non-dialectical position, see J. d'Aspremont and F. Dopagne, "Kadi: The ECJ's reminder of the elementary divide between legal orders", *International Organizations Law Review* (2008); see also J. d'Aspremont and F. Dopagne, "Two constitutionalisms in Europe: pursuing an articulation of the European and international legal orders", *International Organizations Law Review* (2008).

The reconciliation through dialectics that is attempted by international legal scholars sometimes focuses on the way normativity is produced within (and by) international organizations, that is how international organizations produce norms meant to restrict the freedom of international actors that are relevant for the realization of the *objet social* of the organization. According to this dichotomy-avoidance move, it is the dialectical relation between legalism and managerialism that helps to reconcile opposite poles.[48] According to this construction, the exercise of power by international organizations is said to witness an inevitable oscillation between legalism, that is the exercise of authority through rules and managerialism, that is the exercise of authority through groups of experts.[49] The oscillation is explained by the turn to managerialism as a result of the indeterminacy of rules. This turn to managerialism – the argument goes – itself generates the problem of legitimacy, calling for a return to legalism. As a result, the production of normativity by the organization is constantly said to be moving between a rule-based mechanism, that inevitably needs to be anchored in the overarching system of sources of international law, and managerial mechanisms, that leave the autonomy of the organization more or less intact and allow it to escape the constraining effects of sources of international law.[50]

Mention must be made of one last illustration of the dialectical constructions enabling some international legal scholars to flatten the otherwise contradictory paradigmatic framework of the field. This last

---

[48] In this context, deformalization refers to the "process whereby the law retreats solely to the provision of procedures or broadly formulated directives to experts and decision-makers for the purpose of administering international problems by means of functionally effective solutions and 'balancing' interests". See M. Koskenniemi, "Constitutionalism as mindset: reflections on Kantian themes about international law and globalization", 8 in *Theoretical Inquiries in Law* (2006), 9, at 13. For a different meaning of deformalization, see J. d'Aspremont, "The politics of deformalization in international law", *Goettingen Journal of International Law* (2012), 3, 2, (2011), pp. 503–50. See also Chapter 2 above.

[49] See gen. J. Petman, "Deformalization of international organization" in J. Klabbers and A. Wallendahl (eds) *Research Handbooks in International Law* series, 398–429.

[50] For some critical remarks on the relativity of the theory of sources within the legal order of the organizations, see J. d'Aspremont, in "Le processus décisionnel de l'organization internationale" in *Traité de droit des organizations internationales*, (eds) E. Lagrange, H. Ascensio and J.-M. Sorel, (2013), LGDJ, 2013, pp. 402–3.

example brings the attention back to the above-mentioned notion of functionalism, most particularly as Michel Virally has understood it. Indeed, for Virally, the idea of function is the very linchpin of the law of international organizations that allows it to be deployed as a coherent and unitary body of law.[51] By virtue of this idea of function, the dichotomy between contractualism and constitutionalism vanishes and the law of international organizations is left pending between the autonomy and the dependency, as two necessary prerequisites for the fulfilment of the functions assigned to the organizations.[52] Indeed, functions come to underpin both the constitutional existence and autonomy of the organization as well as its contractual limitations and dependency. Functions, for Virally, explain as much as they iron out the tensions between the contractualist and constitutionalist natures of organizations. Virally's functionalist approach can thus be seen as another dialectical move, for the functions become the channel of the oscillation between the two aforementioned divergent poles. It must be noted, however, that to operate as a channel between contractualist and constitutionalist arguments, the functions of the organizations must be kept floating.[53] It is only if the functions of the organization are kept indeterminate that both contractualist and constitutionalist projects can feed therein and that the rules, techniques, narratives and arguments of the law of international organizations can be left in flux between the two.

The four scholarly constructions mentioned here are only a few of those observed in the international legal scholarship which seeks to rationalize the field at the level of its paradigms and reconcile contractualist and constitutionalist approaches. The present observations do not

---

[51] M. Virally, "La notion de fonction dans la théorie de 'l'organization internationales'", in *Mélanges à Charles Rousseau – La Communauté internationale* (1974), Pedone, Paris, pp. 277–300; see also for some critical remarks on the contemporary relevance of M. Virally's work, F. Dopagne, "Retour sur un 'classique'" – M. Virally, "La notion de fonction dans la théorie de 'l'organization internationale'", *Revue Générale de Droit International Public* (2011), pp. 285–7.

[52] For a non-conciliatory understanding of functionalism, see J. Klabbers and A. Wallendahl, *Research Handbook on the Law of International Organizations* (2011), Cheltenham: Edward Elgar; J. Klabbers, "Two Contending Approaches to the Law of International Organizations", in J. Klabbers and Å. Wallendahl (eds), *Research Handbook on International Organizations Law: Between Functionalism and Constitutionalism* (Cheltenham: Edward Elgar, 2010).

[53] In this respect, see the remarks of J. Petman, "Deformalization of international organization" in J. Klabbers and A. Wallendahl (eds) *Research Handbooks in International Law* series, 398–429.

need to exhaustively list the dialectical moves made by international legal scholars to reconcile contractualism and constitutionalism. Instead, this section ends by mentioning yet another type of dichotomy-avoidance strategy which has been relied on by international legal scholars and which extends beyond the refuge in dialectics.

## 3. Beyond the Dialectics: The Search for Grand Reconceptualization

It must be acknowledged that dialectics, even though they constitute the mainstream avenue to avoid the insufferable dichotomy between contractualism and constitutionalism, have not always been seen as the panacea. It happens that international legal scholars sometimes come to acknowledge that the dichotomy – whatever its exact manifestation – cannot be entirely diluted in dialectics.[54] According to that view, turning the dichotomy into dialectics is not sufficient, let alone possible. Yet, because of the irreconcilable character of the dichotomy between these two opposite poles in the present state of the law of international organizations, the only remaining viable option seems to lie with a reconceptualization of the field as a whole. This is the quest for a grand reinvention of the discipline that is occasionally envisaged – albeit never fully realized – in contemporary scholarship.[55] It is argued here that these calls for reconceptualization are manifestations of a similar reconciliatory proclivity to the one that informs the above-mentioned dialectical notions of "dédoublement fonctionnel", "institutional veil" or "functionalism". Interestingly, this quest for reconceptualization – and the accompanying search for conceptual aesthetics – has been more pronounced in Europe than in the United States. While international legal scholars in the former have long been seeking to design paradigmatic watertight systems, the thirst for systemic coherence in the latter has appeared more easily quenchable.[56]

---

[54] C. Brölmann, *The Institutional Veil in Public International Law: International Organizations and the Law of Treaties* (Hart Publishing 2007), p. 1.

[55] C. Brölmann, "A flat earth? International organizations in the system of international law", 70 *Nordic Journal of International Law* (2009) 319, at 340; R. Collins, "Non state actors in international institutional law", in Jean d'Aspremont (ed.) *Participants in the International Legal System: Multiple Perspectives on Non-State Actors in International Law*, (Routledge 2011), p. 313.

[56] D. Bederman, "The souls of international organizations: legal personality and the lighthouse at Cape Spartel", 36 *Virginia Journal of International Law* 275 (1995–1996), p. 278.

While being called for at regular intervals, and irrespective of the above-mentioned geographical variations, there has hardly been any actual attempt to reconceptualize.[57] The international legal scholarship specifically dedicated to the law of international organizations has fallen short of thinking out of the box of the current contractualist and constitutionalist paradigms around which most of the thinking on the subject articulates itself. The only exception to date is probably provided by Global Administrative Law, which has sought to approach problems of global governance by international institutions according to an entirely new perspective.[58] In doing so, it has moved away from mainstream international institutional law, which it considers unhelpful, to solve questions of accountability, participation, and transparency arising in the context of global governance.[59] By virtue of its rupture with the basic formal techniques and discourses of mainstream law of international organizations – which could be well be construed as a paradigmatic revolution from the vantage point of the law of international organizations[60] – it possibly creates space to address some of the problems of the field, as well as its inner tensions.[61] Organizations no longer need to be, once and for all, classified as contractualist or constitutional creatures. It is similarly irrelevant if the relations between them and their members are external or internal, or whether the product of its normative activities is of a domestic or international nature. Global Administrative Law allows the debate to focus on questions of governance deemed more fundamental. This being said, the reconceptualization attempted by

---

[57] Note J. Klabbers' attempt to give a more critical spin to the subject. Yet, this author neither claims nor seeks to "reconceptualize" the law of international organizations. See J. Klabbers, *Introduction to International Institutional Law* (2009), 2nd ed., Cambridge University Press.

[58] For some critical remarks on the dialectic moves between formalization and deformalization made in Global Administrative Law, see J. d'Aspremont, "Droit administratif global et droit international (Global Administrative Law and International Law)" in C. Bories (ed.) *Le Droit Administratif Global* (2012), Paris: Pedone; available at SSRN: http://ssrn.com/abstract=2004699. See also H. Schermers and N. Blokker, *International Institutional Law* (2011), 5th ed., Martinus Nijhoff Publishers, para. 13A.

[59] See the special issue of *International Organizations Law Review* (2009), on Global Administrative Law.

[60] On the notion of paradigm change, see T. Kuhn, *The Structure of Scientific Revolution*, 50th anniversary edition (Chicago, The University of Chicago Press, 2012).

[61] See the special issue of *International Organizations Law Review* (2009), on Global Administrative Law.

Global Administrative Law should not, however, be overvalued, as its primary aim has never been to salvage or reconceptualize the law of international organizations *per se*. Its material scope as well as its normative goals are much broader and, when it comes to the antinomy between contractualism and constitutionalism, its reconciliatory virtues are somewhat "accidental".

## III. "CONSTITUTIVE DICHOTOMY" OR "CONSTITUTIVE QUEST FOR DIALECTICS?"

The previous sections have tried to show that international legal scholars have been caught in a continuous search for conceptual flatness in the field. A few examples of the strategies and techniques they resort to, and especially their refuge in dialectics, have been provided, albeit in a non-exhaustive manner. It must probably have been noted that the previous sections have up to now fallen short of assessing whether such moves have been successful in smothering the paradigmatic incongruences of the law of international organizations. Yet, as it will be argued in this last section, appraising the degree of success of such reconciliatory moves of international legal scholars is not even called for. First, because it is not certain that they can ever succeed. Second, and more importantly, it is very questionable whether such a quest for dialectics is necessary in the first place. Indeed, as is discussed in this last section, the law of international organizations, like international law as a whole,[62] does not need to be saved from its inner tensions. On the contrary, it is contended in these final observations that trying to salvage the law of international organizations from its internal paradigmatic dichotomy may well be counter-productive, for it threatens the distinctiveness as much as the identity[63] of this branch of international law.

---

[62] On the internal contradictions of international law as a whole, see gen. M. Koskenniemi, *From Apology to Utopia: The Structure of International Legal Argument (Reissue with new Epilogue)* (Cambridge: Cambridge University Press, 2005).

[63] It must be acknowledged that the foregoing is not entirely unheard of. C. Brölmann has contended that the tension between the contractualist and constitutive paradigms are constitutive of the identity of the law of international organizations (see C. Brölmann, *The Institutional Veil in Public International Law: International Organizations and the Law of Treaties* (Hart Publishing 2007), p. 30). However, as this section seeks to demonstrate, this argument could

This argument can be explained as follows. The dichotomy between the contractualist and the constitutionalist paradigms is performative in that the coexistence of those two approaches is constitutive of the discipline as a whole. This means that, according to the point defended here, the dichotomy between contractualism and constitutionalism is foundational of the whole subject. In the absence thereof, there would be no law of international organizations as an independent subject of legal studies and the discourses, techniques, arguments and expertise at play in the framework of the law of international organizations would have no distinctiveness whatsoever. On the one hand, should the law of international organizations be exclusively constituted by a contractualist paradigm, questions pertaining to international organizations would eventually be diluted in questions of the law of treaties. On the other hand, should the law of international organizations be exclusively shaped around a constitutionalist paradigm, questions related to international organizations would raise issues of articulation of legal orders of the same nature as those pertaining to the relation between domestic legal orders and the international legal order. In that sense, the contractualist and constitutionalist paradigms should be seen as working in a performative tandem constitutive of the law of international organizations as a whole.

It is true that the weight of textual arguments is often overblown. Yet, in the present case, it is difficult to turn a blind eye to the support for the argument made here that is found in the foundational texts of the discipline. It is undeniable that every branch of international law rests on some mechanically repeated gospels which serve as foundational authoritative texts determinative of the main "values" of the field and of its main narrative. While the sources of international law are famously articulated around Article 38 of the Statute of the International Court of Justice[64] and the so-called law of statehood is built on the 1933 Montevideo Convention on the Rights and Duties of States,[65] one of the

---

be pushed even further. The dichotomy between contractualism and constitutionalism is not only constitutive of the identity of this area of law but also of this area of law itself.

[64] See gen. A. Pellet, "Article 38", in A. Zimmermann, Ch. Tomuschat and K. Oellers-Frahm, *The Statute of the International Court of Justice: a Commentary*, 2nd ed., (Oxford University Press, Oxford, 2012), pp. 731–870. For a critical look at the theory of sources and the idea of rules behind it, see J. d'Aspremont, "The Idea of 'Rules' in the Sources of International Law", 84 *British Yearbook of International Law*, (2014), pp. 103–30.

[65] For some critical remarks on the law of statehood, see Chapter 1.

authoritative texts around which the law of international organizations is built is the above mentioned famous 1949 Advisory Opinion of the International Court of Justice on the *Reparations for Injuries*. This "foundational gospel" of the law of international organizations provides a textual foundation to the performative character of the dichotomy between contractualism and constitutionalism. Indeed, as is widely recognized, this text is known for its paradigmatic inconclusiveness and gives foundations to both contractualist and constitutionalist projects, thereby confirming the foundational character of the tension between them.[66]

The foregoing should certainly not be interpreted as meaning that the paradigmatic antinomy between contractualism and constitutionalism was born with the 1949 Opinion. The foundational character of the dichotomy dates back to the time of inception of the law of international organizations. In fact, in the history of ideas about (the law of) international organizations, there was never a radical shift from one paradigm to the other but rather a concomitant crystallization of each of them. When it was first conceptualized in the international legal scholarship in the nineteenth and twentieth centuries,[67] the idea of international organization was certainly not new.[68] It is nonetheless contractualism that first gave the cognitive categories to apprehend to the phenomenon. Said differently, it is contractualism that first offered a breeding ground for the blossoming of the idea (and the practice) of a law of international

---

[66] D. Bederman, "The souls of international organizations: legal personality and the lighthouse at Cape Spartel", 36 *Virginial Journal of International Law* 275 (1995–1996), at 369; R. Collins, "Non state actors in international institutional law", in J. d'Aspremont (ed.) *Participants in the International Legal System: Multiple Perspectives on Non-State Actors in International Law*, (Routledge 2011), esp. pp. 314–15.

[67] The term was coined by J. Lorimer, *The institutes of the law of nations; a treatise of the jural relations of separate political communities* (Edinburgh and London, W. Blackwood and Sons 1883) 1, at 11; for some critical remarks on the intellectual history about international organizations, see J. Alvarez, *International Organizations as Law-Makers* (2005), Oxford University Press, 17–63.

[68] See gen. B. Reinalda, *The Routledge History of International Organizations from 1815 to the Present Day* (Routledge, London 2009); J.M. Sorel "L'Institutionalization des relations internationales", in E. Lagrange and J.M. Sorel (eds), *Traité de droit des organizations internationales* (LGDJ 2014), 11–34; see A. Peters and S. Peter "International organizations: between technocracy and democracy" in B. Fassbender and A. Peters, *The Oxford Handbook of the History of International Law* (Oxford University Press, 2012), pp. 170–97; D. Bederman, *International Law In Antiquity*, (Cambridge University Press 2001).

organizations. Yet, this contractualism was, from the start, informed by a constitutionalist project, for constitutionalism was its main driving force. At the same time, one could not have set off a move towards constitutionalism from the outset: contractualism was the only possible gateway to constitutionalism.[69] It seems that little has changed ever since, as contractualism remains the main narrative to salvage constitutionalism. This original kinship explains why, until today, contractualism and constitutionalism are to be considered as the inseparable, albeit incongruent, linchpins of the discipline. And this is also how one should understand (the origin of the) blatant similitudes in the justificatory narratives of each of the contractualist and constitutionalist paradigms, and, in particular, the above-mentioned resort to functionalism.[70]

The observations made above certainly do not amount to a call for more cynicism in the scholarship devoted to the law of international organizations. First, because international legal scholars have long been cynical about this area of law. It suffices to recall the extent to which the dominant narrative – and the accompanying belief – that international organizations necessarily serve the public good[71] has been unravelling lately.[72] Second, it does not seem to require much cynicism to come to terms with the fact that the field is not only riven by a dichotomy but also constituted thereby and that one cannot do away with it without risking to imperil, not only the identity and the justificatory narratives of the

---

[69] See A. McNair, *League of Nations as constitutional in substance but still located in inter-state framework*, cited by R. Collins in "Non state actors in international institutional law", in J. d'Aspremont (ed.) *Participants in the International Legal System: Multiple Perspectives on Non-State Actors in International Law* (Routledge 2011), p. 314; A. McNair, "The Functions of Differing Legal Character of Treaties", 11 *British Yearbook of International Law* (1930), 100, at 112.

[70] Cf. *supra*. I.

[71] R. Collins and N.D. White (eds), *International Organizations and the Idea of Autonomy: Institutional Independence in the International Legal Order* (Abingdon: Routledge, 2011), esp. the introduction by R. Collins and N. White: explains that H. Lauterpacht, H. Kelsen, G. Scelle, T. Franck and A. Cassese have all pinned their hopes on autonomous organizations to secure the rule of law in international affairs (p. 2); see also F. Seyersted, *Common Law of International Organizations* (Martinus Nijhoff, 2008).

[72] J. Klabbers "The Changing Image of International Organizations"; in J.-M. Coicaud, V. Heiskanen (eds), *The Legitimacy of International Organizations* (United Nations University Press, 2001). See also the remarks of J. Alvarez, "Constitutional Interpretation in International Organizations," in the same volume, at 104–54.

discipline, but also its mere existence. After all, the law of international organizations is not alone in sharing this fate.[73]

A real cynical argument would contend that the reconciliatory quest for dialectics which was depicted above, more than the dichotomy itself, is constitutive of the foundations of the discipline. Said differently, according to such a sombre view, the essence of the law of international organizations – and thus the goals of studies in this area – would lie, less with the project of unearthing some common rules[74] than with the (vain) moves and techniques which international legal scholars resort to with a view to shrouding a dialectical veil around the dichotomy between the contractualist and constitutionalist projects. That would amount to contend that, short of such a conciliatory proclivity and the quest for dialectics that comes with it, the field would be bereft of its main agenda and even its soul. This view probably constitutes the epitome of cynicism because it would mean that the field owes its existence, distinctiveness and autonomy to a vain and futile craving for coherence through dialectics.

It is hoped that it was made sufficiently clear in the previous paragraphs that the point made here does not go as far as elevating the futility of the epistemological moves by international legal scholars studying the law of international organizations into the decisive parameter of the distinctiveness, autonomy and identity of the latter. The argument put forward in this short chapter should rather be construed as a call for international legal scholars to revisit their abiding inclination to seek refuge in either dialectics or reconceptualization and confront the dichotomous character of the whole subject.[75] Such a call, it seems, is

---

[73] See M. Koskenniemi, *From Apology to Utopia: The Structure of International Legal Argument (Reissue with new Epilogue)* (Cambridge: Cambridge University Press, 2005).

[74] P. Sands and P. Klein, *Bowett's Law of International Institutions* (2009), 6th ed., Sweet & Maxwell, p. 16. See also P. Reuter, *International Institutions* (1961), Praeger; and H. Schermers and N. Blokker, para. 1339. F. Seyersted, *Common Law of International Organizations* (Martinus Nijhoff, 2008). For a critical discussion of that question, see J. Klabbers, "The paradox of international institutional law", 5 *International Organizations Law Review* (2008), pp. 151–73; see H. Schermers and N. Blokker, *International Institutional Law* (2011), 5th ed., Martinus Nijhoff Publishers, para. 22.

[75] It could be argued that coming to terms (and accepting to live) with incongruence may be taken as a sign of maturity. E. Fischer, B. Lange, E. Scotford and C. Carlarne, "Maturity and methodology: starting a debate about environmental law scholarship", 21 *Journal of Environmental Law*, (2009), 22.

anything but cynical. Indeed it presupposes a belief that studying the phenomenon of international organizations from the specific legal perspective inherited from the last century of scholarship on the topic still makes sense today. And there is probably nothing more ingenuous than upholding, as it has been the case in this chapter, a discipline that is shaped by dichotomous paradigms and caught in systemic incoherence.

# 5. Effectivity

This chapter examines the social arrangements pursued by international lawyers through the so-called doctrine of effectivity. Speaking of *a* doctrine of effectivity can itself be subject to discussion, for it seems that effectivity boils down to an aggregate of constructions operating in distinct doctrines: statehood, responsibility, territory, human rights, etc. Even if it seems debatable that there is such a thing as a doctrine of effectivity, the idea of effectivity is so omnipresent in international discourses and practices that it can be approached through a single lens, especially if the intention is to unearth part of the agenda informing its design and deployment. However, because it may not constitute a foundational doctrine properly so-called, this chapter refers to effectivity as an "idea".

## I. EFFECTIVITY AND EFFECTIVENESS

When they think of "effectivity" international lawyers usually come to think of a pragmatic, and factual construction. The idea of "effectivity" is, however, everything but concrete and raises all kinds of questions of legal theory, legal philosophy, epistemology, and theory of knowledge. It should also be highlighted that, from a linguistic standpoint, the word "effectivity" does not exist in British English. The attachment of the International Court of Justice to Her Majesty's English explains why the World Court uses the French word (*effectivité*) when it seeks to refer to "effectivity". These linguistic debates matter less than the semantics and, especially the consensus that "effectivity" ought to be opposed to that of "effectiveness". Effectiveness refers to the *outward* impact of (primary and secondary) rules, institutions and narratives of international law on all international actors and law-appliers.[1] In that sense, one way to see effectiveness is to equate it with the general state of a rule, institution or

---

[1] This is irrespective of whether or not international law is a very powerful instrument of governance. See M. Koskenniemi, "The mystery of legal obligations", 3 *International Theory* (2011), 319, at 321.

narrative in terms of compliance. "Effectivity", for its part, evokes an *inward* process whereby facts are integrated in rules, institutions and narratives as a condition of the operation of law and thus a condition of valid legal reasoning. By virtue of the idea of "effectivity", valid legal reasoning is made contingent on the empirical verification of a certain factual variable. Said differently, "effectivity" refers to the internalization of certain factual variables in the law itself as a result of which valid legal reasoning is conditioned on the demonstration of certain facts.[2]

The types of factual quality that are made a constitutive part of the operation of the rule include (but are not limited to) the finding of an effective government,[3] a certain behavourial practice for the sake of customary law,[4] effective control for the sake of the extraterritorial application of human rights,[5] effective control for the sake of attributing a behaviour to an personified actor,[6] the effective exercise of authority for the sake of belligerent occupation,[7] etc.[8] Valid legal reasoning on the

---

[2] It is true that it may happen that "effectivity" and "effectiveness" overlap when the verification of the factual variable required by the former depends on compliance by certain actors with certain standards.

[3] See *supra* chapter 1.

[4] See *supra* chapter 2.

[5] See gen. M. Milanovic, *Extraterritorial Application of Human Rights Treaties: Law, Principles, and Policy* (Oxford: Oxford University Press, 2011 ).

[6] See the debate about the meaning of effective control for the sake of Article 8 of the Articles on State Responsibility (2001). For some critical remarks, see F. Dopagne, "La responsabilité de l'État du fait des particuliers: les causes d'imputation revisitées par les articles sur la responsabilité de l'État pour fait internationalement illicite", 34, *Revue Belge de Droit International*, (2001), 2, pp. 492–525; B. Montejo, *The Notion of "Effective Control" under the Articles on the Responsibility of International Organizations, Responsibility of International Organizations: Essays in Memory of Sir Ian Brownlie*, edited by M. Ragazzi, Martinus Nijhoff Publishers, 389–404; C. Ryngaert, "Apportioning responsibility between the UN and member states in UN peace-support operations: an inquiry into the application of the effective control standard after Behrami", 45, *Israel Law Review*, (2012), 1, pp. 151–78.

[7] E. Benvenisti, *The International Law of Occupation. Second Edition*, (2012), 43–55; Y. Dinstein, *The International Law of Belligerent Occupation*, (2009), Cambridge University Press, 42–5; A. Roberts, "What is a military occupation?" 55 *British Yearbook of International Law*, (1984), 249–305; see also J. d'Aspremont and J. de Hemptinne, *Droit International Humanitaire*, (2013), chapter 6.

[8] For a recent review of all the doctrines where "effectivity" plays a role, see F.C. Matsumoto, *L'Effectivité en Droit International* (Bruylant, 2014). For a classic, see C. de Visscher, *Les Effectivités du Droit International Public* (Pedone, 1967).

basis of those "effectivity"-based doctrines is thus made contingent on the realization of the factual variable concerned.

It is with such a distinction between "effectivity" and "effectiveness" in mind that this brief chapter formulates three observations on the idea of "effectivity".

## II. THE WORLD OF INTERNATIONAL LAW AND THE OUTSIDE UNIVERSE

The first contention which I venture here is that the idea of "effectivity" operates as a bridge between the world of international law and what I would call an "outside universe". This is premised on the belief that international law creates a world of ideas (some people say "vocabularies"). The main ideas of the world of international law are states, international organizations, treaties, customs, wrongfulness, territory, crimes, etc. Strictly speaking, these ideas do not describe anything. They are ideas.[9]

Unsurprisingly, most international lawyers are unhappy with the world of international law being solely a world of ideas. International lawyers want these ideas to reach out to an outside universe[10] – on which they want to impose their conception of order.[11] This is of course not a new craving.[12] The point made here is rather that this quest to connect with

---

[9] On the relation between international law and ideas and the power of ideas, see gen. P. Allott, "The true function of law in the international community", 5, *Global Legal Studies Journal*, (1998), 391. See also P. Allott, "The concept of international law", 10, *European Journal of International Law*, (1999), 31.

[10] N. Onuf, "Law-making in the global community: a working paper" (1974), in N. Onuf, *International Legal Theory*, 63 at 88: "What international lawyers care to describe as international law is their own invention. It builds the illusion there is an international legal order and they are in charge of it. They see their rules of law as the specific, tangible instrumentalities by which states are made a part of that order and their behavior governed by it ... In this view, law is little more than a set of artifacts. They appear to be germane to international life simply to fulfill their illusory function for lawyers. For their part, lawyers made their artifacts as realistic as possible."

[11] On the "blessed rage for order" of international lawyers, see J. Crawford, "International law as discipline and profession", 106 *ASIL Proceedings*, (2012), at 2.

[12] M. Koskenniemi speaks of Lauterpacht and Oppenheim as a group of cosmopolitan-minded lawyers who tried to translate the diplomacy of states into the administration of legal rules and institutions. See M. Koskenniemi, "The fate

the outside universe is the very reason why they have created another idea, that is, the idea of "effectivity". Needless to say that the idea of "effectivity" created by an international lawyer is itself a mere idea among others. Yet, the idea of "effectivity" allows the above-mentioned "effectivity"-based doctrines of international law to be connected with an outside universe. Said differently, the idea of "effectivity" is what allows those doctrines to operate outside the closed world of ideas of international law. It allows all these foundational doctrines to pierce and beam beyond the atmosphere of the world of international law and relate to the outside universe. It is in this sense that "effectivity", as I understand it here, creates a bridge between the world of international law and an outside universe.

At this stage, it is essential to highlight that the bridge created by "effectivity" between the world of international law and the universe is *bi-directional*. While "effectivity" creates a bridge between international law and the outside universe by making valid legal reasoning dependent on factual variables, it does not follow that the world of international law is automatically and unilaterally shaped after such an imported outside universe. Although global actors constantly shape international law in a way that allows the pursuit of certain agendas that they see as in their self interest, it is important to realize that the universe which is imported into the world of international law by virtue of "effectivity" simultaneously is, to a significant extent, constructed along the lines of the ideas (and descriptive categories) of the very same world of international law.[13] In other words, this outside universe (made of effective government, effective control, behavioral practice, etc.), despite heavily bearing on the design of international law, is itself partly molded after the categories of the world of international law.[14] At any time, this imported outside

---

of public international law: between technique and politics", 207 *The Modern Law Review*, (2007), 1, at 2.

[13] For a discussion on the idea of "out-there-ness" see chapter 6. See also gen. J. Law, *After Method. Mess in Social Science Research*, (Routledge, 2004), at 19–25. On the idea that facts are interpretive, see S. Fish, *Doing What Comes Naturally*, (Duke University Press, 1989), at 157.

[14] See P. Allott, "The idealist's dilemma: re-imagining international society", EJIL-Talk! ("Nation and state and government are notorious fictions, metaphysical entities existing only in and for the human mind. The whole of the law is a vast work of fiction, a masterpiece of the human imagination, creating its own entirely artificial reality."). P. Allott goes as far as saying that it is the ideas of international lawyers that have created disorder in the world. See also J. Crawford, "International law as discipline and profession", 106 *ASIL Proceedings*, (2012), at 16: "We are collectively part of the makers of that world".

universe is simultaneously a projection of the world of ideas of international law. The importation of the outside world as a result of "effectivity" is thus one facet of what constitutes an intricate dialectic process, for any import in the world of international law and its main doctrines by virtue of effectivity is equally shaped by a projection of the latter. The world that is imported into international law by virtue of effectivity is as much constitutive of and constituted by international law.

This is, of course, not to say that the ideas by virtue of which international law constitutes the outside universe are universally shared among international lawyers themselves. Discourses and practices about the categories of international law, as was explained in chapter 1, are also battles over the description and re-description of the world.[15] This is however not something on which this chapter needs to elaborate. It only matters here to emphasize that effectivity is a tool that allows international lawyers to project their world of – contested – ideas on the outside world.

## III. THE THERAPEUTIC DIMENSION OF THE IDEA OF "EFFECTIVITY"

The contention made here that "effectivity" constitutes a connecting tool between the world of international law and an outside universe immediately raises some questions: why make the foundational doctrines of international law (and the legal reasoning in connection with each of them) dependent on factual determination? Why expressly make space in legal argumentation for factual determinations? Why not restrict legal reasoning to a purely normative or semantic exercise? Why do certain professionals of international law feel the need to connect the world of ideas of international law with an outside (albeit self-created) universe?

It is argued here that part of the answer lies with the profession of international legal academics. More specifically, it is submitted here that the idea of "effectivity" alleviates a terrible fear of those professionals that are not confronted with practice, that is the fear of being sequestered in their own world of ideas.[16] In other words, "effectivity" soothes the

---

[15] See the introduction of this book. See also M. Koskenniemi, "The fate of public international law: between technique and politics", 207 *The Modern Law Review*, (2007), 1, at 7.

[16] G. Simpson, "On the magic mountain: teaching public international law", 10, *European Journal of International Law*, (1999), 70, at 74: "We are often delighted when judges take notice of international law".

fear of certain professionals of being cloistered in a world of abstract ideas (states, borders, sources, wrongfulness, crimes, etc.) without being able to reach out to the universe.[17] Said even more explicitly, "effectivity" allows international academics to elude a self-perception that their profession boils down to theology and reassures them that they are not theologians.[18] The idea of "effectivity" can accordingly be considered as a powerful drug against epistemological claustrophobia for certain categories of professionals, and especially legal academics. It helps turn international law into a body of knowledge about the practice going on in the outside universe and, simultaneously, the experts of the ideas of international law into the experts of the outside universe of states, effective governments, customs, territory, wrongfulness. As a result, after having been cured from their claustrophobic anxieties, legal academics, thanks to the idea of effectivity are in a position to self-appoint themselves as astronauts in the outside universe.[19]

## IV. THE DECEITFUL IDEA OF EFFECTIVITY

It is important to conclude by emphasizing that this image of international law as the social science pertaining to what is going on in this self-created outside universe can be deceitful, at least when confronted

---

[17] On some critical remarks on the pitfall of self-referentiality, see the introductory speech of the 5th Research Forum of the *European Society of International Law* by J. d'Aspremont, "International lawyers live!" available at SSRN: http://ssrn.com/abstract=2271115.

[18] This does not exclude that they have some awareness of the risk of failure and can include what M. Koskenniemi calls a "commitment", that is a sentimental attachment to the field's constitutive rhetoric and traditions with some awareness of the risk of failure. See M. Koskenniemi, "Between commitment and cynicism; outline of a theory of international law as practice," in *Collection of Essays by Legal Advisors*, (United Nations, 1999), 493. It is interesting to note that the charge of theology has been raised against those perceived as formalist in other circumstances. For an example in the American jurisprudential debate, see N. Duxbury, *Patterns of American Jurisprudence*, (1997), OUP, at 37.

[19] This finding is irrespective of the fact that international lawyers do not need international law to exist as an object to warrant their existence as a professional discipline. See, J. Crawford, "International law as discipline and profession", 106 *ASIL Proceedings*, (2012), at 2 ("One does not have to believe in the existence of God to credit the existence of the clergy"). See also the introductory speech of the 5th Research Forum of the *European Society of International Law* by J. d'Aspremont, "International lawyers live!" available at SSRN: http://ssrn.com/abstract=2271115.

with a – somewhat ideal – external perspective. Indeed, because the idea of "effectivity" bridges the world of international law with an outside universe, it makes practitioners look as if, from an external perspective, they are in control of the universe that is imported into the world of international law. From an external perspective, practitioners are in the driver's seat in the outside universe and hence in international law. From such an external perspective, those who decide in the outside universe are policy-makers, legal advisers, counsels, and judges, legal academics only occupying a back seat. From an external perspective, legal academics have, at best, spiritual authority.[20] This external imagery brought about by the idea of "effectivity" reveals the deceitfulness inherent therein. As was explained earlier, the idea of "effectivity" makes certain categories of professionals feel they are not theologians while making them look as if they are having nothing more than spiritual authority. However, as the above remarks also pointed out, the idea of "effectivity" simultaneously endows some of these professionals, and especially legal academics, with architectural responsibilities in the construction of the outside universe.

The foregoing should suffice to make clear that, for certain professionals of international law, there could not be a more comfortable position. Those professionals define the vocabularies and ideas that are projected in the universe while being simultaneously portrayed, from an external perspective, as solely wielding spiritual authority about what is going on in this universe. Their position is that of immense authority, all of it veiled and concealed by the idea of "effectivity". It does not seem controversial to hold that it is in definition and description that lies the greatest power.[21] By virtue of the smokescreen provided by the idea of "effectivity", certain professionals of international law, and especially legal academics, thus exert such a definitional power in all secrecy and without much formal accountability but reputational.

Against this backdrop, there seems to be no doubt that the idea of "effectivity" will continue to prosper and inform scholarly debates and representations of the world for future decades. Indeed, as was argued here, "effectivity" alleviates the fear of certain categories of professionals, and especially legal academics, of being relegated to the periphery as well as their fear of theology. It provides them with a powerful drug

---

[20] As is well-known, this is an image that has been the object of compelling contestations over the last decades. See e.g. M. Koskenniemi, *The Gentle Civilizer of Nations*, (CUP, 2004).

[21] See gen. S. Singh, "Appendix 2: international law as a technical discipline: critical perspectives on the narrative structure of a theory" in J. d'Aspremont, *Formalism and the Sources of International Law*, (Oxford: OUP, 2013), 236.

against epistemological claustrophobia. Most importantly, it empowers these professionals with definitional power while allowing them to be perceived as being in the back seat. If those professionals relish power (as I believe they do), they would be foolish to forsake the idea of "effectivity".

# PART II

The argumentative techniques

# 6. Methodology

This chapter is premised on the idea that methodological choices are most conducive to the persuasiveness of legal arguments and thus play a very central role in the social validation thereof. After formulating some general considerations on the relationship between theory and methodology as well as the social constraints on methodological choices (I), this chapter offers a handful of critical observations on methodological debates in contemporary legal studies (II).

## I. GENERAL CONSIDERATIONS

The following sections discuss the relation between methodology and theory as well as the concept of the methodological package (1), the freedom to choose, customize and use methodological packages (2), the social constraints on methodological choices (3) and the possibility to evaluate methodological choices from a functional and social perspective (4).

### 1. Methodology, Theory and Methodological Packages

The following observations are premised on the idea that it is vain to seek to distinguish legal methods and theories of law, for none is really independent from the other.[1] Theories of (international) law come with certain methodological moves while the various sets of legal methods found in the literature and the practice imply and presuppose certain choices in terms of theory of law.[2] Said differently, the choice for a given concept of (international) law involves the adoption of certain investigative and conceptual methods while the choice for certain methods can only be evaluated within the framework of certain theories of law. This

---

[1] See gen. A. Halpin, "The methodology of jurisprudence: thirty years off the point", 19 *Canadian Journal of Law and Jurisprudence*, (2006), 67, esp. 75.

[2] M. Hesselink, "A European Legal Science?", Centre for the study of European contract law working paper series, No. 2008/02, at 23; "Adopting a legal method implies, in particular, adopting a theory of law (and adjudication) and probably (depending on the theory of law) also a theory of justice".

means that the theories of law and methodology cannot be estranged from one another and, thus, cannot be thought about and discussed separately.[3]

This preliminary argument could be pushed even further. It is submitted in this chapter that legal theories are better construed as methodological packages. Methodological packages, for the sake of the following observations, must be understood as a set of cognitive tools, techniques of argumentation, evaluative criteria and communicative protocols meant to secure persuasiveness within a certain audience adhering to a certain concept of law.[4] It is thus an all-embracing set of methods, theories, narratives, techniques and moves of different kinds that is geared towards the production of arguments for a given audience. Each of them represents a different "legal style"[5] which will only be appreciated and valued by the audience trained to that style.

There is another premise to the observations that follow which should be spelled out. It is commonplace to recognize that any theory of law is performative in that it creates its own realities[6] and that the theories do not describe what it is out there but rather produce what they seek to understand or regulate.[7] This is a point that was discussed in Chapter 5. It is argued here that such a common view requires to be nuanced. The

---

[3] For a challenge to this view, see J. Coleman, "The architecture of jurisprudence", 121 *The Yale Law Journal*, (2011), 2, esp. 34–40.

[4] Albeit broader, this conception of methodology echoes the understanding of M. Koskenniemi. See M. Koskenniemi, "Methodology of international law", *Max Planck Encyclopedia of Public International Law*, para. 1.

[5] M. Koskenniemi, "Letter to the editors of the symposium", 93 *AJIL*, 351 (1999), at 358–9. See also M. Prost, *The Concept of Unity in Public International Law*, (Hart, 2011), at 153 ("To be 'in the truth' of international law, that is, to be validated by the members of the 'invisible college', a statement must refer to a full, rightly packed, continuous, geographically well-defined field of objects; it must use a well-defined alphabet of notions; it must be located within a recognizable thematic horizon; and lastly, it must adhere to a certain aesthetics of argument (that is, a certain 'style')").

[6] P. Allott, "Language, method and the nature of international law", 45 *BYBIL*, 79, (1971), at 118; M. Koskenniemi, "Letter to the editors of the symposium", 93 *AJIL*, 351, (1999), at 360. This had long been recognized by Kelsen: see Kelsen, *Reine Rechtslehre* (2nd ed. Vienna: Deuticke 1960) 239 (trans. by J. Kammerhofer, "Law-making by scholars"), 74–5.

[7] For a more general discussion of the long move away from the intuitive empiricist understanding of knowledge production as embodied by Merton and the rejection of the idea of "out-thereness", "anteriority", "definiteness" and "universalism", see gen. John Law, *After Method. Mess in Social Science Research*, Routledge, (2004), at 5 and 22–5.

performativeness of theories of law is better explained by virtue of the above-mentioned idea of methodological packages. It is when they are construed as methodological packages that theories can be said to be performative and constitutive of the world they try to apprehend, explain and regulate.[8] A choice of particular methodological packages produces a certain vision of the world.[9]

Needless to say that such methodological packages are "not hermetically sealed" and are "fluid and negotiable".[10] Indeed, there is no agreement on what the dominant and universally accepted methodological packages are.[11] But even the very mainstream and dominant methodological packages like positivism and naturalism remain very indeterminate, everyone understanding these bundles of theories and methods in a very different way.[12] In that sense, the contents of methodological packages fluctuate according to intersubjective dynamics and are never fixed.

## 2. The Freedom to Choose, Customize and Use Methodological Packages

Methodological packages only hold their existence from a choice.[13] Indeed, methodological packages do not have any objective existence

---

[8] For P. Allott, by virtue of this performativeness, the writer about international law has a correspondingly responsible task: his generalization must do justice to the evidence that is known to him. See gen P. Allott, "Language, method and the nature of international law", 45 *BYBIL*, 79, (1971), at 119. See also Chapter 5, above.

[9] Q. Skinner, *The Foundation of Modern Political Thought*, (Cambridge, Cambridge University Press, 1978), at xi.

[10] R. Cryer, T. Hervey and B. Sokhi-Bulley, *Research Methodologies in EU and International Law*, Hart, 2011, at 14.

[11] It is interesting to note for instance that, as far as international law is concerned, the list of methodologies examined in the famous 1999 AJIL symposium differs significantly from the list of methodologies studied in Cryer, Hervey and Sokhi-Bulley. On these variations, see R. van Gestel, H.-W. Micklitz and M.P. Maduro, "Methodology in the New Legal World", EUI Working Paper LAW 2012/13, at p. 1.

[12] On the indeterminate character of the notion of legal positivism in international legal scholarship, see J. d'Aspremont and J. Kammerhofer, "The future of international legal positivism", in J. Kammerhofer and J. d'Aspremont (eds), *International Legal Positivism in a Postmodern World* (CUP, 2014) 1.

[13] R. Cryer, T. Hervey and B. Sokhi-Bulley, *Research Methodologies in EU and International Law*, Hart, 2011, at 9; R. van Gestel, H.-W. Micklitz and M.P. Maduro, "Methodology in the New Legal World", EUI Working Paper LAW

(nor validity) but through their espousal by the professionals of the community concerned. In that sense there is no methodological package that is, a priori, endowed with more validity or force than another. There are just a multitude of methodological packages which, in practice, are endorsed by professionals without any of them having any methodological or theoretical ascendancy over the other.[14] It follows that professionals choose, customize and use methodological packages in the way that fits their expertise, the socialization process they have been through, the social group they belong to and/or speak to, their agendas and, more generally, the circumstances in which they seek persuasiveness.

The result of such a freedom is an inherent possibility to customize one's methodological package(s). Indeed, subject to the social constraints mentioned below as well as traditions, no one is committed to stick to one single methodological package. In other words, no one, at least at face value, is obliged to adhere to one single package. The abiding freedom to choose one's methodology also implies a freedom to customize the methodological package(s) one relies on. It seems rather uncontested that methodological choices and theories involve "a mixture of unarticulated formalism (here are the rules, learn these texts), legal realism (texts do not matter, state practice matters), political realism (states are nasty and break the rules), and various forms of cosmopolitanism (states are irrelevant, globalization of human rights or civil society is what counts)".[15]

## 3. Choices of Methodological Packages as a Socially and Functionally Constrained Act

Needless to say that this multi-dimensional freedom – the freedom to choose one's methodological packages and to customize them – is not totally unbridled, for such choices are necessarily socially situated. Although there is no a-methodological standpoint from which a hierarchy of methodological packages could be established as was indicated above, it seems uncontested that some methodological packages are held "in

---

2012/13; see also O. Corten, *Méthodologie du Droit international public*, Editions de L'Université Libre de Bruxelles, 2009 pp. 45–6.

[14] M. Koskenniemi, "Letter to the editors of the symposium", 93 *AJIL*, 351, (1999), at 352; A. Orford, "On International Legal Method", 1 *London Review of International Law*, (2013), 166–97, at 167.

[15] G. Simpson, "On the magic mountain: teaching public international law", 10 *EJIL*, 1999, 70–92, at 79.

higher esteem" than others.[16] There are thus no a priori conceptual or theoretical hierarchies among methodological packages but fluctuating perceptions of how methodological packages are received in a given community. As has already been highlighted on numerous occasions in this book, validation is thus not theoretical but social, for it hinges on the assent of the relevant community.[17] For the choice of a methodological package to be made efficiently, a "(m)astery of the international legal methods require close acquaintance with the preferences and biases of the institutions at which one is arguing",[18] as well as a realization that such preferences constantly change over time.[19] This includes knowledge of the fluctuating aesthetics sought by the community concerned.[20]

It will come as no surprise that choices of methodological packages are not always made in full awareness of such social constraints. It happens that social constraints are so strong and overwhelming that the choice for a certain methodological package may even be made without any self-awareness and boils down to the mechanical repetition of an inherited style.[21]

It would probably be too reductive to construe the choice for methodological packages as being solely subject to social constraints. When choosing, customizing or using a methodological package, any professional will take into account the purpose of the activity for the sake of which the choice is made. In other words, a methodological package is

---

[16] M. Koskenniemi, "Letter to the editors of the symposium", 93 *AJIL*, 351, (1999), p. 356 ("The final arbiter of what works is nothing other than the context (academic or professional) in which one argues").

[17] On the idea of social validation, see gen. T. Kuhn, *The Structure of Scientific Revolutions*, The University of Chicago Press, 50th anniversary ed., 2012, 94. See also S. Fish, "Fish v. Fiss", 36 *Stanford Law Review*, (1984), pp. 1325–47, at 1331.

[18] M. Koskenniemi, "Methodology of international law", *Max Planck Encyclopedia of Public International Law*, para. 13. At para. 24, M. Koskenniemi adds: "While different institutions highlight one or the other of the legal argument's constitutive poles – it is sometimes better to argue in terms of formal rules, at other times in terms of the policy-objectives of decision-makers – neither of them can be fully preferred over the other".

[19] M. Koskenniemi, "Methodology of international law", *Max Planck Encyclopedia of Public International Law*, para. 25.

[20] T. Kuhn, *The Structure of Scientific Revolutions*, The University of Chicago Press, 50th anniversary edition, 2012, at 155.

[21] S. Fish, "Fish v. Fiss", 36 *Stanford Law Review*, (1984), pp. 1325–47, at 1331.

also chosen to perform a certain function, that function being determined by the agenda pursued by the author of that choice.

It is important to realize that these social and functional dimensions of methodological choices are those that make evaluation of these choice at all possible. This is the object of the next section.

## 4. The Possibility of a Social and Functional Evaluation of Methodological Choices

It has been recalled above that there is no meta-methodological position from which hierarchies between methodological packages could be established, all of them having a priori the same validity. This truism does not necessarily mean that the choice of a methodological package cannot be evaluated. It remains possible to evaluate such choices according to the corresponding social and functional evaluative yardsticks. In other words, the choice of the methodological package can be confronted with the preferences and biases of the community, or at least with how they are understood, as well as its fulfilling of the agenda pursued by the author of the choice.

It is true that the functional evaluation of methodology probably rests on more stable yardsticks. It will always be difficult to determine the preferences of the community concerned, not less because such preferences are very fluctuating. In contrast, functional evaluation requires to confront the declared aim of the project with the methodological packages that it embraces.[22] This presupposes of course that there is self-awareness about what one is trying to achieve. Be that as it may, legal argumentation, especially when it is carried out in an academic context, can potentially be geared towards the performance of a wide variety of functions. Among those functional yardsticks on the basis of which methodological choices can be evaluated, one finds predictability, intelligibility and complexity-reduction, as well as progressive development of the law.[23] The adequacy of any methodological choice can always be assessed – or at least discussed – in the light of any of these goals, especially since one can no longer find a shelter behind an allegedly objective descriptive project.[24]

---

[22] J. Smits, *The Mind and Method of the Legal Academic*, Edward Elgar, (2012), at 119.

[23] On the choices between intelligibility and predictability, see A. Rosenberg, *Philosophy of Social Science*, 4th ed., Westview Press, (2012), 295

[24] On the traditional debate on the evaluative dimension of description in jurisprudence, see V.R. Blanco, "The methodological problem in legal theory:

It has been argued by some authors that, besides social and functional yardsticks, evaluation of methodological choices could also be carried out on the basis of other criteria, like the scientific nature of the methodological package chosen or its conformity with certain formal values.[25] It is not certain that, as far as international law is concerned, there is any consensus on the scientific nature of scholarly inquiries or legal argumentation. It is true that it cannot be excluded that choices for methodological packages are evaluated on the basis of formal criteria, but such criteria are themselves the result of a social validation process. Indeed, only those formal criteria valued and validated by the community concerned will be taken into account when appraising the choice of a given methodological package. The social and functional dimensions seem to be the only standpoints from which methodological choices can be evaluated.

## II. CHOICES OF METHODOLOGICAL PACKAGES IN INTERNATIONAL LAW

After a few considerations on the institutional environment against the backdrop of which methodological choices in international law are made (1), the rest of this chapter discusses induction and the idea of system (2), the turn to empiricism (3), interdisciplinarity and multidisciplinarity (4), the need for paradigmatic revolution (5), pluralism (6) and critical attitudes (7).

### 1. The Institutional Background of Methodological Choices in International Law

Debates in international law take place in a rather liberal environment. Since international law was elevated into an academic discipline more than a century ago, no single interpretive authority has been able to empower itself as a monopolistic setter of the interpretation of international legal rules. Neither the establishment of a World Court nor that of an *Institut de Droit International* – meant to mirror "the legal

---

normative and descriptive jurisprudence revisited", 19 *Ratio Juris*, (2006), 26–54; see more generally, S. Perry, "Hart's methodological positivism", 4 *Legal Theory*, (1998), 427–67 or J. Dickson, *Evaluation and Legal Theory*, Oxford, Hart, (2001).

[25] D. Feldman, "The nature of legal scholarship", 52 *The Modern Law Review*, (1989), at 498.

conscience of the civilized world"[26] – has come to offset the absence of a supreme guardian of interpretation in the community of international lawyers. That is not to say that the field is not structured nor hierarchical. It is simply that interpretive power in international law has remained extremely diffused. Structures and hierarchies are not institutionalized, but not less powerful and compelling. It is nowadays scattered between influential prolific minds affiliated with prestigious research institutions, domestic and international courts, international and regional law-codifying bodies, and, more occasionally, non-governmental organizations (NGOs), which compete with one another for interpretive authority and persuasiveness.

In this context, the battle for power is primarily a battle to impose certain interpretive postures and methodological choices.[27] Who wins the battle over interpretation and methodological packages is in a position to dictate the agenda, a certain vision of the world as well as some societal choices.[28] In contrast to the domestic scene,[29] conquering institutional sites of power in international law, although it may provide a decisive advantage, is often only secondary to the imposition of interpretive and methodological choices. This being said, there remains a clear advantage associated with belonging to a clan or a school,[30] as each of these social groupings deploys a whole apparatus and various tactics, strategies,

---

[26] It is interesting to note that the French text that is the only authoritative version goes as follows: "Il a pour but de favoriser le progrès du droit international ... En travaillant à formuler les principes généraux de la science de manière à répondre à la conscience juridique du monde civilisé." For some critical insights, see M. Koskenniemi, *The Gentle Civilizer of Nations: The Rise and Fall of International Law 1870–1960* (CUP, 2001), 39.

[27] See gen. S. Fish, *Doing What comes Naturally*, Duke University Press, 1989.

[28] M. Hesselink, "A European Legal Science?" Centre for the Study of European Contract Law Working Paper Series, No. 2008/02, at 20.

[29] For a superb historical account of the battle of methodological packages along institutional lines, see N. Duxbury, *Patterns of American Jurisprudence*, (OUP, 1995).

[30] D. Feldman, "The nature of legal scholarship", 52 *The Modern Law Review*, (1989), 498, at 513; see also A. Rasulov, "New approaches to international law: images of a genealogy", in J.M. Beneyto and D. Kennedy (eds), *New Approaches to International Law: the European and the American Experiences*, (TMC Asser-Springer, 2012), pp. 151–91.

networks at the service of the imposition of interpretive and methodological choices.[31]

It is with these specific features of the arena where methodological battles are fought that a few remarks on some of the dominant or successful methodological packages must now be formulated.

## 2. Induction and the Idea of System

Inductive methods have long been a common component of the dominant methodological package found in international legal studies. For instance, when one refers to the dominant school of positivism, what is actually often meant is the choice for inductive methods. The choice for inductive methods is, itself, often accompanied by the idea of system. Systemic thinking and induction function on the basis of an internal perspective.[32] Taken together, inductive methods and the idea of systems, cloak legal argumentation with the trappings of science and give it an aura of objectivity.[33]

Although dominant in Europe,[34] such systemic conceptions of international law and inductive methods are usually more contested in the American tradition of international law.[35] This is not to say that the idea of system and inductive methods is unknown to the American tradition of international law. According to the common law tradition that pervades the American approach of international law, every adjudicatory case creates (and contributes to) a precedent-based system.[36] In that sense, the

---

[31] See gen. R. Debray, *Transmitting Culture*, Columbia University Press, (1997). For an application to the Critical Legal Studies Movement, see A. Rasulov, "New approaches to international law: images of a genealogy", in J.M. Beneyto and D. Kennedy (eds), *New Approaches to International Law: the European and the American Experiences*, (TMC Asser-Springer, 2012), pp. 151–91.

[32] M. Hesselink, "How many systems of private law are there in Europe? On plural legal sources, multiple identities and the Unity of Law", Amsterdam Law School Legal Studies Research Paper No. 2012-59, at 5.

[33] D. Feldman, "The nature of legal scholarship", 52 *The Modern Law Review*, (1989) 498, at 499.

[34] J.M. Smits, *The Mind and Method of the Legal Academic*, (Edward Elgar, 2012), at 18.

[35] E. Benvenisti, "Comments on the systemic vision of national courts as part of an international rule of law", 4 *Jerusalem Review of Legal Studies*, (2012), 42.

[36] A. Somek, "The Indelible Science of Law", University of Iowa Legal Studies Research Paper, Number 09-18, June 2010, 21 (according to whom

difference between the European and the American traditions lies more with the nature of their respective systemic and inductive approaches to international law.[37]

It is noteworthy that, despite some resilience in some parts of the world, inductive and systemic methods have endured serious discredit over the last decades. It has become mundane to lay bare the deductive moves at work behind inductive methodological choices.[38] It is now also more commonly accepted that international law rests on doctrines that are a blend of deduction and induction obfuscating one another.[39] Some of these doctrines have been analyzed in the previous chapters. The same discredit has hit the idea of system. Although international lawyers are very much aware of the advantages associated with construing international law as a system,[40] systemic and inductive methods are no longer

---

every case creates its own legal science). See also G. Simpson who claims that, very often, by giving international law the appearance of the common law, we seek to transform it into a system. See G. Simpson, "On the magic mountain: teaching public international law", 10 *European Journal of International Law*, (1999), 70, 75.

[37] This is not to say that European approaches to the international legal system are homogeneous. There exist variations about the concept of legal system between German and French international lawyers. It suffices to compare the German intellectual origins of the idea of international legal system and the dominant systemic view in the French legal scholarship. Comp. J. von Bernstorff, "German intellectual historical origins of international legal positivism", in, *International Legal Positivism in a Post-Modern World*, 50, J. Kammerhofer and J. d'Aspremont (eds), (2014) and J. Combacau, "Le droit international: bric-à-brac ou système?", 31 *Archives de Philosophie du Droit*, (1986), 85.

[38] See M. Koskenniemi, *From Apology to Utopia*, (CUP, 2005).

[39] The best example probably is the doctrine on the establishment of customary international law. See J. d'Aspremont, *Customary International Law as a Dance Floor: Part I* at http://www.ejiltalk.org/customary-international-law-as-a-dance-floor-part-i/ and J. d'Aspremont, *Customary International Law as a Dance Floor: Part II*, at http://www.ejiltalk.org/customary-international-law-as-a-dance-floor-part-ii/; see also W. Worster, "The inductive and deductive methods in customary international law analysis: traditional and modern approaches", 45 *Georgetown Journal of International Law*, (2014),445; see also S.A.G. Talmon, "Determining customary international law: the ICJ's methodology between induction, deduction and assertion", 25 *European Journal of International Law* (2014) (forthcoming).

[40] E. Benvenisti, "Comments on the systemic vision of national courts as part of an international rule of law", 4 *Jerusalem Review of Legal Studies*, (2012), 42, 43 ("The systemic vision of international law suited an evolving and meandering legal order because it provided room for both the continuity and change: continuity of the basic principles like sovereignty and the doctrine of

reified in present international legal scholarship. The disrepute of induction inherited from Hume's skeptical account of causality has finally reached international legal studies.[41] Likewise, systemic approaches to international law are nowadays seen as pathological manifestations of the natural inclination of the human mind to find patterns in heterogeneous practices and materials[42] or as a makeshift tool to quench the taxonomical gluttony of legal academics.[43]

## 3. The Turn to Empiricism

After coming to terms with the limits of acquiring knowledge through induction and systematic thinking, international lawyers have increasingly been embracing empiricism (knowledge from experience). This is a tendency particularly conspicuous in American scholarship. This is certainly not new. It is well known that after the turn to instrumentalism by the New Haven Law School in the 1950s and 1960s, one witnessed a subsequent turn to liberal individualism through global institutionalism, as was strongly advocated by the Manhattan Law School in the 1970s and 1980s,[44] the 1990s brought a turn to legitimacy and empiricism. This turn to legitimacy, notoriously spearheaded by Thomas Franck,[45] has generated deep structural consequences on Anglo-American scholarship and practice, notably because it allowed empirical inquiries (why do states comply with international law) to conveniently converge with

---

sources, and change though opportunities for state actors to adjust specific norms by practice or consent and an opportunity for judges to assert changes in the law through adjudication").

[41] P. Allott, "Language, method and the nature of international law", 45 *British Yearbook of International Law*, (1971), 79, 101.

[42] P. Allott, *Language, Method and the Nature of International Law*, 45 *British Yearbook of International Law*, (1971), 79, 104. See also S. Singh, "Appendix 2: international law as a technical discipline: critical perspectives on the narrative structure of a theory", reproduced in J. d'Aspremont, *Formalism and the Sources of International Law*, 236 (2013) (available at SSRN: http://ssrn.com/abstract=2270415).

[43] J. Coleman, "The architecture of jurisprudence", 121 *The Yale Law Journal*, (2011), 2, 2.

[44] M. Koskenniemi, "Law, teleology and international relations: an essay in counterdisciplinarity", 26, *International Relations*, (2012), 3, 15.

[45] See T. Franck, *Fairness in International Law and Institutions*, (1995), 6.

definitional inquiries (what is international law).[46] The quest for legitimacy (and thus the study of those dynamics that uphold each of them) has, ever since, ranked high on the agenda of international lawyers and especially legal academics, in the US. More recently, this legitimacy school has gradually ceded pride of place to the empirical school of international law that more radically prioritized the study of the conditions under which international law is formed and produces effects.[47]

The above-mentioned success of the turn to empiricism can be explained in many ways. It is not only by virtue of the disenchantment with induction and scientific methods. The turn to empiricism rests on an attempt to develop a new authoritative coding[48] which is not bound to be inductive[49] and which seems to be within the reach of international lawyers. The popularity of empiricism among international lawyers also originates in what is often perceived as a healthy pragmatism[50] as well as the desire to be taken seriously by political and judicial authorities.[51]

It should be made clear that, albeit carrying a feeling of factual objectivism, empiricism has certainly not stripped international law – and international legal studies – of their normative and ideological dimensions. It now seems widely accepted among international lawyers that there is not such a thing as un-prejudiced empirical observations made under a veil of ignorance.[52] It is often the false objectivism that lies at the origin of empiricism that has justified the most severe criticisms leveled against it. But the turn to empiricism has also been disapproved for the

---

[46] On this aspect of the turn to legitimacy, see D. Bederman, *The Spirit of International Law*, 3 (Georgia University Press, 2002).

[47] G. Shaffer and T. Ginsburg, "The empirical turn in international legal scholarship", 106 *American Journal of International Law*, (2012), 1, 1.

[48] L. Epstein and A.D. Martin, "Quantitatives to empirical legal research", in P. Cane and H. Kritzer (eds), *The Oxford Handbook on Empirical Legal Research*, (OUP, 2010), 910–25, at 911.

[49] Developing the coding scheme can be inductive or deductive. L. Epstein and A.D. Martin, "Quantitatives to empirical legal research", in P. Cane and H. Kritzer (eds), *The Oxford Handbook on Empirical Legal Research*, (OUP, 2010), 910–25, at 911.

[50] For some critical remarks, see A. Somek, "Legal science as a source of law: a late reply by Puchta to Kantorowicz", University of Iowa Legal Studies Research Paper Series, (2012), Number 13-7, at 4.

[51] J. Klabbers, "The relative autonomy of international law and the forgotten politics of interdisciplinarity", 1 *Journal of International Law and International Relations*, (2005), 35, at 41.

[52] There are no pre-conceptual or even pre-theoretical data that exist outside any conceptual and descriptive framework. See A. MacIntyre, *Whose Justice? Which Rationality?* (Duckworth, 1988), 333.

interdisciplinary moves that it seems to call for. As interdisciplinary – and its other variant: multidisciplinary – are not inherent in empiricism but can be potential components of other methodological packages, they are discussed in a separate section.

## 4. Interdisciplinarity and Multidisciplinarity

Strictly speaking, multidisciplinary research refers to a non-integrative blend of methods in that each of them keeps its distinctiveness without alteration within the multidisciplinary relationship. In contrast, interdisciplinary research refers to a more integrative mixture of methods without clearly upholding the distinctiveness of each of them, resulting in aggregated methodological packages without a clear DNA. In practice, however, it is very difficult to distinguish between multidisciplinary and interdisciplinary methodological packages. The terms are accordingly often used interchangeably to refer to methodological packages that depart from the classical model known in the discipline and include a methodological component borrowed from (or practiced in) other disciplines.

Interdisciplinary and multidisciplinary methodological packages are, by definition, very heterogeneous and presuppose resort to a blend of very different methods. The importation of methods practiced elsewhere into the methodological packages of international lawyers requires some inevitable distortion and decontextualization. Indeed, those "foreign" methods are translated (that is decoded and recoded) to remain intelligible in the context of international legal studies and adjusted to uphold their usefulness when applied to an object of inquiry that is different from the object for which they were originally designed.

It is submitted here that part of the success of interdisciplinary and multidisciplinary methodological packages can be traced back, not only to the above-mentioned success of empiricism but also to their opening up of new avenues of research or new types of legal argumentation. Interdisciplinary and multidisciplinary methodological packages simultaneously assuage the unquenchable thirst of international lawyers for new materials.[53] Such popularity can also be explained by virtue of the

---

[53] I have argued elsewhere that some of the methodological choices behind soft law are informed by the same rationale. See J. d'Aspremont, "Softness in international law: a self-serving quest for new legal materials", 19 *European Journal of International Law*, (2008), 1075–93. See also chapter 2 above. For a discussion of that methodological tendency in International Environmental Law,

methodological obscurantism which protects against social invalidation. Indeed, other members of the community of international lawyers are not always in a position to verify the accuracy and consistency of the "foreign" methods that are borrowed from other disciplines. In that sense, substantive review of such imports is not always possible, thereby shielding such methodological packages from being faulted and invalidated.

The resort to interdisciplinary and multidisciplinary methodological packages has of course not remained immune from criticism. As is well known, such choices have been lambasted for their hegemonic "imposition of empirical political science ... as a world tribunal assisting whoever is in charge",[54] for promoting "a single limited apparition of interdisciplinarity"[55], for being limited to bringing together two or more people from the neighbouring disciplines,[56] or for exposing international lawyers to "doing merely history, or economics, or ethics, or international relations, under a thin veneer of international law".[57]

It is argued here that the most compelling charge against such interdisciplinary and multidisciplinary methodological packages probably lies elsewhere. Strictly speaking, such a choice, if it is done seriously, requires methodological multilingualism.[58] Indeed, it presupposes the acquisition of full command of these foreign methods. However, it is not certain that, when it comes to methodology, it is possible to acquire a

---

see E. Fisher, B. Lange, E. Scotford and C. Carlarne, "Maturity and methodology: starting a debate about environmental law scholarship" 21 *Journal of Environmental Law*, (2009), at 224–5.

[54] Martti Koskenniemi, "Constitutionalism as mindset: reflections on Kantian themes about international law and globalization", 8 *Theoretical Inquiries in Law*, (2006), 9, at 14 ; see also Martti Koskenniemi, "The mystery of legal obligation", 3 *International Theory*, (2011), 319–25, at 319.

[55] Jan Klabbers, "The relative autonomy of international law and the forgotten politics of interdisciplinarity", 1 *Journal of International Law and International Relations*, (2005), 35, 38.

[56] Jan Klabbers, "The relative autonomy of international law and the forgotten politics of interdisciplinarity", 1 *Journal of International Law and International Relations*, (2005), 35, 45.

[57] Jan Klabbers, "The relative autonomy of international law and the forgotten politics of interdisciplinarity", 1 *Journal of International Law and International Relations*, (2005), 35, 38.

[58] On this notion, see Rob van Gestel, Hans-W. Micklitz and Miguel Poiares Maduro, "Methodology in the New Legal World", EUI Working Paper LAW, 2012/13 1, 14 (2012).

new mother tongue.[59] By definition, and as it was recalled above, distortions are inevitable and methods from other fields are inevitably decoded and recoded according to the codes which international lawyers have acquired through the socialization discussed in the Introduction of this book. It is not certain, however, that after having been socialized, international lawyers can possibly borrow from other disciplines with a veil of ignorance. What they borrow and integrate in their methodological package is necessarily the result of their own projection and reconstruction.

There probably is another – equally fundamental – objection against multidisciplinary and interdisciplinary methodological packages. It pertains to the above-mentioned (in)validation of legal argumentation. In the case of multidisciplinary and interdisciplinary methodological packages, the social (in)validation of legal argumentation grows more intricate, if not impossible. Indeed, peers and other professionals are incapable to verify how these foreign methods are deployed and integrated in the methodological package concerned. This is one of the greatest appeals of such methodological packages. Yet, this is also what makes multidisciplinarity and interdisciplinarity akin to an intimidating tactic very detrimental to the social validation process itself.[60] If methodological packages cannot be socially (in)validated, like all other parts of legal arguments, the very dynamics constitutive of the argumentative practice of international law are jeopardized.[61] This is probably a peril which proponents of multidisciplinary and interdisciplinary research have yet to appreciate.

## 5. The Abiding (Need for) Methodological Revolution

Another feature of methodological debates in international law must be mentioned here. It pertains to the constant expectation in international legal studies of a renewal of methodological choices. Indeed, in the community of international lawyers, revolution is valued. It constitutes a source of recognition for their architects as well as a welcome means for the rejuvenation of legal arguments and the rise of new research space. Such revolutions are supposed to occur through the discovery of new

---

[59] A. MacIntyre, *Whose Justice? Which Rationality?*, Duckworth, 1988, at 375.
[60] Similar academic tactics found in the practice of academic writing are discussed in chapter 8.
[61] See *supra* Introduction. M. Bodig however suggested to me that interdisciplinarity, can, in some circumstances, enhance epistemic validation.

facts or behaviours or through the adoption of new conceptual frameworks. In both cases, revolutions thus come by virtue of revolutionary methodological packages, be they descriptive, evaluative or explanatory. It is the possibility of describing new factual developments, shedding light on new facets of a phenomenon or providing new evaluative or explanatory tools that is applauded by the community of international lawyers as a welcome revolution. Some of these revolutionary moves have been discussed in the first part of this book in connection with subjects, sources and law-making.[62]

The foregoing thus means that the paradigmatic revolution that international lawyers commonly seek to foment usually takes the form of a specific methodological package. More precisely, the revolution is seen as the imposition of a specific – and innovative – package. What is more, although often more diffused and diluted than commonly perceived, these revolutions witness the return to the same key – albeit slightly adjusted – methodological packages that had been repudiated in the past but that are rehabilitated through revolution. The recurrence of some methodological packages in this constant revolutionary environment is the phenomenon at work behind the finding made by many authors that theoretical debates are moving in circles. This idea that the renewal repeats and that the scholarly debates oscillate between paradigms as a pendulum[63] is nothing more than the expression of the seesawing dynamics within this constant quest for changes of methodological packages.

This quest for methodological revolutions, be it through new descriptive, evaluative or explanatory models, can be explained as follows. First, it can be traced back to the dominant reformist attitude of international lawyers[64] for the great majority of whom international law is a (good) tool for societal reforms.[65] But there is probably another – more

---

[62] See chapters 1–3.

[63] D. Kennedy, "When renewal repeats: thinking against the box", 32 *New York University Journal of Law and Politics*, (2000), 335–499; D. Bederman, *The Spirit of International Law*, The University of Georgia Press, (2002), 7–9; G. Shaffer and T. Ginsburg, "The empirical turn in international legal scholarship" 106 AJIL, (2012), at 11.

[64] These scholars have been dubbed the idealists by F. Megret. See F. Megret, "International law as law", in J. Crawford and M. Koskenniemi (eds), *Cambridge Companion to International Law*, (CUP, 2011), available at http://papers.ssrn.com/sol3/papers.cfm?abstract_id=1672824, pp. 8–9.

[65] On the various dimensions of this enthusiasm for the international, see D. Kennedy, "A new world order: yesterday, today and tomorrow", 4 *Transnational Legal and Contemporary Problems*, (1994), 329–75, 336; see also S. Marks, *The Riddle of All Constitutions* (2003), 146.

fundamental – reason for this thirst for methodological revolution. This second reason pertains to the plight (and fear) of non-remembrance with which international lawyers are – consciously or unconsciously – confronted and the correlative search for recognition.

It must be noted that the recognition that international lawyers generally seek to secure is, to a large extent, peer-recognition. Few international lawyers are interested in recognition by the general public – which often is simply out of reach despite its possible penetration in the political discourse.[66] They may at times be seeking the recognition they could earn from domestic or international courts and tribunals in the form of an endorsement of an argument through an explicit or vague reference. Yet, because the practice of international law cannot be reduced to adjudicatory practice, recognition by law-applying bodies is only a limited part of the recognition they may be seeking. In sharp contrast to domestic legal scholars,[67] recognition by courts is a limited drive in the profession which has primarily remained geared towards peer-recognition. Be that as it may, this inextricable quest for recognition stimulates the need for methodological revolution[68] and explains why international law is permeated by a constant search for renewal.

It must be acknowledged that this revolutionary mindset is sometimes attenuated. For instance, there are geographical variations in the need for permanent revolution. For instance, methodological revolution is a more structural dynamic in the US legal scholarship than in the European legal scholarship which could be seen as more stable. In Europe, it is even fair to say that methodological revolutions are sometimes regarded dimly. Young international lawyers are often judged on the basis of their ability to reproduce the methodological packages in force and not on their capacity to devise a new methodological framework. This being said, and although more conservative and more resistant to methodological change, even in the European tradition, methodological revolutions are valued.

---

[66] See e.g. P. Sands, *Lawless World: America and the Making and Breaking of Global Rules*, (Penguin, 2005).
[67] M. Hesselink, "A European legal science?", Centre for the Study of European Contract Law Working Paper Series, No. 2008/02, p. 14.
[68] See F. Ost and M. van de Kerchove, "De la scène au balcon. D'où vient la science du droit?" in F. Chazel and J. Commaille (eds), *Normes Juridiques et Régulation Sociale*, (Paris, L.G.D.J., 1991), p. 68 ff.; S. Santos, *Towards A New Common Sense: Law, Science and Politics in the Paradigmatic Transition*, New York, Routledge, 1995; see also M. Hesselink, "A European Legal Science?", Centre for the Study of European Contract Law Working Paper Series, No. 2008/02, p. 20.

This constant quest for methodological revolution is not something that ought to be praised or bemoaned. It is rather a driving force of methodological debates in international law that one should be aware of. It is also important to realize that those revolutionary moves are not as radical and contrasted as is often portrayed. Methodological oscillations are much softer and protracted than one may think.[69] Moreover, revolutions always unfold within a – albeit remote – similar tradition.[70] There cannot be any methodological revolution if there is not some continuity between commensurable methodological fundamentals. In that sense, the revolutionary narrative that dominates and infuses methodological debates should be seen as nothing more than a welcome self-regenerating dynamism that keeps international legal thinking in motion.

## 6. Pluralism and Methodological Perspectivism

International lawyers have often found in pluralism the magic elixir to fix the contradictions of their doctrines or those of the international legal order as a whole. Indeed, once it is accepted that a doctrine or the legal order is pluralistic, it can no longer be faulted for its false coherence.[71] This pluralistic mantra is repeatedly professed to offer a counterweight to the traditional – and now often discredited – "rage for order"[72] or formalistic structures[73] of international lawyers. It is argued here that pluralism should not be considered any different from methodological perspectivism. Perspectivism "puts into question the possibility of making truth-claims from within any one tradition"[74] and presupposes that "no one tradition is entitled to arrogate to itself an exclusive title; no one

---

[69] This is one of the central arguments of the study of N. Duxbury on American jurisprudence. See also N. Duxbury, *Patterns of American Jurisprudence*, OUP, 1997.

[70] A. MacIntyre, *Whose Justice? Which Rationality?*, Duckworth, (1988), 352–53.

[71] For an example, see P.S. Berman, "A pluralist approach to international law", 32 *The Yale Journal of International Law*, (2007), 301.

[72] J. Crawford, "International law as discipline and profession", 105 *ASIL Proceedings*, (2012), 1.

[73] On the possibility of withholding a rule of recognition and safeguarding pluralism, see however S. Besson, "Theorizing the sources of international law", in S. Besson and J. Tasioulas (eds), *The Philosophy of International Law*, (OUP, Oxford, 2010), 163, at 184.

[74] A. MacIntyre, *Whose Justice? Which Rationality?*, Duckworth, (1988), 352–53, 352.

tradition can deny legitimacy to its rival".[75] The problem with methodological perspectivism (and thus with pluralism) is not only that it may be a conceptual impossibility for it is inconceivable to be outside all traditions.[76] It is also that it ceases to pose demands on the world.[77] In these circumstances, it is not certain that the pluralistic project can seriously be upheld. Rather than letting themselves be lured by pluralistic avoidance strategies, international lawyers should, more simply, come to terms with the inexorable contradictory nature of international lawyers' doctrines and of the international legal order as a whole.[78]

## 7. Deconstruction, Structuralism and the Critical Attitude

Despite fundamental differences, deconstruction and (post-)structuralism are often used interchangeably in mainstream international legal literature to refer to the works of David Kennedy and Martti Koskenniemi. In that sense, there is a fair deal of imprecision as to how those influential works are referred. As has been aptly discussed by Sahib Singh,[79] David Kennedy, and even more conspicuously, Martti Koskenniemi,[80] are works of structuralism and not of deconstruction,[81] for deconstruction is

---

[75] Ibid.

[76] A. MacIntyre, *Whose Justice? Which Rationality?*, Duckworth, (1988), 352–53

[77] M. Koskenniemi, "The fate of public international law: between technique and politics", 70 *The Modern Law Review*, (2007), 1–30, 23.

[78] See the example discussed in chapter 4 above.

[79] S. Singh, "International legal positivism and new approaches to international law" in J. Kammerhofer and J. d'Aspremont (eds), *International Legal Positivism in a Postmodern World*, (CUP, 2014), 291–316. See also O. Korhonen, "New international law: silence, defence or deliverance?" 7 *EJIL*, (1996), 1–28, at 19–21.

[80] See M. Koskenniemi, *From Apology to Utopia*, (CUP, 2005), especially chapter 8. See also the notion of cultural formalism discussed in chapter 2 above.

[81] These are works of structuralism because they take roots in Saussurean structural linguistics and assume that words have no inner meaning but that originating in – and being left fluctuating in – its relationship with other words. On deconstruction in general, see R. Cotterrell, *The Politics of Jurisprudence. A Critical Introduction to Legal Philosophy*, 2nd ed., (OUP, 2011), at 239 ("Deconstruction is, strictly speaking, neither a method nor a technique but an event, a transcending of the limited understanding of modern thought in various ways, though without the possibility of reaching any complete knowledge or understanding. But the term is often used to refer generally to approaches that aim at this transcending by critically interpreting texts or ideas").

consciously discontinued.[82] In the light of these important differences between structuralism and deconstruction, others have preferred to speak of "postmodernism" or "critical legal studies" without any further nuance. This is how "postmodernism" and "critical legal studies" have become catchwords that embrace a host of different concepts and attitudes.[83] Besides being associated with some (perceived) (post-) structuralism and deconstruction, these catchwords are often used to refer to anti-liberal and anti-universal approaches, the rejection of reasoned narrative, the instability of knowledge, the move away from universal grand theories, the deconstruction of "metanarratives", the empowerment of the rule-applier, the politics of language, general textual indeterminacy, etc.

This heterogeneity explains why the critical attitude cannot be identified as a separate, self-conscious and monolithic movement.[84] Rather, it is better seen as a self-reflective attitude or a mindset in the sense that it seeks to undo the "false consciousness" of mainstream scholarship.[85] It is more about debunking than reforming.[86] At the same time, postmodernism does not annihilate normative legal theory's projects.[87] As

---

[82] On this idea of a termination of deconstruction see P. Schlag, "'Le hors de texte, c'est moi': the politics of form and the domestication of deconstruction" 11 *Cardozo Law Review*, (1989–1990), 1631–74; P. Schlag, "The problem of the subject" 69 *Texas Law Review*, (1991), 1627–743; P. Schlag, "A brief survey of deconstruction" 27 *Cardozo Law Review*, (2005) 741–52; and P. Dews, *Logics of Disintegration. Post-Structuralist Thought and the Claims of Critical Theory* (Verso 1987) 33–44, 200–19.

[83] D. Patterson argues that "the discussion of postmodernism has fallen into the hands of those who use it as a vehicle for the propagation of specious ideas". See D. Patterson, "Postmodernism", in D. Patterson (ed.),. *A Companion to Philosophy of Law and Legal Theory*, (Blackwell Publishers Ltd, Oxford, 1999) 375.

[84] D. Kennedy, "Critical theory, structuralism and contemporary legal scholarship", 21 *New England Law Review*, (1985–1986), 209, at 277. On the history of this movement, see M. Kelman, *A Guide to Critical Legal Studies*, (Harvard University Press, 1987).

[85] D. Kennedy, "Critical theory, structuralism and contemporary legal scholarship", 21 *New England Law Review*, (1985–1986), 209, at 223.

[86] N. Duxburry, *Patterns of American Jurisprudence*, (OUP, 1997) at 422.

[87] R. Cotterrell, *The Politics of Jurisprudence. A Critical Introduction to Legal Philosophy*, 2nd ed., (OUP, 2011).

was mentioned above, Martti Koskenniemi, for instance, is famous for discontinuing deconstruction by virtue of a neo-Kantian posture.[88]

It is not the ambition of this short section to explore further the various – and sometimes contradictory[89] – facets of the critical attitude. The point which this section seeks to make is simpler. Although a complex, heterogeneous, and often misunderstood attitude, the critical attitude has borne an immense impact on the international legal scholarship, and especially on methodological debates.[90] Their impact on methodological debates is not without paradox as the critical attitude has never promoted anything like a certain methodological package.[91] However, the critical attitude has contributed to the generalization of the use of binomes for explanatory purposes as well as socio-historical situationalism.[92] Moreover, they have infused the consciousness of international lawyers with a critical edge which had been absent so far. They have more specifically contributed to a growing acceptance of findings – long made by non-lawyers[93] – that a universal perspective is a contradiction in terms and that there is not such a thing as a meta-standpoint "that allows that method or politics to be discussed from the outside of particular

---

[88] On the culture of formalism, see chapter 2 above. See also M. Koskenniemi, "Miserable comforters: international relations as new nature law", 15 *European Journal of International Relations*, (2009), 395–422.

[89] According to Kennedy, it is impossible to combine structuralism with critical theory, each of them setting the other aside. As a result, both structuralism and critical legal theory fail to provide the sort of definitive security which legal scholars have sought. See D. Kennedy, "Critical theory, structuralism and contemporary legal scholarship", 21 *New England Law Review*, (1985–1986), 209, at 275, and at 287. For a similar argument, see J.M. Balkin, "Deconstruction", in D. Patterson (ed.) *A Companion to Philosophy of Law and Legal Theory*, (Blackwell, Oxford, 1999) 367–74.

[90] D. Bederman, "Appraising a century of scholarship in the American Journal of International Law", 100 *AJIL*, (2006), 20–63, at 48 ("In my view, the most surprising intellectual turn of the AJIL's past decade has been the self-conscious renewal of interest in the methods and techniques of international legal scholarship itself.").

[91] M. Koskenniemi, "Letter to the editors of the symposium", 93 *AJIL*, (1999), 351, at 352–3.

[92] See *supra* Introduction. See also J. Dunoff, "From interdisciplinarity to counterdisciplinarity: is there madness in Martti's method?", 27 *Temple Journal of International and Comparative Law*, (2013), 309.

[93] S. Fish, *Doing What comes Naturally*, Duke University Press, (1989), 11 and 488.

methodological or political controversies".[94] In the same vein, they have convinced a great number of international lawyers that disorder is as much a creation as order,[95] just like, in Kuhn's terms, anomaly is created by the paradigm in place.[96] There is nowadays much more (personal search for and interest in) self-awareness, especially when it comes to methodological choices. This is not to say that self-awareness is ever achieved (or achievable) by those self-aware international lawyers.[97] It is simply that being socialized as an international lawyer today also includes an overture for methodological self-awareness.

It cannot be excluded that this welcome legacy comes with some unexpected unfavorable consequences. The greater use of semantic instability in legal argumentation and the resort to intimidating tactics in academic writing – as will be discussed in chapter 8 – can constitute a possible fallout of the success of critical works for reasons that are still a little unclear. In the same vein, it cannot be excluded that, in the future, international legal studies grow akin to international relations literature where a great deal of the cerebral efforts are deployed to (self-)reflect about choices and designs of methodological packages. While methodological self-awareness is surely a welcome addition to the argumentative techniques which international lawyers acquire through socialization, turning it into an obsession would be very detrimental to the sustainability of international law as an argumentative practice.

---

[94] M. Koskenniemi, "Letter to the editors of the symposium", 93 *AJIL*, (1999), 351, at 352; A. Orford, "On international legal method", 1 *London Review of International Law*, (2013), 166–197, at 167.

[95] S. Singh, "International law as a technical discipline: critical perspectives on the narrative structure of a theory" (May 26, 2013). Appendix 2 in J. d'Aspremont, *Formalism and the Sources of International Law*, (Oxford: OUP, 2013), 236–61.

[96] T. Kuhn, *The Structure of Scientific Revolutions*, The University of Chicago Press, 50th anniversary edition, 2012.

[97] S. Singh, "International law as a technical discipline: critical perspectives on the narrative structure of a theory" (May 26, 2013). Appendix 2 in J. d'Aspremont, *Formalism and the Sources of International Law*, (Oxford: OUP, 2013), 236–61; University of Cambridge Faculty of Law Research Paper No. 22/2013. Available at SSRN: http://ssrn.com/abstract=2270415.

# 7. Interpretation

International law is understood in this book as an argumentative practice constituted of fundamental doctrines and argumentative techniques. Those doctrines and techniques are deployed with a view to securing validation of legal arguments according to modes that have been inherited from a socialization process.[1] Yet, as has already been pointed out, the distinction between foundational doctrines and argumentative techniques is not always self-evident. Interpretation is a good illustration thereof. The codification of the so-called "rules on interpretation" in the two Vienna Conventions on the Law of Treaties may indeed convey an image of interpretation as a foundational doctrine. Clearly, this book takes the opposite view and considers interpretation to be an argumentative technique. This is probably not controversial. This being said, whether interpretation qualifies as a foundational doctrine or an argumentative technique is probably a debate of little relevance. It seems more important to look into the conceptual choices made by international lawyers to organize and constrain content-determination in international law. This means reflecting on the way in which interpretation (and its supposed rules) have been construed and designed. This is the object of this chapter.

## I. COMMITMENT AND INTERPRETIVE PROCESSES IN THE NORMATIVE UNIVERSE OF INTERNATIONAL LAW

For the sake of this chapter, it is submitted that the world any human or corporate person operates in is an aggregation of normative universes which are all individually structured around the possibility of right or wrong, of permissible or impermissible, of valid or invalid.[2] International

---

[1] See *supra* Introduction.
[2] Comp. with R. Cover, "The Supreme Court 1982 term – foreword: nomos and narrative", 97 *Harvard Law Review*, (1983), 4, at 4–5 (for whom there is only one single normative universe which we all inhabit and where the

law constitutes one of these normative universes. Like other normative universes, international law is a vehicle for methods and narratives that construct a certain reality and validate or invalidate certain practices. This particular universe is inhabited by international lawyers, whose membership of the universe is not only institutional or professional.[3] It is also the result of a commitment, namely a commitment to the field's rhetoric and traditions,[4] and to the system of knowledge and argumentation that comes with it. Such a commitment is the primary cement and the main constitutive element of the universe of international law. Indeed, as was already discussed in the Introduction of this book, it is by virtue of this commitment that interpretation of international law is not totally unbridled and operates within the framework of pre-existing social constraints.

This commitment by international lawyers to the normative universe of international law manifests itself in very different ways. This chapter grapples specifically with two of the main expressions of international lawyers' commitment towards international law, which they embrace: (i) the methods to determine the content of legal rules; and (ii) the methods to identify legal rules that are made available by the normative universe of international law. This chapter is premised on the idea that international lawyers, while trying to give meaning to legal rules (content-determination) or while engaging in the identification of rules (law-ascertainment), necessarily commit themselves to certain techniques, rhetoric and traditions that are provided by the normative universe of international law. In doing so, this chapter argues that interpretation should be seen as multi-dimensional. Interpretation consists not only of attributing meaning to the rules (content-determination), but also of ascertaining what is and what is not law (law ascertainment).

It is true that the two interpretive processes referred to here can easily be indistinguishable, as they both manifest a commitment to the techniques, rhetoric and traditions of the normative universe of international

---

dichotomies of "right and wrong, of lawful and unlawful, of valid and void" are constantly at play).

[3] On membership of the international law profession, see J. d'Aspremont, "Wording in international law", 25 *Leiden Journal of International Law*, (2012), 575.

[4] M. Koskenniemi argues that such a commitment necessarily comes with a countervailing professional doubt about the identity of international law and that of the profession organized around it. See. M. Koskenniemi, "Between commitment and cynicism: outline for a theory of international law as practice", in *Collection of Essays by Legal Advisers of States, Legal Advisers of International Organizations and Practitioners in the Field of International Law*, (Office of Legal Affairs, United Nations, NY, 1999), 495–523, esp. 496.

law. Practice often makes them part of the same intellectual operation, illustrated by the way in which the mainstream theory of customary international law is applied by international courts and tribunals.[5] Yet the gist of the argument here is that, although the processes are both committal and interpretive in nature, law-ascertainment and content-determination must be clearly distinguished. Each of them engages different questions of law, power and authority. Moreover, each of them also comes with a distinct approach to controlling indeterminacy and arbitrariness in adjudication.

This chapter is structured as follows. Section II discloses the understanding of interpretation that the subsequent argument is premised on. Section III sets out the central distinction between content-determination and law-ascertainment as interpretive processes. Both the common and distinctive features of law-ascertainment and content-determination processes are discussed here, with a focus on the type of constraints that have been put in place to domesticate them. While constraints on content-determination processes have usually been envisaged as "rules" in mainstream international legal scholarship, constraints on law-ascertainment processes, although often referred to as "secondary rules", are better seen as indicative of a professional community's practices and traditions. Section IV concludes with a few epistemological remarks on the place and the state of the debate on interpretation in contemporary international legal scholarship.

In seeking to analyze the relationship between these two interpretive processes, this chapter neither purports to vindicate any particular method of interpretation, nor seeks to offer a general theory of interpretation.[6] Rather, it aims to raise awareness of the multidimensional character of interpretation, and to shed light on the theoretical and practical implications of distinguishing content-determination and law-ascertainment interpretive processes in relation to interpretation in international law.

---

[5] For a classical account, see H. Thirlway, *International Customary Law and Codification: An Examination of the Continuing Role of Custom in the Present Period of Codification of International Law*, (Sijthoff, 1972). See also the literature, cited and discussed in J. d'Aspremont, *Formalism and the Sources of International Law*, (OUP, 2011), chapter 7, esp. 161–74.

[6] Indeed, it is not clear that such a theorization is possible from the vantage point of international legal theory. However, see G. Hernandez, "Interpretation", in J. Kammerhofer and J. d'Aspremont (eds), *International Legal Positivism in a Postmodern World*, (CUP, 2014), 317–48.

## II. COMMITTED INTERPRETATION AND THE NECESSARY FEELING OF "OUT-THERE-NESS"

For the purposes of this chapter, interpretation is a performative and constitutive activity in that it contributes to the making of what it purports to find.[7] This means that interpretation is constitutive of international law and the world which international law is supposed to apply to. In the specific context of adjudication, for instance,[8] this understanding implies that interpretation produces both law and fact and the relation between them. The constitutive and performative character of interpretation is uncontroversial,[9] and it is therefore not necessary to dwell upon it. More noteworthy is the contention that, by being constitutive of both the law itself and the world to which the law is meant to apply, interpretation can be either broad or restrictive. Indeed, interpretation can expand the realm of international law by qualifying norms that were previously considered alien to the international legal order as rules of international law. Interpretation can also broaden the ambit of international law by fleshing out the content of existing rules.[10] Conversely, interpretation can be restrictive in that it can strip a rule of law of any meaningful content. Interpretation can also go as far as to deprive a rule of any legal pedigree. Understanding interpretation this way presupposes that international law ought to be construed not only as a set of rules,[11]

---

[7] See I. Venzke, "Post-modern perspectives on orthodox positivism", in J. Kammerhofer and J. d'Aspremont (eds), *International Legal Positivism in a Postmodern World* (CUP, 2014, 182–210); N. Onuf, "Constructivism: a user's manual", in V. Kublakova, N. Onuf, and P. Kowert (eds), *International Relations in a Constructed World*, (Sharpe, New York, 1998) 59: "Saying is doing; talking is undoubtedly the most important way that we go about making the world what it is".

[8] For some critical remarks on the tendency of international lawyers to reflect on interpretation solely from the perspective of the judge, see A. Bianchi, D. Peat and M.R. Windsor (eds), *Interpretation in International Law* (Oxford University Press, 2015) (forthcoming).

[9] See H.L.A. Hart, *The Concept of Law* (2nd ed., OUP, 1994), 144–50; H. Kelsen, *Pure Theory of Law* (Max Knight trans., University of California Press, 1967), 348–56.

[10] On the possible agenda behind the expansionist use of interpretation, see J. d'Aspremont, "The politics of deformalization in international law", 3 *Goettingen Journal of International Law*, (2011), 503.

[11] J. d'Aspremont, *Formalism and the Sources of International Law*, (OUP, 2011).

but also as an argumentative practice aimed at persuading target audiences.[12] Seen in this way, interpretation is a ubiquitous phenomenon,[13] with all practices and discourses about international law having an interpretive dimension.[14]

The ever-present nature of interpretation explains the confrontational character of the discipline of international law. First, as was discussed in Chapter 6 this is because there is no independent meta-criterion allowing the interpreter to choose between methods of interpretation and to validate one as being superior to the other.[15] Whether the question is one of content-determination, law-ascertainment, or establishment of the facts to which these rules are meant to apply, "it is the consensus in the profession – the invisible college of international lawyers – that determines, at any moment, whether a particular argument is or is not persuasive".[16] Indeed, there is no validating standard other than the assent of the relevant community.[17] Some choices are held in higher esteem than others in the specific community where they are made,[18] depending on the constant fluctuation of accepted aesthetics and institutional and political dynamics.[19] This is why interpretation should be seen as an act

---

[12] M. Koskenniemi, "Methodology of international law", (2007) in *Max Plank Encyclopedia of Public International Law*, http://opil.ouplaw.com/home/EPIL, para 1; A. Bianchi, D. Peat and M.R. Windsor (eds), *Interpretation in International Law* (Oxford University Press, 2015) (forthcoming).

[13] R. Cover, "The Supreme Court 1982 term – foreword: nomos and narrative", 97 *Harvard Law Review*, (1983), 4, 4–5.

[14] Interpretation, in that sense, is said to permeate all of legal life. See G. Hernandez, "Interpretation" in J. Kammerhofer and J. d'Aspremont (eds), *International Legal Positivism in a Postmodern World*, (CUP, 2014), 317–48. However, see the claims that legal reasoning and interpretation cannot be conflated and that not all legal reasoning involves interpretation: T. Endicott, "Legal interpretation", in A. Marmor (ed.), *Routledge Companion to Philosophy of Law*, (Routledge, 2012), 109.

[15] It has been argued that a purely perspectivist attitude is impossible. See A. MacIntyre, *Whose Justice? Which Rationality?*, (Duckworth, 1988), at 351–2

[16] M. Koskenniemi, "Methodology of international law", (2007) in *Max Plank Encyclopedia of Public International Law*, http://opil.ouplaw.com/home/EPIL, para. 1.

[17] See M. Kuhn, *The Structure of Scientific Revolutions*, University of Chicago Press, 50th anniversary, 2012.

[18] M. Koskenniemi, "Letter to the editors of the symposium", 93 *American Journal of International Law* (1999), 351–61, p. 353.

[19] M. Kuhn, *The Structure of Scientific Revolutions*, University of Chicago Press, 50th anniversary, 2012, p. 155. See also J. d'Aspremont, "Wording in international law", 25 *Leiden Journal of International Law*, (2012), 575.

of authority dependent on its ability to induce acceptance by way of argument or persuasion.[20]

Second, the confrontational character of interpretation stems from the fact that each method of interpretation remains unstable and can produce a variety of rules, meanings, or discourses. Indeed, it is a truism that none of the traditional methods of interpretation, whether textualism, intentionalism or purposivism,[21] can mechanically produce one single stable meaning. Nor can the doctrine of sources provide full stability in the process of law-ascertainment.[22] In this sense, there seems to be a wide agreement that meaning is constructed and not extracted through interpretation. In other words, interpretation should be seen as evaluative and normative rather than empirical.[23]

A third source of confrontation is the absence of any authority in a position to produce a single authoritative interpretation and impose it on all professionals. Indeed, since international law emerged as an academic discipline more than a century ago, no interpretive authority has been able to empower itself as a monopolistic interpretive standard setter for international legal rules. Neither the establishment of a world court nor the *Institut de Droit international*, intended to mirror "the legal conscience of the civilized world",[24] came to offset the absence of a supreme guardian of interpretation in the epistemic community of international lawyers. Interpretive power in international law has accordingly remained extremely diffuse. It is nowadays scattered between influential and

---

[20] G. Hernandez, "Interpretation" in J. Kammerhofer and J. d'Aspremont (eds), *International Legal Positivism in a Postmodern World*, (CUP, 2014), 317–48.

[21] Textualism resorts heavily to inductive technique, allowing the interpreter to infer the command from the text itself. According to intentionalism, the interpreter strives to reconstruct the actual intention of the lawmaker. In adopting a purposivist approach, the interpreter purports to continue the legislative task based on the purpose pursued by an idealized legislator in order to give effect to the policy goals pursued in the specific case concerned. See A. Marmor, "Textualism in context", *USC Gould School of Law Legal Studies Research Paper Series* No. 12–13 July 18, 2012.

[22] J. d'Aspremont, *Formalism and the Sources of International Law*, (OUP, 2011).

[23] G. Letsas, "Strasbourg's interpretive ethic: lessons for the international lawyer", 21 *European Journal of International Law*, (2010), p. 535.

[24] The authoritative French text reads as follows: "Il a pour but de favoriser le progrès du droit international. En travaillant à formuler les principes généraux de la science de manière à répondre à la conscience juridique du monde civilisé." For some critical insights, see M. Koskenniemi, *The Gentle Civilizer of Nations: The Rise and Fall of International Law 1870–1960* (2001), 39.

prolific minds affiliated with prestigious research institutions, domestic and international courts, international and regional law-codifying bodies, and, more occasionally, non-governmental organizations (NGOs), which compete with one another for interpretive authority and persuasiveness. As a result, all the interpreters are involved in a difficult and sometimes ruthless struggle,[25] each of them trying to bar the interpretive superiority of the other.[26] The fragmented state of the interpretive space in the argumentative arena of international law inevitably fuels the confrontational nature of the discipline.

For these reasons, one can argue that interpretative disagreements are inherent in the normative universe of international law and that the normative universe of international law is bound to be confrontational.[27] Put shortly, interpretation necessarily yields confrontation in the whole discipline. It makes the profession and the production of knowledge in international law very confrontational at the level of normative and substantive values and at the level of form and procedure.[28]

What is particularly noteworthy is that this confrontation unfolds behind the veil of a quest for what could be termed "*out-there-ness*". Indeed, there seems to be consensus on the necessity of perpetuating an intuitive, empiricist and inductive understanding of interpretation as an activity geared towards unearthing what is already *out there*. Accordingly, observers of (and stakeholders in) international adjudicatory processes feel bound to perpetuate the Montesquieuan or Blackstonian myth of the mechanical extraction of meaning. In other words, everyone repeats that courts do not fight for semantic authority but simply unearth the

---

[25] See A. Bianchi, D. Peat and M.R. Windsor (eds), *Interpretation in International Law* (Oxford University Press, 2015) (forthcoming).

[26] On the role of legal science and checks and balances, see A. Somek, "The indelible science of law", 7(3) *International Journal of Constitutional Law*, (2009), 424.

[27] For some remarks on the confrontational nature of the discipline, see S. Singh, "International law as a technical discipline: critical perspectives on the narrative structure of a theory", Appendix 2 in J. d'Aspremont, *Formalism and the Sources of International Law*, (Oxford: OUP, 2013), pp. 236–61.

[28] See G. Simpson, "On the magic mountain: teaching public international law", 10 *European Journal of International Law*, (1999), 70, 78: "At one time, when societies were relatively homogeneous, law could secure agreement through appeal to fundamental shared values or cultural practices or comprehensive moralities. Now the appeal to procedural values or decision-making processes as legitimating devices has replaced the search for substantive agreement on higher order goals".

semantics that are already in the text.[29] The rules of interpretation in the Vienna Convention on the Law of Treaties that enjoy almost universal social consensus[30] further buoy this fiction.[31] At least as far as adjudicatory processes are concerned, the above-mentioned confrontation is presented in mechanical and inductive terms, probably because this is a necessary twist to preserve the authority and legitimacy of such processes.[32] Yet it remains that, for the purposes of this chapter, the confrontation at stake in the whole discipline, including in adjudicatory processes, is better understood as an argumentative battle for semantic authority.[33]

Interpretation is thus discussed in this chapter in its multifaceted manifestations: as a commitment; as being constitutive of the world to which it purports to apply; as being omnipresent in the practice of international law; as breeding a pervasive confrontation between professionals; and as an activity geared toward the extraction of the meaning *out there*. The central argument, however, remains that interpretation is not a homogeneous and one-dimensional phenomenon. Tearing off the veil of unicity in which interpretation is too often shrouded constitutes a necessary prerequisite to grasp the most fascinating and challenging theoretical, doctrinal and normative issues which the game of interpretation in international law raises.

---

[29] For a compelling contemporary challenge of this mainstream view, see I. Venzke, *How Interpretation Makes International Law: On Semantic Change and Normative Twists*, (OUP, 2012).

[30] See section IV below.

[31] For some critical remarks in this respect, see G. Hernandez, "Interpretation", in J. Kammerhofer and J. d'Aspremont eds, *International Legal Positivism in a Postmodern World*, (CUP, 2014), 317–48.

[32] That does not mean that the formalist position is necessarily an easy or convenient one. It "is not merely a linguistic doctrine, but a doctrine that implies, in addition to a theory of language, a theory of the self, of community, of rationality, of practice, of politics". S. Fish, *Doing What Comes Naturally*, (Duke University Press, 1989) (referring to R. Unger).

[33] See J. d'Aspremont, "Wording in international law" 25 *Leiden Journal of International Law*, (2012), 575; I. Venzke, *How the Practice of Interpretation Makes International Law: On Semantic Change and Normative Twists*, (OUP, 2012).

## III. A DICHOTOMOUS VIEW ON INTERPRETATION IN INTERNATIONAL LAW

This section puts forward a conceptual dichotomy that helps foster a multi-dimensional understanding of interpretation. This dichotomy calls for a move away from a monolithic concept of interpretation in international law and reveals – as much as it creates – a whole new range of questions and issues of law, power and authority, as well as indeterminacy-mitigating techniques. This means that the dichotomy put forward here simultaneously carries the epistemological project of redefining the agenda of studies on interpretation in international law, as is explained in the last section of this chapter.[34]

As was argued in the previous section, interpretation is a ubiquitous, performative and constitutive activity conducive to the confrontational nature of the discipline. It produces the law as well as the facts, and the relation (and potential conflicts) between them. Yet even if it is taken as a ubiquitous activity constitutive of the whole discipline, it does not mean that interpretation is a homogeneous and unitary phenomenon. Rather, the central argument of this chapter is that two specific types of interpretive processes must be distinguished: interpretive processes geared towards the determination of the content of rules and interpretive processes aimed at the ascertainment of the rules themselves.

According to the first of these interpretive processes, a judge interprets the law which she is empowered to apply, with a view to determining – or creating according to a Kelsenian account – the applicable standard of behaviour or the normative guideline for the case of which she is seized. This is interpretation for content-determination purposes, which is certainly not an activity reserved to the judge. Any professional dealing with international law will engage in content-determination.[35] Yet it is within the context of adjudication that content-determination interpretation is the most visible.

---

[34] It should be noted that the multi-dimensional approach to interpretation advocated here is not fundamentally groundbreaking. R. Dworkin famously identified several interpretative stages: *Law's Empire*, (Harvard, 1986), 65–7. See also D. Hollis, "The existential function of interpretation in international law", in A. Bianchi, D. Peat and M.R. Windsor (eds), *Interpretation in International Law* (Oxford University Press, 2015) (forthcoming).

[35] On some of the cross-cutting professional dynamics affecting all those who are involved in the business of argumentation about international law, see J. d'Aspremont, "Wording in international law", 25 *Leiden Journal of International Law*, (2012), 575.

There is a distinct interpretive process whereby any professional is also called upon to interpret the pedigree of rules in order to ascertain whether a given rule can claim to be part of the international legal order. This will usually involve the interpretation of a doctrine of sources of law. Significantly, this interpretive process of rule-ascertainment cannot be conflated with that of content-determination. The main point to be made here is that our understanding of interpretation should not be limited to content-determination.

This particular distinction between content-determination processes and law-ascertainment processes is crucial to understand the concept and the practice of interpretation as well as international law as a whole. Mainstream studies of interpretation in international law look almost exclusively at the content-determination interpretation process. However, interpretation should not be understood as a content-determination technique only. What qualifies as law itself involves an act of interpretation. When ascertaining the law, the judge, counsel, academic, activist, adviser or even the remote observer necessarily interprets some pre-existing – and sometimes unconsciously inherited – standards of identification of law.

Readers may find that the above-mentioned dichotomy is reminiscent of another distinction, namely that the interpretation of primary norms must be distinguished from the interpretation of the rules of recognition.[36] The resemblance to the distinction between primary and secondary rules further confirms – rather than contradicts – the possibility and necessity of distinguishing between the interpretation of primary standards (content-determination) and those standards that determine what constitutes valid law to interpret (law-ascertainment).

It must again be highlighted that singling out these two specific interpretive processes is not meant to exhaust and capture the whole phenomenon of interpretation. For example, facts are also the object of

---

[36] On the traditional use of this classical distinction made by H.L.A. Hart in international law, see J. Combacau and D. Alland, "Primary and secondary rules in the law of state responsibility categorizing international obligations", 16 *Netherlands Yearbook of International Law*, (1985), 81–109. For some critical remarks on Hart and International Law, see J. d'Aspremont, "Herbert Hart in Today's International Legal Scholarship", in J. Kammerhofer and J. d'Aspremont (eds), *International Legal Positivism in a Post-Modern World*, (CUP, 2014), 114–50.

several types of interpretive processes.[37] The facts falling within the scope of the exercise of authority of a judge must be apprehended and given a meaning in relation to the rule that is invoked and for which the judge concerned has authority. This chapter excludes interpretation of facts, even if such interpretation of facts sometimes comes with an existential dimension, as is the case with the determination of state practice in relation to customary international law. When this chapter refers to law-ascertainment interpretation, it means interpretation of the formal or non-formal law-ascertainment yardsticks according to which international legal rules are identified, to the exclusion of the interpretation of facts having a law-ascertaining value.

Although not groundbreaking, the dichotomy presented here is far from being self-evident. It often remains tempting to conflate content-determination and law-ascertainment, or at least to approach them as being part of exactly the same interpretive phenomenon. This is not surprising, for these two interpretive processes have much in common. Section 1 sketches out some of the elements of resemblance between the two interpretive processes. However, these elements of resemblance do not at all put into question the overarching dichotomy. Section 2 goes on to review the main distinguishing factors between content-determination and law-ascertainment.

## 1. Elements of Resemblance: Behaviour, Authority, Power, Formalization, Instability of Meaning

Content-determination and law-ascertainment interpretations share many similar features. These common characteristics explain why they cannot always be easily distinguished. The difficulty in distinguishing them is exacerbated by the fact that they may operate simultaneously in practice. This is true with respect to application of the mainstream doctrine of customary international law, whereby the ascertainment of customary law and the determination of its content are simultaneous operations. It could even be argued that when the ascertainment of law is a matter of ascertainment of facts, like in the mainstream doctrine of customary international law, the distinction loses its explanatory force.

The main areas of resemblance between content-determination and law-ascertainment interpretation processes are the following. First, both content-determination and law-ascertainment processes are interpretive

---

[37] See J. d'Aspremont and M.M. Mbengue, "Strategies of engagement with scientific fact-finding in international adjudication", *Journal of International Dispute Settlement* (2014), 240–72.

activities of a delineating and definitional nature with respect to the type of behaviour allowed in the international legal order. In other words, these two interpretive processes seek to define the lawful and the non-lawful, reflecting what Fleur Johns describes as "the tendency to try to confer upon international law some delimited time, space and subject matter for its 'proper' (albeit not autonomous) operation".[38] They are part of the "practices of references, spatialization and temporalization through which international lawyers convey a sense of what may be opposed to international legal compliance".[39]

Second, both content-determination and law-ascertainment processes are instrumental in the constitution of the authority of both international law and international legal arguments. Indeed, the theories and techniques that are used in a content-determination or law-ascertainment operation – that is usually a theory of interpretation for the former and a theory of sources for the latter – are conducive to determining the authority of legal argumentation in general, and that of scholarly studies and judicial decisions in particular. In that sense, exactly like methods[40], style and aesthetics, they are constitutive elements of the "machine for the production of statements" in international law.[41] They both provide "rules of discourse-production"[42] that will locate and validate an argument in the discipline's order of truth, within the normative universe of international law.

Third, both processes are the theatre of a power struggle as much as they are manifestations of power. Both content-determination and law-ascertainment processes are constituted by and constitutive of power. This Foucauldian and Marxist understanding of content-determination and law-ascertainment interpretive processes is probably not controversial.[43] It has long been recognized that it is in formal categories that real power resides despite them seeming "simply descriptive of independent realities".[44] This means that there is an inherent hegemonic dimension in each of these

---

[38] F. Johns, *Non-Legality in International Law – Unruly Law*, (CUP, 2013), p. 8.
[39] Ibid. p. 22.
[40] See Chapter 6 above.
[41] M. Prost, *The Concept of Unity in Public International Law*, (Oxford, Hart Publishing, 2012), p. 149.
[42] Ibid. p. 149.
[43] W. Brown, "Power after Foucault", in *Oxford Handbook of Political Theory*, (OUP, 2008), at 65.
[44] S. Fish, *Doing What Comes Naturally*, (Duke University Press, 1989), pp. 23–4.

interpretive processes. Each of them seeks the universalization of meaning in relation to the specific context in which interpretation occurs.[45] The winner of the interpretive confrontation succeeds in establishing her own rule-of-use for the specific community where the interpretation takes place.[46]

Fourth, both processes fail to create stable meaning and knowledge about what law prescribes and to rein in indeterminacy. This is not to say that they leave the indeterminacy of the law unaffected.[47] It is more that both content-determination and law-ascertainment contribute to creating indeterminacy itself. Indeed, indeterminacy is not determinable in the abstract.[48] There is no such thing as context-less indeterminacy, that is the simple corollary of the absence of an a priori meaning of language. Indeterminacy is itself a product of interpretation and as such it is derived from the individual and collective context as well as the predispositions of the interpreter.[49]

Fifth, since they fail to produce stable meaning, both content-determination and law-ascertainment processes have been the objects of formalization by international lawyers. International legal scholars have long tried to offset the instability of the meaning of rules by a sometimes naïve formalization of the techniques and methods attendant on the interpretive process. It is noteworthy that this attempted formalization has not been the same for content-determination and law-ascertainment, demonstrating the extent to which the two processes are distinct. As far

---

[45] For some remarks see M. Koskenniemi, "Hegemonic regimes", in M. Young (ed.), *Regime Interaction in International Law* (CUP, 2012), at 305–24.

[46] See D. Busse, "Semantic strategies as a means of politics" in P. Ahonen (ed.) *Tracing the Semiotic Boundaries of Politics*, (Berlin, de Gruyter, 1993), pp. 121–8, esp. 122–3. See the discussion by I. Venzke, "Post-modern perspectives on orthodox positivism", in J. Kammerhofer and J. d'Aspremont, *International Legal Positivism in a Postmodern World* (CUP, 2014), 182–210.

[47] For a taxonomy of different types of indeterminacy, see the distinction made between ordinary vagueness, transparent vagueness and extravagant vagueness: A. Marmor, "Varieties of vagueness in the law", *USC Legal Studies Research Paper No. 12-8*. (2013).

[48] S. Singh, "International law as a technical discipline: critical perspectives on the narrative structure of a theory", Appendix 2 in J. d'Aspremont, *Formalism and the Sources of International Law*, (OUP, 2013), pp. 236–61.

[49] A. Bianchi argues that the interpretive process is "deeply embedded in a societal context where different actors interact with one another". See A. Bianchi, "Textual interpretation and (international) law reading: The myth of (in)determinacy and the genealogy of meaning", in P. Bekker (ed.) *Making Transnational Law Work in the Global Economy – Essays in Honour of Detlev Vagts*, (Cambridge University Press, 2010), p. 35.

as content-determination is concerned, attempts to formalize such a process have manifested themselves in theories of interpretation hinging upon a subtle balance between textualist, intentionalist and purposivist methods. The Vienna Conventions on the Law of Treaties can be seen as the embodiment of such an attempt to formalize the methods and techniques of content-determination.[50] In the case of law-ascertainment, formalization has materialized in the doctrine of sources being portrayed as a formal enunciation of the pedigree of rules despite the contradictory but uncontested resort to intent or state practice as law-ascertainment yardsticks.[51] None of the attempts to formalize the methods or techniques of content-determination or law-ascertainment have been very successful.[52]

While there are important elements of resemblance, the endeavor to formalize the constraints on these two interpretive processes point to structural and systemic differences between content-determination and law-ascertainment interpretive processes. Indeed, irrespective of their practical impact, the nature of the constraints envisaged by international lawyers for each of these interpretive processes varies fundamentally. This is the subject of the next subsection.

## 2. Elements of Dissimilarity: Functions and Constraints

It goes without saying that the semantics of the proposed dichotomy already indicates a functional divergence between content-determination and law-ascertainment. Even though both content-determination and law-ascertainment processes are interpretive activities of a delineating and definitional nature, each process performs a different function. The former purports to elucidate the content of rules with a view to determining the standard of behaviour or normative guidance provided by them. The latter seeks to determine whether a given norm qualifies as a

---

[50] Textualism is probably the most mainstream interpretive method. See A. Bianchi, "Textual interpretation and (international) law reading: The myth of (in)determinacy and the genealogy of meaning", in P. Bekker (ed.) *Making Transnational Law Work in the Global Economy – Essays in Honour of Detlev Vagts*, (Cambridge University Press, 2010), p. 35.

[51] J. d'Aspremont, *Formalism and the Sources of International Law* (OUP, 2011), especially chapter 7 (arguing that in the mainstream theory of sources, ascertainment is not properly formal as, for both custom-identification and treaty-identification, it rests on non-formal criteria like intent or state practice)

[52] I have argued that the formalization attempted by the mainstream theory of sources was a sham. See J. d'Aspremont, *Formalism and the Sources of International Law*, (OUP, 2011), especially chapter 7.

legal rule and can claim to be part of the international legal order. In other words, the former is intended to produce meaning and a standard of conduct, while the latter is intended to produce a binary structure of ascertainment that distinguishes between law and non-law.[53]

The distinction between content-determination and rule-ascertainment needs not only be upheld in functional terms. The varying argumentative authority among international law professionals may also be explained in terms of this distinction. In particular, the authority that one may enjoy with respect to content-determination may not necessarily be the same as far as law-ascertainment is concerned. For instance, the voice of the activist might be heard when it comes to the content of international legal rules while her interpretive influence in terms of ascertaining international legal rules may be very thin. The international legal scholar may find herself in exactly the opposite situation. The international judge, in turn, may enjoy distinct clout with respect to both interpretive processes, not to mention the interpretation of facts. The same probably holds true for the International Law Commission. This should suffice to show that each interpretive process comes with a different distribution of authority among professionals involved in the interpretation of international law.

However, the main structural difference between content-determination and law-ascertainment lies in the very nature of the constraints curtailing the interpreter's interpretive freedom. More specifically, it is submitted that the constraints on content-determination interpretation have usually been construed as disciplining rules in mainstream legal scholarship, whereas those restricting law-ascertainment interpretation proceed from practice and tradition.

This structural tension between disciplining rules and social practices and traditions is certainly not new. It is reminiscent of a debate that goes well beyond the study of interpretation in international law, epitomized by the famous disagreement between Owen Fiss[54] and Stanley Fish,[55] which Ronald Dworkin[56] and Pierre Schlag[57] later contributed to.

---

[53] This functional criterion is the one which Duncan Hollis has used to ground the distinction between the two interpretive processes. See D. Hollis, "The existential function of interpretation in international law", A. Bianchi, D. Peat and M. Windsor (eds), *Interpretation in International Law*, (OUP, 2015).

[54] O. Fiss "Objectivity and interpretation", 34 *Stanford Law Review*, (1982), 739; O. Fiss, "The jurisprudence (!) of Stanley Fish", 80 *ADE Bulletin*, (1985).

[55] S. Fish, "Fish v. Fiss", 36 *Stanford Law Review*, (1984), 1325–47.

[56] R. Dworkin, "My reply to Stanley Fish (and Walter Benn Michaels): Please don't talk about objectivity any more", in W.J.T. Mitchell (ed.), *The Politics of Interpretation* (University of Chicago Press 1983), 287.

Needless to say, it would be of no avail to rehash those classic arguments here. This chapter only seeks to make the point that the structural differences between content-determination and law-ascertainment hinge upon the same contours of that debate. As a result, references to this traditional confrontation are inevitable.

One last remark must be made before the constraints on content-determination and law-ascertainment are spelt out. Although the constraints imposed upon each process diverge, there seems to be some consensus as to the origin of those constraints. Subject to some notable exceptions,[58] the constraints on each interpretive process are largely the product of a community. Yet despite ample support for the idea that constraints on each interpretive process originate in the professional community of international law discussed in the Introduction of this book, there is much disagreement as to the form that such constraints should take.

## 2.1 The disciplining rules constraining content-determination interpretation

As noted above, mainstream international legal scholarship has always promoted a predominantly rule-based approach to interpretation, in the sense that the interpretive process of content-determination must be based on formal rules. This is the overall model provided by the Vienna Convention on the Law of Treaties, which purports to provide formal rules for the interpretation of treaties. Although other international legal acts are subject to different and specific regimes of content-determination interpretation,[59] a rule-based approach has also prevailed when it comes to the content-determination of non-treaty legal acts. These rules are meant to operate as formal constraints on interpretive freedom. As

---

[57] P. Schlag, "Fish v. Zapp, the case of the relatively autonomous self", 76 *Georgetown Law Journal*, (1987), 36.
[58] See I. Venzke, "Is interpretation in international law a game?", in A. Bianchi, D. Peat and M. Windsor (eds), *Interpretation in International Law*, (OUP, 2015) (forthcoming).
[59] ICJ, *Accordance with international law of the unilateral declaration of independence in respect of Kosovo*, (Request for Advisory Opinion), Advisory Opinion of 22 July 2010, para. 94. See E. Papstavridis, "Interpretation of security council resolutions under chapter vii in the aftermath of the Iraqi crisis", *International and Comparative Law Quarterly*, (2007), 83.

Andrea Bianchi puts it, the "current reflection of mainstream international legal scholarship remains imbued with traditional rule-based approaches to legal interpretation".[60]

Formal constraints on content-determination interpretation can be of several types. In mainstream international legal scholarship, these formal constraints can be either textualist, intentionalist, purposivist, or a combination of the three, as put forward by the Vienna Convention on the Law of Treaties.[61] It is of no avail to dwell on the substance of the constraints that these rules seek to impose on the interpreter. Likewise, for the purposes of our analysis, it does not matter whether they are *legal* rules properly so-called, or merely guiding principles or directives,[62] as their legal force is unlikely to affect their potential for yielding constraints. The doubts expressed by some of the drafters of the 1969 Vienna Convention on the Law of Treaties are worth recalling in this respect. For instance, Alfred Verdross raised the question of the nature of the rules of interpretation which the International Law Commission intended to codify, arguing that "the Commission ought first to decide whether it recognized the existence of such rules".[63] In his view, "it was highly controversial whether the rules established by the case-law of arbitral tribunals and international courts were general rules of international law or merely technical rules".[64] In the same vein, Sir Humphrey Waldock conceded that he "was decidedly lukewarm on rules on interpretation,

---

[60] A. Bianchi, "Textual interpretation and (international) law reading: the myth of (in)determinacy and the genealogy of meaning", in P. Bekker (ed.) *Making Transnational Law Work in the Global Economy – Essays in Honour of Detlev Vagts*, (Cambridge University Press, 2010) 35. This presupposes some *horror vacui* argument according to J. Klabbers: "Reluctant grundnormen: article 31(3)(c) and 42 of the Vienna Convention on the Law of Treaties and the fragmentation of international law", in M. Craven, M. Fitzmaurice and M. Vogiatzi (eds), *Time, History and International Law*, (Brill, 2007), 141, 160.

[61] These constraints are primarily linguistic: A. Bianchi, "Textual interpretation and (international) law reading: the myth of (in)determinacy and the genealogy of meaning", in P. Bekker (ed.) *Making Transnational Law Work in the Global Economy – Essays in Honour of Detlev Vagts*, (Cambridge University Press, 2010), 36.

[62] I. Van Damme, *Treaty Interpretation by the WTO Appellate Body*, (OUP, 2009), p. 35.

[63] ILC, 726th Meeting, A/CN.4/167) reproduced in *YILC* (1964), vol. I: 20–21, para. 15.

[64] Ibid.

including them more because he thought this was expected of him than out of genuine expectation that rules on interpretation would be of much use".[65]

Rather than the substance or binding character of such rules, what matters for the sake of the argument made here is the *format* of the constraints on content-determination interpretation. They are largely thought of as rules by mainstream international law scholarship. This is precisely where one is bound to revive the debate between Owen Fiss and Stanley Fish mentioned above. Indeed, if construed as rules by the mainstream international legal scholarship, such constraints on content-determination interpretation correspond to what Fiss calls "disciplining rules".[66]

Yet, if they are thought of as "disciplining rules", irrespective of their substance and binding character, such constraints on content-determination meet the fundamental objection of an infinite regress made by Fish, according to which such rules themselves need interpretive constraints which in turn also need another set of interpretive constraints.[67] The objection against disciplining rules of interpretation is that the criteria to which rules of interpretation refer cannot themselves be exempted from interpretation.[68] For Fish, such rules "are in need of interpretation and cannot themselves serve as constraints on interpretation".[69] This objection led Fish to understand constraints on interpretation not as rules but as practices of an "interpretive community". This is

---

[65] J. Klabbers, "Virtuous interpretation", in M. Fitzmaurice, O. Elias and P. Merkouris (eds) *Treaty Interpretation and the Vienna Convention on the Law of Treaties: 30 Years on*, Vol. 1 (Leiden and Boston: Martinus Nijhoff Publishers, 2010) 17, at 18.

[66] O. Fiss "Objectivity and interpretation", 34 *Stanford Law Review*, 739 (1982).

[67] See I. Venzke, "Language games: topography and traction of a metaphor"; I. Venzke, "Post-modern perspectives on orthodox positivism", in J. Kammerhofer and J. d'Aspremont (eds), *International Legal Positivism in a Postmodern World* (CUP, 2014), 182–210. See also G. Letsas, "Strasbourg's interpretive ethic: lessons for the international lawyer", 21 *EJIL*, (2010), 509–41, 534.

[68] A. Bianchi, "Textual interpretation and (international) law reading: the myth of (in)determinacy and the genealogy of meaning", in P. Bekker (ed.) *Making Transnational Law Work in the Global Economy – Essays in Honour of Detlev Vagts*, (Cambridge University Press, 2010) p. 48. This is a criticism made by H.L.A. Hart, *The Concept of Law*, (2nd edition, 1994, OUP), at 126. For some mitigating factors, see G. Hernandez, "Interpretation", in J. Kammerhofer and J. d'Aspremont (eds), *International Legal Positivism in a Postmodern World* (CUP, 2014), 317–48.

[69] S. Fish, "Fish v. Fiss", 36 *Stanford Law Review*, (1984), 1325–47, 1336.

also what allows us to differentiate constraints on content-determination interpretation from constraints on law-ascertainment interpretation, as explained below.

## 2.2 The social practice and tradition constraining law-ascertainment interpretation

In contrast to the rule-based approach to binding constraints on content-determination interpretation, questions about the nature of constraints on law-ascertainment have been almost ignored by mainstream international legal scholarship.[70] It is as if international legal scholarship had decided to restrict interpretation to content-determination processes.[71] Constraints on law-ascertainment processes have only been the object of attention in relation to the argument that they cannot be distinguished from content-determination interpretation.[72]

In the absence of any studies to rely on, one could be tempted to construe constraints on law-ascertainment interpretation similarly to the mainstream understanding of constraints placed on content-determination interpretation. This rule-based understanding of constraints on law-ascertainment interpretation would correspond to the common wisdom that the theory of sources constitute a set of "secondary rules" of international law, which, at face-value, seems to equate these systemic principles to rules properly so-called. This is also the impression generated by Article 38 of the Statute of the International Court of Justice, which is often regarded as the gospel in terms of law-ascertainment.[73] This type of constraint would engender the infinite regress objection, given the need for rules on the interpretation of secondary rules in international law.[74] The argument offered here is that constraints on law-ascertainment interpretation should rather be construed as a communitarian practice.

---

[70] See also D. Hollis, "The existential function of interpretation in international law", in A. Bianchi, D. Peat and M.R. Windsor (eds), *Interpretation in International Law* (Oxford University Press, 2015) (forthcoming).

[71] I have not engaged with interpretation in my study of law-ascertainment: *Formalism and the Sources of International Law*, (OUP, 2011).

[72] See e.g., O. Corten, *Méthodologie du droit international public*, (Editions de l'Université Libre de Bruxelles, 2009), at 213–15.

[73] See gen. A. Pellet, "Article 38", in A. Zimmermann, C. Tomuschat and K. Oellers-Frahm, *The Statute of the International Court of Justice: A Commentary*, (Oxford University Press, 2006), 677.

[74] See I. Venzke, "Post-modern perspectives on orthodox positivism", in J. Kammerhofer and J. d'Aspremont (eds), *International Legal Positivism in a Postmodern World* (CUP, 2014), 182–210.

I have argued elsewhere that the pedigree requirements prescribed by the doctrine of sources, which provides the criteria by which law-ascertainment interpretation is carried out, originates in social practice.[75] Law-ascertainment is a practice whereby the community of law-applying authorities shares some linguistic signs to determine its object of study, and its objects of agreement and disagreement. The social practice of law-applying authorities is thus embedded in a larger community sharing common signs of communication. I would like to extend this argument by submitting that this specific social understanding of the sources of international law allows one to move away from a rule-based understanding of constraints on law-ascertainment interpretation (and hence a rule-based understanding of the sources themselves).

This notion of a community in which the social practice of law-applying authorities takes place is where the objections raised by Fish against Fiss have real purchase. Fish famously contended that rules are not necessary to constrain interpretation processes.[76] For him, it is a mistake "to think of interpretation as an activity in need of constraints, when in fact interpretation is a structure of constraints".[77] Fish considered that "practice is already principled, since at every moment it is ordered by an understanding of what is practice (the law, basketball), an understanding that can always be put into the form of rules – rules that will be opaque to the outsider – but is not produced by them".[78] He suggests that meanings "do not proceed from an isolated individual but from a public and conventional point of view".[79] This public and

---

[75] J. d'Aspremont, *Formalism and the Sources of International Law*, (OUP, 2011), esp. chapter 7.

[76] Stanley Fish objects to disciplining rules on the basis that they are not necessary because the reader and texts are not in need of the constraints that disciplining rules would provide: "The trainee is not only possessed of but possessed by a knowledge of the ropes, by a tacit knowledge that tells him not so much what to do, but already has him doing it as a condition of perception and even of thought". See S. Fish, "Fish v. Fiss", 36 *Stanford Law Review*, (1984), 1325–47, at 1333.

[77] S. Fish, *Is there a text in this class?*, (Harvard University Press, 1980), p. 356.

[78] S. Fish, "Fish v. Fiss", 36 *Stanford Law Review*, (1984), 1325–47, at 1331–2.

[79] S. Fish, *Is there a text in this class?*, (Harvard University Press, 1980), p. 14.

conventional point of view is what Fish has famously identified with the "interpretive community".[80]

The concept of interpretive community does not need to be addressed at great length here. What is worth mentioning is that the idea of interpretive communities makes constraints on interpretation a question of "knowledge", rather than being referable to a "list" of rules.[81] At the same time, the concept of interpretive community allows one to understand the social practice in which constraints on law-ascertainment interpretation originate as being principled, without falling into the indeterminacy and infinite regress of rules argument.[82] In other words, it makes it possible to reject rule-based constraints on law-ascertainment interpretation while avoiding complete skeptical or relativist positions concerning interpretation.[83]

It is true that the community and the constraints it produces are "not fixed and finite",[84] thereby making constraints on law-ascertainment rather unstable. Fish writes that "interpretive communities are no more

---

[80] S. Fish, *Is there a text in this class?*, (Harvard University Press, 1980): "The relationship between interpretation and text is thus reversed: interpretive strategies are not put into execution after reading; they are the shape of reading, and because they are the shape of reading, they give texts their shape, making them rather than, as is usually assumed, arising from them" (p. 13). According to Fish, these "interpretive strategies" do not make the reader an independent agent. They "proceed not from him but from the interpretive community of which he is a member" (p. 14).

[81] S. Fish, "Fish v. Fiss", 36 *Stanford Law Review*, (1984), 1325–47, 1329. Cf. J. Schelly, "Interpretation in law: the Dworkin–Fish debate (or soccer amongst the Gahuku-Gama)", 73 *California Law Review*, (1985), 158, 163–4. According to Schelly, Fish and Dworkin both agree that authority for interpretation derives from a process that is complex, communal, and political. The ultimate difference between them is that, for Dworkin, morality ultimately constrains interpretation, whereas for Fish, epistemic communities are subject to political rather than moral constraints.

[82] Dworkin famously conceived of interpretation as a social and communitarian practice, likening the role of the interpreter to a chain novelist. See R. Dworkin, "Law as interpretation", 9 *Critical Inquiry*, (1982), 179. However, Fish argues that the interpreter is not constrained by the past but recreates it. See S. Fish, "Working on the chain gang: interpretation in the law and in literary criticism", 9 *Critical Inquiry*, (1982), 201.

[83] In the same vein, see A. MacIntyre, *Whose Justice? Which Rationality?*, (Duckworth, 1988), p. 352.

[84] S. Fish, "Fish v. Fiss", 36 *Stanford Law Review* (1984) 1325–47, 1329

stable than texts because interpretive strategies are not natural or universal, but learned".[85] However, this community-constraining practice is not fully indeterminate and inevitably comes with an element of continuity. Indeed, communitarian practice comes with an element of tradition "which involves both the practice of the past and its constant re-writing, as a way of projecting oneself into the future". According to that view, each actor "contributes to the content of the tradition that develops" and continuously adjusts it to the needs of the time.[86] Interpretation is accordingly anchored in a pattern inherited from the past which is then reconstructed.[87]

This relative instability of social constraints on interpretation could be seen as conferring a welcome flexibility that "allows for [a] significant degree of conflict and dissent".[88] As Mark Mitchell contends when commenting on MacIntyre's and Michael Polanyi's concept of tradition, "entering into a tradition requires an act of submission to an authority".[89] One's submission to authority, however, does not need to be absolute or completely unquestioning. According to that view, tradition leaves intact the possibility of dissent.[90] Understanding the origin of constraints on law-ascertainment interpretation thus allows such constraints to accommodate uncertainty without putting communication between professionals in peril. What is more, it is this lack of complete certainty about the maxims of conversation that enables the success of communication in spite of certain divergences in communicative expectations or intentions. The lack of certainty "leaves certain content hanging in the air, as it were,

---

[85] S. Fish, *Is there a text in this class?*, (Harvard University Press, 1980), p. 172.

[86] M. Mitchell, "Michael Polanyi, Alasdair MacIntyre, and the Role of Tradition", 19 *Humanitas*, (2006), 97, 104–5 (referring to M. Polanyi, *Personal Knowledge. Towards a Post-Critical Philosophy*, Routledge, (1958), p. 160).

[87] M. Koskenniemi, "Constitutionalism as mindset: reflections on Kantian themes about international law and globalization", 8 *Theoretical Inquiries in Law*, (2006), 9, at 22: "This is what traditions do: they try to accommodate new phenomena in patterned, familiar understandings, seeking to balance reverence for the past with openness to the future, with innovators sometimes rejected as degraders, sometimes celebrated as regenerators".

[88] M. Polanyi as described by M. Mitchell, "Michael Polanyi, Alasdair MacIntyre, and the Role of Tradition", 19 *Humanitas*, (2006), 97 at 106.

[89] Ibid.

[90] Ibid.

leaving each party to the conversation with an option of understanding the full communicated content somewhat differently".[91]

The social approach to constraints on law-ascertainment interpretation advocated here, grounded in practice and tradition, is neither conceptually watertight nor a theoretical panacea. This account, like the rule-based approach to content-determination, has not been spared from controversy. For instance, Fiss has famously objected that "[j]ust as one cannot understand or formulate rules unless one is a participant in the practice, so one cannot participate successfully within the practice known as law ... unless one is able to understand or formulate the rules governing the practice".[92] This alludes to the impossibility of standardizing the constraints. Fiss goes on to suggest that, since Fish "rejects the disciplining rules – or any general normative standards – he is left without any basis for resolving conflicting interpretations in any principled way".[93] Schlag has also denounced the failure by Fish to define the set of constraints generated by the interpretive community. According to Schlag, Fish shies away from such a definition because such a descriptive exercise would condemn Fish to produce a text which would give a contradictory spin to his argument. For Schlag, Fish's notion of interpretive community is a pure convenience as it allows him to resist deconstruction.[94] Dennis Patterson, for his part, has alleged that the concept of interpretive community was unstable as it was constantly oscillating between a homogeneous variant and a pluralistic variant to explain diverging interpretations.[95] Others have also seen an element of circularity in the concept of interpretive community.[96]

---

[91] A. Marmor, "Can the law imply more than it says? On some pragmatic aspects of strategic speech", *USC Law Legal Studies Paper* No. 09-43, p. 14.

[92] O. Fiss, "The Jurisprudence (!) of Stanley Fish", 80 *ADE Bulletin*, (1985), 1, at 2.

[93] Ibid.

[94] P. Schlag, "Fish v. Zapp, The case of the relatively autonomous self", 76 *Georgetown Law Journal*, (1987), 36, at 42–9. See also D. Patterson, "You made me do it: my reply to Stanley Fish", 72 *Texas Law Review*, (1993), 67, esp. 76–7, esp. 72.

[95] D. Patterson, "You made me do it: my reply to Stanley Fish", 72 *Texas Law Review*, (1993), 67, esp. 76–7.

[96] For both M. Polanyi and A. MacIntyre, "belief must necessarily precede knowing". This necessarily brings about circularity because one must commit oneself to certain premises and the conclusions one reaches are necessarily entailed by the premises embraced. See M. Mitchell, "Michael Polanyi, Alasdair MacIntyre, and the Role of Tradition", 19 *Humanitas*, (2006), 97, 109–11.

This is certainly not the place to resolve such controversies or salvage either Fiss' or Fish's accounts of constraints on interpretation. For present purposes, the point is that the non-rule-based conception of constraints on law-ascertainment seems the only viable direction in which law-ascertainment can possibly operate. If constraints on law-ascertainment were to be construed as rules, that would condemn the identification of international law (and, in my view, the discipline as a whole) to remain in a state of flux, thereby precluding the possibility of communication between professionals.[97]

In the end, the way in which constraints on content-determination and law-ascertainment interpretation are understood and operate does not matter much for the purposes of the dichotomy put forward in this chapter. The mere fact that constraints on content-determination and law-ascertainment can be construed differently, at least from a theoretical perspective, suffices to show interpretation must be regarded as multi-dimensional. And this bears epistemological consquences.

## IV. CONCLUDING REMARKS

Dichotomies, like the one described in this chapter, are by their very nature exclusive and constitutive. They rest on a binary construction of the world and reject a more all-inclusive approach to the phenomenon of interpretation. Moreover, the embrace of such a dichotomy is not neutral but is informed by conceptual and methodological choices, which, in turn, are determined by some normative agenda and by intellectual preferences. Some of these preferences have been disclosed in the previous sections. In particular, it should now be clear to the reader that the reason for inviting international legal theorists to distinguish between content-determination and law-ascertainment interpretive processes is derived from an overarching normative desire to preserve the possibility of communication between professionals involved in argumentation about international law. It is a desire to make the game of interpretation possible in the first place.

As this chapter draws to a close, another dimension of the distinction between content-determination and law-ascertainment interpretive processes is worth addressing, namely its particular epistemological agenda.

---

[97] See J. d'Aspremont, *Formalism and the Sources of International Law*, (OUP, 2011), especially chapters 1 and 2.

The dichotomy advocated here has the ambition to bring a new dimension to the debate about interpretation in international law. As was repeatedly indicated above, international legal scholarship has long restricted its study of interpretation to content-determination, thereby failing to pay any attention to the interpretive processes at play in law-ascertainment. This restrictive focus on content-determination interpretation in international legal studies – and thus on only one aspect of the object of the game of interpretation – is what prompts the following final observations.

Content-determination interpretation continues to occupy a prominent place in the research agenda of international lawyers. Half a dozen monographs have been produced on interpretation in international law in recent years.[98] This is not to mention scholarly articles and book chapters. Unsurprisingly, most of them continue to be prejudiced by the rule-based approach fostered by the Vienna Conventions on the Law of Treaties, discussed above. These studies on the content-determination interpretive process continue to be caught in the infinite regress affecting the rule-based approach.[99] Interestingly, such an objection does not seem to suffice to prompt a paradigmatic change in international legal studies. International legal scholars continue, generation after generation, to study content-determination interpretation from a rule-based perspective, thereby repeating the same inconclusive paradigmatic move made by previous generations. In my view, broadening the scope of international legal studies on interpretation by including law-ascertainment interpretive processes would help international lawyers emancipate themselves from the prison of a rule-based approach to constraints on interpretation, and could help them both realize the limits of their current conceptual framework and engage in a critical reflection about the paradigms they use.

Refusal to engage with this broader view of interpretive processes risks relegating international legal scholarship to the hamster wheel of studies on content-determination interpretation, where the rules, rather than the

---

[98] See M. Waibel, "Demystifying the art of interpretation", 22 *European Journal of International Law*, (2011), 571–88. See also the works cited by A. Bianchi, D. Peat and M.R. Windsor (eds), *Interpretation in International Law* (Oxford University Press, 2015) (forthcoming).

[99] A. Bianchi, "Textual interpretation and (international) law reading: the myth of (in)determinacy and the genealogy of meaning", in P. Bekker (ed.) *Making Transnational Law Work in the Global Economy – Essays in Honour of Detlev Vagts*, (Cambridge University Press, 2010), p. 35.

practice of, interpretation, is the perpetual focus.[100] It must be acknowledged that training and exercising one's skills has self-educational virtue in itself. By running indefinitely in the hamster wheel of content-determination interpretation, the techniques to secure persuasiveness and argumentative authority within the professional community of international law may be enhanced. Furthermore, this may provide international lawyers with thoughts, insights, and self-reflection on foundational questions in the social sciences like the relationship between fact and norm, the performativity of language, the tensions between textualism and arbitrariness, and some aspects of a theory of knowledge.

Irrespective of the undisputed virtues of exercising in the hamster wheel, however, one may wonder whether it is worth continuing to write articles, research papers, monographs and edited collections on the theme of interpretation if the only resulting virtue is self-education. It only makes sense for studies on interpretation in international law to remain on the research agenda if international lawyers are prepared to open their eyes to other interpretive processes at work in international law, thereby seizing a chance to emancipate themselves from the circularity of rule-based approaches to interpretation. This is a necessary step if one wants to salvage studies about interpretation in international law.

---

[100] See generally, D. Kennedy, "When renewal repeats: thinking against the box", 32 *New York University Journal of International Law and Politics*, (2000), 335.

# 8. Academic writing

This chapter examines contemporary practices pertaining to academic writing and the writing tactics that international lawyers deploy in their pursuit of the social arrangements they contemplate. Academic writing is taken here as one of the key argumentative techniques in any social science. It is certainly not a fully autonomous argumentative technique that can be completely severed from methodology and interpretation which have been examined in the two previous chapters. Methodological and interpretive choices – as much as foundational doctrines – materialize in judgements, pleadings, position papers, as well as scholarly writing. In that sense, academic writing is one of the modes of expression through which foundational doctrines as well as methodological and interpretive choices manifest themselves. Yet, academic writing also comes with its own self-standing tactics distinguishable from foundational doctrines as well as methodological and interpretive choices. Those tactics of academic writing that are distinguishable from interpretation and methodology are of an argumentative nature. In that sense, this chapter should be seen as grappling with practices of argumentation. And there is no doubt that acquiring the mastery of those writing tactics as much as the capacity to decipher their deployment is part of the socialization of international lawyers.[1] Although the socialization of international lawyers includes the mastery of some of the following writing tactics, those tactics are individual as much as collective skills.[2] In other words, they are inherited from the collectivity but the mastery of their technique remains dependent on individual performances.

---

[1] A. MacIntyre, *Whose Justice? Which Rationality?*, Duckworth, 1988, at 5 ("Arguments, that is to say, have come to be understood in some circles not as expressions of rationality, but as weapons, the techniques for deploying which furnish a key part of the professional skills of lawyers, academics, economists, and journalists who thereby dominate the dialectically unfluent and inarticulate").

[2] D. Feldman, "The nature of legal scholarship", 52 *Modern Law Review*, (1989), 498–517, at 508.

The writing tactics which are discussed in this chapter constitute what I have called elsewhere "wording" tactics.[3] These tactics are resorted to, as was argued in the introduction, to secure social validation of argumentation.[4] It is against the backdrop of the idea that legal argumentation is socially validated within the community of international lawyers that the following tactics must be appraised. Each of them is a means used, besides interpretive and methodological choices, to acquire or consolidate assent of the (part of the) community of international lawyers to which the argument is addressed.

The following sections sketch out some of the most common writing practices in the contemporary production of scholarly ideas. Mention is specifically made of those writing tactics deployed to create textual economy (I), generate semantic instability (II), enhance textual aesthetics (III), yield empiricism (IV), create strawmen in order to preserve the argumentative character of scholarly ideas (V), gratify oneself (VI), rough out and hone scholarly ideas (VII), magnify erudition (VIII), make new idioms or neologisms (IX), and, eventually, intimidate peers (X).

Before embarking on such a – quick – overview of contemporary academic writing tactics, three caveats must be formulated. First, it should be noted that all the following writing tactics found in contemporary legal scholarship often overlap. They should accordingly not be taken in isolation from one another. Second, such practices vary according to the sub-groups of the community of international legal scholars, and especially according to the subject that they study. Scholars engaged in international legal theory will not usually resort to the same writing tactics as those who study – and are trying to develop – international criminal law for instance. Third, there is inevitably a great dose of oversimplification in the account made in this chapter. The strategies driving contemporary academic writing are certainly more subtle than is depicted here. However, despite the broad strokes with which this chapter ventures to delineate some of the most common writing tactics in the production of knowledge about international law, the following – cursory – observations should suffice to invite further reflection on the textual tactics of the profession.

---

[3] J. d'Aspremont, "Wording in international law", 25 *Leiden Journal of International Law*, (2012), 575–602.

[4] See *supra* Introduction, section 5.

## I. PROTECTIVE TEXTUAL ECONOMY

One of the most common writing tactics is laconism. Being succinct is time-saving. Indeed, laconism allows the author to float ideas without unveiling the lack of ripeness thereof. But textual economy can simultaneously be very self-protective. Indeed, words define the surface of scholarly arguments and, by the same token, determine the surface of legal scholars' engagement in the argumentative competition for naming. The less scholars say, the less they expose themselves. Said differently, the less scholars say, the less they venture into the argumentative fray. Textual stinginess can prove an extremely protective measure as it reduces the surface of argumentation exposed by its author. In that sense, textual economy can prove an efficient argumentative conflict-avoidance strategy. It is important to note that textual economy is however not always resorted to for argumentative-avoidance purposes. It may also help create semantic instability which must be examined separately.

## II. THE PURSUIT OF SEMANTIC INSTABILITY

Words express concepts which, by definition, have an economizing function, for they refer to a given state of affairs. The greater the state of affairs referred to by words, the more economizing they are.[5] As a matter of fact, words of international law are becoming more and more economizing. Indeed, international law constitutes cumulative knowledge. It is ever-growing and self-enriching. Indeed, as a result of continuous application and interpretation, each concept enriches itself as do the semantics of the words through which they are translated. Thus, the semantic load of words in international law grows unabated. This is an important point for, the more economical words are, the more room for semantic instability is generated.

The use of highly economical words to yield semantic instability is a growing practice. Word semantics are purposely kept open to allow semantic oscillation. It can take various forms including the borrowing of words and idioms from social or hard sciences, for those words and idioms will usually not be entirely fathomable by other members of the community of international legal scholars, thereby allowing a wide space

---

[5] A. Ross, "Tû-tû", 70 *Harvard Law Review*, (1956–57), 812, esp. 813. For a contemporary translation of that idea and a critical evaluation thereof by U. Linderfalk, "On the many functions of the international legal concepts, part one", available at http://papers.ssrn.com/sol3/papers.cfm?abstract_id=1863048.

for semantic fluctuation. Semantic instability allows the destabilization of fellow scholars. Indeed, it confuses the reader who can never clearly delineate or grasp an ever-changing and unstable argument. It bars any argumentative backfire while allowing the author to dodge most counter-arguments by taking refuge under a semantic shelter. It simultaneously allows magnificent textual acrobatics and wordplays. Such benefits make semantic instability a textual tool of great convenience. It is because of their instrumentality to semantic instability that some of the buzz words permeating the current literature on international law[6] have proved so successful. Some strands of the community of international legal scholars have even made semantic instability their principal and systematic text-making tool.[7]

## III. THE AESTHETICS OF SCHOLARLY ARGUMENTS

It seems hard to deny that nowadays the aesthetics of scholarly construction are often as important as the substantive argument that is pursued therewith. That is because international legal scholars think that the aesthetics contribute to the persuasiveness of their argument. As was mentioned in the introduction, this is a consideration the structure of this book is not alien to.[8] Besides providing a buttress of the authority of an argument, footnoting has long played such an aesthetic-enhancing role. The amount of references as well as the names that are referred to – the so-called "cult of citation"[9] – have always been contributing to embellishing a scholarly piece. This has even constituted an institutional prerequisite for an article to be deemed publishable. Yet, in their quest for aesthetics, international legal scholars now also systematically use words to embellish what can otherwise be perceived as a rather monotonous and insipid construction. At the price of being sometimes pompous, international legal scholars have a much greater inclination to infuse their texts with what they perceive as the most impeccable locution or idioms.

---

[6] One of the best illustrations is probably the semantic instability that has been nurtured around the idiom of legal pluralism.

[7] On the use of semantic instability in the work of J. Derrida, see F. Kastner, "The paradoxes of justice: the ultimate difference between a philosophical and sociological observation of law", in O. Perez and G. Teubner, *Paradoxes and Inconsistencies in the Law*, (Hart, 2005), 168–70.

[8] See *supra* Introduction, section 6.

[9] D. Bederman, "Appraising a century of scholarship in the American Journal of International Law", 100 *AJIL*, (2006), 20–63, at 55.

They accordingly spend hours finding the finest textual ornament. Thesauruses become the indispensable tool of scholars in the quest for the most textually embellishing expression. This can also manifest itself in the borrowing of words and idioms which are deemed of great aesthetic virtue from social or hard sciences or from foreign languages. Needless to say that like all judgements of aesthetic value, the decorative effect of their words still depends on the sensory, affective and emotional predisposition of the reader. Yet, they sufficiently flatter authors themselves. This textual pompousness has grown more common among the new generation of international legal scholars, often prompting the previous generation to bemoan what they see as artificial textual bodybuilding. Although I believe that international legal scholars have at their disposal a greater panoply of concepts – and hence of words, this criticism is not always ill-founded. Textual body-building and the quest for aesthetics are nowadays epidemic in the international legal scholarship. And that phenomenon has been exacerbated by some strands of the community which systematically resort to aesthetic-enhancing mechanisms.

## IV. THE CONSTRUCTION OF EMPIRICAL DATA

In chapter 5 above, it has been recalled the extent to which international law constitutes a set of ideas that are projected on (and constitutive of) the outside world. It has also been highlighted on that occasion how much empiricism has been deemed necessary for international lawyers to secure both self-esteem and authority in the eyes of policy-makers.[10] Empiricism is conducive to the creation of "out there-ness" which is deemed indispensable for the establishment of the authority of legal arguments as well as the authority of international lawyers themselves.[11] This is what explains why an important part of the international legal scholarship has enthusiastically embraced empiricism as a central paradigm of legal studies.[12]

It is of an embarrassing conspicuity to recall there is not such a thing as empirical objectivism. Concepts are the tools with which reality is

---

[10] See *supra* chapter 5.
[11] On this idea, see also chapter 7 on "Interpretation".
[12] See Chapter 6 above. See also the critical remarks on the turn to empiricism in Anglo-American scholarship formulated by J. d'Aspremont, "Send back the lifeboats: confronting the project of the saving of international law", *American Journal of International Law*, (2014).

observed and constructed.[13] That means that descriptive facts cannot determine their own rational significance and "value facts" are necessary to bring practice to life.[14] Said again differently, thought categories contribute to the construction of the world.[15] Data collection is necessarily data construction. This is why empirical methodology is always inevitably conceptual and normative.[16]

While it is traditionally the concepts – and not the words into which they are translated – which construct reality, international legal scholars more often succumb to the temptation of letting their empirical data be exclusively built on words. Indeed, catchy words or idioms, without any conceptual flesh, are elevated in empirical lenses. This means that it is the word that drives empiricism. Empiricism is instrumentalized to serve the aesthetics. It is the elegant or graceful word or idiom that is elevated into a reality-constructing tool. The word, rather than the concept, becomes the building block of empirical data. When this is the case, the conceptual fleshing is usually postponed until the flashy word has secured sufficient popularity and has been adopted or espoused by a great number of members of the community. It is however at the conceptual fleshing-out stage that the data-constructive role of words comes to light and that one realizes the empirical power of words, occasionally requiring some face-saving ruses.

---

[13] See the famous and oft-quoted assertion by P. Allott, *Eunomia*, (Oxford University Press, 2001), p. xxvii: "We make the human world, including human institutions through the power of the human mind. What we have made by thinking we can make new by new thinking". On this point, see the remarks of J. Beckett, "Countering uncertainty and ending up/down arguments: prolegomena to a response to NAIL", 16 *EJIL*, (2005), 213, esp. pp. 214–16. See also J. Raz, "Between authority and interpretation", p. 31: "In large measure what we study when we study the nature of law is the nature of our own self-understandings ... It is part of the self-consciousness of our society to see certain institutions as legal. And that consciousness is part of what we study when we inquire into the nature of law".

[14] M. Greenberg, "How facts make law", UCLA School of Law, *Public Law & Legal Theory Research Paper No. 05-22*, p. 173.

[15] P. Bourdieu, "The force of law: toward a sociology of the juridical field", 38 *Hastings Law Journal*, (1987), 814–53, p. 839. According to Bourdieu, this is the "creative power of representation" (ibid.).

[16] See Chapter 6 above.

## V. THE CONSTRUCTION OF STRAWMEN

As was explained above, adversity is inherent in the making of arguments.[17] It is in that sense that the international legal scholarship is inherently adversarial. Arguments are built on (and geared towards) peers' stances on – seemingly – similar questions. If an idea built by an international legal scholar does not respond to a pre-existing one, it fails to qualify as an argument in the first place and the question of its persuasiveness or semantic authority does not even arise. Seeking persuasiveness and semantic authority thus presupposes a conflict of thought. Yet, often in making and fine-tuning their scholarly constructions, international legal scholars find out that the argumentative conflict they had presupposed was nothing more than a mirage.[18] When this is the case, it often happens that they feel already too wedded to their own idea – or have already invested too much time therein – to be able to backtrack or trash their whole construction. In such a case, they feel pressed – to create an argumentative strawman which they can subsequently batter at whim, allowing their idea to become an argument in its own right. There are several ways to build strawmen. One can fabricate empirical data as was explained above, or one can fabricate semantics. One can also choose to carry out arbitrary stereotypical grouping of scholars.[19]

## VI. THE "ROUGHING OUT" PROCESS OF SCHOLARLY IDEAS

The following use of words is more unconscious. Following the developments of new technologies and writing materials, scholars have changed their thought-forming processes. While the previous generations were constrained to work out any idea mentally before couching it on paper, new technologies allow scholars to carve their ideas directly on the screen. In that sense, the screen has become the drawing board of

---

[17] See Introduction above.
[18] See J. Nijman, P. Ricoeur, "International Law: Beyond 'The End of the Subject'. Towards a Reconceptualization of International Legal Personality", 20 *LJIL*, (2007), 25–64, at 850, (she argues that there are more law professors than there are good scholarly topics that they are capable of addressing).
[19] For D. Kennedy, this sort of grouping is an act of violence. See D. Kennedy, "Primitive legal scholarship", 27 *Harvard Journal of International Law*, (1986), 1, at 12.

scholarly constructions, directly impacting on how scholarly thoughts are carved.[20] It is true that thought-forming processes vary and there probably are as many of them as members of the community. Yet, new technologies have made writing look like action painting. Rough ideas are thrown on the screen before being subjected to several stages of refinement. Scholars will begin by spewing their ideas on the drawing board before knocking off the large portions of unwanted words. In this pitching operation, words will be eliminated. Those portions of words that are eliminated constitute the testing ground where the refined idea takes shape. In that sense, a large portion of words used by international legal scholars are simply testing materials meant to be subsequently refined by their scholarly mallet in a "roughing out" process. It remains that not all the words that were specifically thrown on the screen as building materials are eliminated by the "roughing out" process. Some of them continue to infuse the texts that are finally transformed in portable document format. In that sense, as a result of new technologies, texts about international law bear much more manifestly than before the imprints of the earlier stages of scholars' thought-forming processes.

---

[20] Elsewhere I have elaborated on other transformation of the thought-forming processes in our epistemic community as a result of new technologies: "Debating – and the culture of the critique that comes along with it – are now an integral part of the activity of being an international legal scholar. Debate has become an essential component of the production of legal thoughts. Ideas are no longer mulled over for years in an – often dusty and messy – isolated study and kept secret until the day of their solemn revelation through publication in a top-tier international law journal. While still being the product of a long individual cerebral effort, ideas are now shared, tested and further refined through peer-to-peer experimentation at an earlier stage of the scholarly thought-making process ... legal scholars of the 21st century have grown more faithful in the Socratic virtues of the exchange of ideas which they now see as instrumental in the mutual development and sharpening of legal thinking as a whole ... thanks to the new means of transfer of knowledge, scholarly debates have simultaneously undergone a process of deformalization. Lack of seniority no longer bars access to the experts' debate and the implicit hierarchies of the profession have ceased to constitute compelling barriers to the expression of disagreement. Legal blogging has been both the cause and the consequence of these fundamental changes in the debating culture – and the thought-making process – of the international legal scholarship of the 21st century." See J. d'Aspremont, "In defense of the hazardous tool of legal blogging", EJIL: Talk!, 6 January 2011, http://www.ejiltalk.org/in-defense-of-the-hazardous-tool-of-legal-blogging/.

## VII. SCHOLARLY SELF-GRATIFICATION

International legal scholars can be a bit fetishist. They worship their own textual production. This is inherent in the action of producing and publishing. It is difficult to imagine a scholar publishing a text which he or she would be appalled by. Sometimes under the strain of insane deadlines because of recurrent and imprudent over-commitment, international legal scholars happen to submit scholarly pieces they are not entirely satisfied with and which, because of lack of time or lack of passion, they could not sharpen and deepen sufficiently. Yet, it seems that pride is a constitutive element of pushing an idea out in the argumentative arena. It is not only until the words and the articulation thereof generate a feeling of satisfaction that international legal scholars venture to float them in the argumentative arena. International legal scholars would hardly publish and let disseminate their textual creation if they did not feel any satisfaction with the words they have couched on their screen. In that sense, words are self-gratifying. They redeem international legal scholars with a self-constructed satisfaction without which they would not feel sufficiently self-confident to step into the argumentative fray.

## VIII. THE MAGNIFYING OF ERUDITION

Sharing some kinship with the wording for self-gratifying purposes, the techniques geared towards the promotion of erudition are rife in the literature about international law. Indeed, through words, international legal scholars can easily display their knowledge about areas which are unrelated to international law. Indeed, words and idioms help them convey the impression of knowledge on disciplines or culture alien to (international) law. Preferred areas of knowledge about which (international) legal scholars relish manifesting erudition are of all kinds. They include other humanities as well as social and hard sciences.[21] They also include references to the names of scholars unknown to the discipline –

---

[21] It is interesting to note that for Thomas Kuhn the turn to philosophy may also be seen as ushering in a paradigmatic change. See, T. Kuhn, *The Structure of Scientific Revolutions*, University of Chicago Press, 4th ed., 2012, "The proliferation of competing articulations, the willingness to try anything, the expression of explicit discontent, the recourse to philosophy and to debate over fundamentals, all these are symptoms of a transition from normal to extraordinary research" (p. 91).

which will often be accompanied by citations taken out of their context and artfully rebranded to provide authority to an argument about international law. Using words of a language foreign to that in which the scholarly work is written is similarly a common erudition-enhancing technique, Latin or French often being the languages *à la mode*. Such promoting techniques are popular because of their efficiency. Just one word or idiom suffices to impart a feeling of great erudition. Actually, the more alien or technical the word is, the more erudite the author thinks he or she will sound. The use of such a technique is often accompanied by the abovementioned care for the aesthetics of the text and the self-gratifying attitude described earlier. By the same token, it happens that such boasting practice is instrumental to the intimidating tactics which are discussed below.

## IX. THE MAKING OF NEW IDIOMS OR NEOLOGISM

In one's quest for social validation of one's argument, being in a position to claim ownership of a particular word, idiom or neologism naturally provides extra authority in the argumentative struggle which inevitably ensues over the semantics of that word, idiom or neologism. Fighting for the semantics of existing concepts is far more strenuous and arduous than defending one's textual turf. It goes without saying that coining a new buzzword may take various forms. It may be the creation of a catchy neologism. It may be the use of a particular semantic. It can amount to unearthing a word or idiom in ancient texts of the discipline. Or it can boil down to borrowing words and idioms in sister disciplines and importing them in the argumentative arena of international law. Because of the tactical advantage that such paternity provides, the coining of new words or idioms often constitutes a passport to the hall of fame, usually ensuring greater prospects of career-promotion. Unsurprisingly, this fame-enhancing effect of a magic formula has led international legal scholars to be extremely creative. Everyone ventures into new words or idioms every now and then with the hope that it will be picked up by peers. As a result, the literature is continuously imbued with new neologisms and idioms.[22] Needless to say that most such endeavors falter. It is noteworthy that international legal scholars are not the only group of the interpretative community of international law to make such linguistic

---

[22] For some critical remarks on the use of neologisms, see R. Debray, *Transmitting Culture*, (Columbia University Press, 1997), at viii.

experiments. So do international judges whose linguistic creativity probably has a higher chance of success given the visibility and authority traditionally attached to their functions.[23]

## X. SCHOLARLY INTIMIDATING TACTICS

In a crammed and teeming argumentative arena of international law,[24] keeping other participants at distance and preserving one's breathing space have turned existential. In this struggle for breathing space, semantic intimidation has proved a convenient and efficacious tool. Indeed, words – especially those one borrows from other fields and which may be unknown to peers – can be used as heavy artillery that one makes appear on adversaries' radar to intimidate the latter. Such a practice is grounded in the belief that argumentative adversaries will accordingly be deterred from directly engaging with one's argument, which can, in turn, create some comforting distance. Interestingly, there is even a tendency to cling to such heavy artillery when the argumentative turbulences are particularly violent. In that sense, the more unchartered the water of the debate, the greater the temptation to make use of such intimidating turn-outs. Such a wording can manifest itself in various ways. Like many other of the abovementioned tactics, it can take the form of a transplant of words and idioms from social or hard sciences which are often unfathomable for peers. It can also express itself through conceptual "obscurantism"[25] or semantic instability.[26]

All the foregoing tactics are deployed to enhance persuasiveness of legal argumentation with a view to securing social validation. It is not excluded that such tactics may at time prove counter-productive and undermine the realization of the very objective towards which they are geared. One may think of the semantic instability, the convenience of neologism or the intimidating tactics that may resonate well in certain specific circles of the community of international legal scholars while faring poorly among other groups of international legal scholars. It is not the place to comment on the respective virtues of each of the

---

[23] See the classical examples of praetor-created idioms of "erga omnes obligations" or "counter-measures" which were immediately picked up by the international community.

[24] On this aspect, see the Introduction.

[25] D. Feldman, "The nature of legal scholarship", 52 *Modern Law Review*, (1989), 498–517.

[26] See *supra* section 2.

above-mentioned tactics. It is not even certain that they can be measured, for they depend as much on the talent of the individual scholars as the community to which the piece of writing is addressed. What matters to stress, in conclusion, is simply that this wide variety of academic writing tactics are deployed for the same, unique goal, that is to secure persuasiveness and hence validation of legal argumentation by (a part of) the community of international legal scholars.

# 9. Dissemination*

Opinions, information, and legal arguments about international law cannot be received, taken into account, debated, and eventually validated within the community of international lawyers as long as they have not been disseminated.[1] Dissemination ensures that opinions, information, and legal arguments are received by the addressees who then find themselves in a position to evaluate as well as (in)validate them on the basis of the criteria they have acquired through socialization.[2] These various steps are inherent in the political knowledge-production process in international law.[3] Drawing from Regis Debray's famous distinction between communication and transmission, the foregoing amounts to saying that dissemination is a material act of a communicative nature that allows the political phenomenon of transmission to take place.[4] This holds for all types of opinions, informations, legal arguments, be they produced by political authorities, judicial bodies, governmental advisers or academics. For all of them, dissemination is essential for their product

---

\* This chapter orginates in an editorial of the *Leiden Journal of International Law*, written with Larissa van den Herik.

[1] See B. Latour, *Science in Action*, (Harvard University Press, 1987), pp. 40–41 ("You may have written a paper that settles a fierce controversy once and for all, but if readers ignore it, it cannot be turned into fact; it simply cannot. You may protest against the injustice; you may treasure the certitude of being right in your inner heart; but it will never go further than your inner heart; you will never go further in certitude without the help of others. Fact construction is so much a collective process that an isolated person builds only dreams, claims and feelings, not facts").

[2] On the process of socialization and social validation, see above Introduction.

[3] Knowledge is understood here as established patterns of information which can be of a factual or argumentative nature. See gen. P. Allott, "Language, method and the nature of international law", 45 *BYBIL*, (1971), 79, at 105. On the inherent communicable dimension of knowledge, see P. Baert and A. Shipman, "Transforming the intellectual", in F.D. Rubio and P. Baert (eds), *The Politics of Knowledge*, (Routledge, 2012), 179, at 179.

[4] See gen. R. Debray, *Transmitting Culture*, Columbia University Press (1997).

to be received and (in)validated by the addressees – and possibly the whole community of international lawyers – they seek to convince. In that sense, dissemination encapsulates a variety of techniques that are essential in the social validation process of international legal arguments. It is against the backdrop of the contribution of dissemination to the social validation of legal arguments that a short chapter of this book is devoted to contemporary practices of dissemination.

It does not seem contested that dissemination takes place through highly organized communicative networks and routes.[5] These networks and routes must be those accepted, recognized, and consulted by the community of professionals to whom opinions, information, and legal arguments are addressed.[6] It may be that for certain categories of international lawyers those networks or routes are less convoluted. For instance, the dissemination of a court's decisions will usually follow a rather straightforward and simple process of dissemination.[7] In contrast, dissemination of academic products of thoughts will be subjected to a more intricate process that involves the resort to a wide variety of academic publishing and disseminating tools. Continuing the reflection on academic writing of the previous chapter, this chapter zeroes in on the role of academic publishing in the process of dissemination, and especially that of law journals. The focus on law journals, rather than other tools of dissemination, is informed by the assumption that law journals continue to constitute a cardinal instrument of dissemination in contemporary international legal debates.[8] This chapter is followed by a chapter on the technique of blogging that is similarly part of the dissemination indispensable for the transmission, reception, and (in)validation of legal arguments. These two final chapters examine the way in which international lawyers use techniques of dissemination as well as the (perceived) purposes for which they are deployed.

---

[5] Ibid., at 14.

[6] R.L. Bard, "Advocacy masquerading as scholarship; or, why legal scholars cannot be trusted", 55 *Brooklyn Law Review*, (1989), 853, at 854.

[7] On the importance of communicative tools of judges to secure persuasiveness, see G. Davidov and M. Davidov, "How judges use weapons of influence: the social psychology of courts", 46 *Israel Law Review*, (2013), 7–24.

[8] On the earlier disseminating role of the *American Journal of International Law*, see the critical remarks by D. Bederman, "Appraising a century of scholarship in the American Journal of International Law", 100 *AJIL*, (2006), 20–63, 134–5.

## I. THE EXTERNALITIES OF ACADEMIC PUBLISHING

The externalities of academic publishing are well-known. It generates billions of tons of carbon dioxide by virtue of production, shipping or even online access,[9] exacerbates egos of authors, leads to over-commitment of all stakeholders – whether authors, reviewers, editors or publishers – and contributes to the proliferation of legal thinking,[10] which, in social sciences, can be extremely harmful for the discipline as a whole. This – often underestimated – fallout of academic publishing is obfuscated by the public good associated therewith. Indeed, academic publishing is almost unanimously elevated into a lofty and noble activity performed in the public interest, if not of the society as a whole, at least of the professional community concerned. There seems to be unanimity that academic publishing serves the public good.

It goes without saying that perceptions of what the public good of academic publishing is are extremely diverse and aplenty, if not in contradiction. Every member of the epistemic community of international law has a particular own take on what type(s) of public good academic publishing supposedly serves. The primary public good of academic publishing – and thus the main mitigating parameter of the above-mentioned externalities – lies in the above-mentioned social validation of legal arguments and the crystallization of knowledge about law that it contributes to make possible. More specifically, by selecting, ensuring (a given) quality, marrying name and reputation to certain authors and themes and disseminating scholarly works, law journals permit the information and opinions of members of the epistemic community of international law to be disseminated and subsequently validated within that community. In that sense, it is widely believed among international lawyers that in the intricate social process from information to knowledge, law journals constitute an essential medium.[11] Said differently, law journals are an important part of the assembly line for the validation of legal arguments and knowledge about international law.

---

[9] On the unsettling carbon footprints of data centers, see J. Glanz, "Power, pollution and the internet", *New York Times*, 22 September 2012.

[10] On this idea of proliferation of international legal thinking, see J. d'Aspremont, "Softness in international law: a rejoinder to A. D'Amato", 20 *European Journal of International Law*, (2009), 911–17.

[11] On the concept of knowledge-formation in international law, see J. d'Aspremont, "Wording in international law", 25 *Leiden Journal of International Law*, (2012), 575–602.

## II. THE ASSEMBLY LINE OF KNOWLEDGE ABOUT INTERNATIONAL LAW

It goes without saying that law journals cannot themselves improvise assembly lines of knowledge about international law. The alchemy necessary to allow the above-mentioned crystallizing and validating effect to take place requires a few carefully fine-tuned operations which are briefly mentioned here. Two particular techniques must be found on the assembly line for it to generate crystallization and validation effect. These necessary techniques primarily pertain to quality and order. A few words need to be said about each of these two central features of law journals in each of the two following sections. Yet, it is preliminary of importance to recall that quality and order are respectively the cause and the consequence of one inherent feature of law journals: selectiveness. Indeed, albeit the proliferation of law journals – whether paper or electronic – has significantly eased access to professional publication, law journals select the information and opinions they disseminate. This is hardly surprising. Given their current format, journals cannot materially publish everything. Even for exclusively online journals, selectiveness is a central feature short of which they would simply be no different from databases. It is true that selectiveness is a feature which law journals share with blogs, although, given their nature and assigned functions, the latter have usually been less selective than law journals.[12] However, the understanding of selectiveness by law journals is key to how they contribute to the crystallization of knowledge about international law. Indeed, the yardstick for selection (quality) and the way in which selection manifests itself (order) are very determinative of the crystallization effect that will transform opinion and information into legal knowledge.

## III. QUALITY CONTROL AND CERTIFICATION

Certainly, the most central technique that allows a law journal to contribute to the crystallization and validation of the information, opinions, and legal arguments is the certification of quality of the scholarship

---

[12] On expert blogging, see chapter 10.

that is published. Knowledge – and thus validated arguments – necessitates verification procedures.[13] Needless to say that quality is not an objective finding and remains contingent on those criteria which are *in abstracto* elevated into yardsticks of quality as well as the way in which they are applied *in concreto* by those to whom quality-evaluation is delegated. The quality-indicators to which journals may be resorting can be of an extremely wide variety. Practices in international law academic publishing can vary enormously between journals but also between cultural and geographical lines. For instance, quality-control is strictly defined in continental Europe or in Asia and will usually take the form of peer-review. On the contrary, in the United States, quality-control is more loosely defined, alternative criteria like sources, originality and impact being commonly resorted to by those in charge of law journals.[14] It is certainly not the place to discuss the value and merit of each of these quality indicators and the practices of quality-evaluation. What matters to highlight here is that, whatever quality-indicators they embrace, law journals (and their editorial boards) are (seeing themselves as) endowed with the responsibility of tracing and certifying quality. The reason thereof is because quality is a constitutive element of social validation of legal arguments as was discussed in the Introduction above. If the quality of the scholarly opinions and information disseminated by journals could not be certified, such scholarly output would have little chance to be socially validated.

## IV. ORDER AND SEQUENCE IN DISSEMINATION

It is not controversial to say that the gargantuan flow of information and opinions about law cannot be digested and made sense of by the members of the professional community of international law. It is also true that law journals contribute to the deluge caused by prolific scholarly production. Yet, they simultaneously help structure these floods. In particular, they frame and set a pace for the stream of opinions and information that are constantly produced about international law. By ordering the production of information and opinions about international law, journals enhance the possibility of such scholarly work being

---

[13] P. Allott, "Language, method and the nature of international law", 45 *BYBIL*, (1971), 79, at 117.

[14] It is important to note that very different standards apply with respect to the publication of monographs where quality-indicators resemble those used in Europe.

received and validated by peers as legal knowledge. The attention of those members of the professional community is spared and only drawn to those scholarly opinions and information which the editors of a journal deem worthy of their attention. This, in turn, increases the chance of peer-reception and peer-validation, indispensable for such information and opinions to be socially validated.

## V. DIGITALIZING THE ASSEMBLY LINE

Needless to say that quality-control (and certification) as well as ordering – and the way they are practiced by law journals – are being seriously affected by the rise of new actors in academic publishing.[15] Indeed, academic publishing is undergoing a pluralization as a result of new technologies. New actors have gained a foothold therein. Interestingly, the above-mentioned two features of law journals are precisely those aspects by virtue of which these new actors distinguish themselves from law journals. Other media, like blogs and open access databases operate on the basis of methods of dissemination radically more liberal when it comes to order and quality.[16]

While it seems a foregone conclusion that the era of paper journals is coming to an end, it remains open to question whether (someday exclusively online) law journals will be able to preserve the two above-mentioned distinctive features. This chapter argues that vindicating such two techniques is vital if law journals want to remain a central medium in the assembly line of knowledge-production and social validation of legal arguments. It should be made clear, however, that it is not that the existence of the law journal should be vindicated for the sake of law journals themselves. Vindicating these two features of academic publishing should thus not be construed as a – dogmatic – defense of law journals but as a plea for the preservation of the two central features of the law journal – quality-control and order. The ebbing away of quality-control and certification as well as order would not only lead to a dilution of law journals but it would also severely erode the social validation process.

---

[15] On these challenges, see L. van den Herik, "LJIL in the age of cyberspace", 25 *Leiden Journal of International Law*, (2012), 1. More generally on the impact of the new technologies on the production of knowledge, see F.D. Rubio and P. Baert, *The Politics of Knowledge*, (Routledge, 2012).

[16] See Chapter 10 below.

## VI. THE FIVE RIDDLES ABOUT THE ROLE OF LAW JOURNALS IN FUTURE SOCIAL VALIDATION PROCESSES

This short chapter concludes with a few final observations. These observations are phrased in the form of questions in that they are meant to invite all the stakeholders in the business of academic publishing to reflect upon five central questions for the public good of knowledge production and social validation of tomorrow. The answers thereto are likely to determine the design and nomenclature of the assembly line of knowledge production and social validation in the decades to come, especially in relation to law journals or those tools of dissemination that could someday replace them.

First, quality control – in the form of peer-review as it is usually organized in Europe – is free of charge in the professional community of international law in contrast with other disciplines. Indeed, reviewers are not remunerated for evaluating scholarly works of others. Quality-evaluation thus depends on the sense of responsibility and civism of the members of the epistemic community of international law. Cost incurred by journals instead relate to their secretariat and their website. In this context, the question of the affiliation of journals with major publishing houses necessarily arise for both publishers and journals. Given the multiplication of open-access database and the skyrocketing amount of articles uploaded on these databases by authors themselves, will publishers still find it sufficiently profitable to publish law journals in the future? Conversely, will law journals still find an interest in being affiliated to (and subject to the rules of) a major publisher if they can finance their overhead costs through other channels?

Second, while the question of the kinship between law journals and publishers will come to the fore, that of the suitability of the creation of new journals will too. For instance, just in the professional community of international law, there is not a single year which does not witness the creation of a new journal. Despite the uncontested emergence of new areas of research both from empirical and epistemological standpoints, the creation of new – often ultra-specialized and narrowly focused – journals, supposedly serving the public good of the epistemic community of international law, raises two fundamental questions. First, doesn't the creation of new journals contribute to the proliferation of international legal thinking which, as was said, undermines the assembly line of knowledge-production? Second, don't law journals of a general ambit continue to offer an appropriate platform for publication of specialized work and contribute more usefully to the crystallization of information and opinion into knowledge?

Third, because quality-control operates on a voluntary basis and hinges on the civic obligations of all members of the epistemic community, securing reviewers has become an uphill battle. Peer-review has rightly been said to be in crisis.[17] That difficulty is growing in proportion with the enormous need for peer-evaluation in the profession of international lawyer. Indeed, as a result of the proliferation of law journals as well as the financing of research through state-supported foundation of peer-evaluated research projects, international legal scholars are constantly solicited to evaluate the work of one another. In these circumstances, the individual feelings of responsibility no longer suffice to entice members of that community to contribute to the evaluation of the works of peers. Additional incitements are necessary to convince members of the community to engage in peer-evaluation and do so seriously. In this context, will international lawyers and other stake-holders be forced to move towards a paid-evaluation model as in nature sciences? Will they be in need of discarding the current anonymity paradigm of peer-review processes and disclose the names of reviewers for each volume of journals as a token of recognition for their work?

Fourth, quality-control does not necessarily mean peer-review processes. In the light of the abovementioned crisis of the peer review model and the fact that peer-review is not a panacea – for peer-review processes are often politically loaded – the question of the resort to other quality-indicators will arise more compellingly. Will international lawyers and other stakeholders be tempted to embrace other quality indicators like impact – in the form of citation indexes or downloads – or footnoting and sources?

Fifth, in the same vein, going-on-line does not necessarily mean turning to gratuity and open-access. Law journals can choose to be exclusively on-line publications while still limiting access to paying (individual or institutional) subscribers. Restricted access remains question-begging from the vantage point of public finances, as most authors and peer-reviewers in this profession are paid by virtue of public funding. Indeed, public institutions are also most often those paying access to the databases or financing open-access. The current model thus shows that a few (mostly private) actors benefiting from repeated and multi-layered public support. In the context of strained public finances,

---

[17] On the crisis of peer-review, see J. Weiler, "Peer review in crisis", EJIL: Talk!, 12 July 2012, http://www.ejiltalk.org/peer-review-in-crisis/

the question of open access will grow more pressing and with it the need to revisit the whole business model of academic publishing. If this were the case, will international lawyers and other stakeholders be able to preserve the linchpins of the assembly line of knowledge production and social validation of legal arguments which have been briefly discussed here? This question touches directly on the viability of argument-validating processes.

# 10. Expert blogging

In the quest for persuasiveness and social validation of their legal arguments, certain professions of international lawyers will consider the resort to legal blogging as a communicative tool geared towards dissemination (transmission).[1] Such a resort will usually be supplementary and will not replace other communicative tools. Legal blogging on current (legal) developments undoubtedly remains a hazardous exercise in which one should engage with the greatest care in one's quest for persuasiveness and social validation – if not with the greatest self-restraint. At the same time, it comes with important virtues. This chapter reviews the pros and cons of expert blogging in the light of the common misunderstandings thereof found among international lawyers, with a special emphasis on its role in the social validation of legal exponents.

## I. LEGAL BLOGGING AND ITS DETRACTORS

In some strands of the international legal scholarship, many still resent blogging – and hence tend to despise those who engage in blogging – for two main reasons. First, legal blogging is scorned for the superficiality of the analyses and the absurd ideas it disseminates. Second, it is berated for disinhibiting scholars and bolstering their disregard of the – unwritten – codes and hierarchies of the profession.

These two objections are surely not ill-founded. Indeed, posts on legal blogs are often quickly written notes on current legal developments without much critical distance and replete with unfinished thoughts. Likewise, posts on legal blogs allow direct confrontations between legal scholars at odds with the traditional non-confrontational debates conducted by the intermediary of international law journals. Yet, these criticisms rest on a misunderstanding of what legal blogging is all about and, more fundamentally, a negation of the cultural evolution witnessed in the international legal scholarship over the last two decades. First, as

---

[1] On R. Debray's distinction between communication and transmission, see chapter 9 above.

is further discussed below, legal blogging is neither meant to be proper legal scholarship nor does it seek to replace it. Posts on blogs do not claim to be long matured thoughts benefiting from hindsight. They are simply and modestly meant to be informative. This is the first main virtue of legal blogging.

As to the second objection, it seems to stem from a more fundamental ignorance as to how ideas are formed, exchanged and discussed in the contemporary international legal scholarship. Nowadays, the fora of our scholarly debates have ceased to rest exclusively with the non-polemical, non-confrontational, aseptic and cozy framework offered by international law journals. Instead, scholarly debates are multifold and ubiquitous. They are taking place everywhere, all the time and, in various forms. Scholarly debates have even ceased to be accidental. Differences of opinion are no longer stifled or concealed but they are consciously unearthed. Debating – and the culture of the critique that comes along with it – are now an integral part of the activity of being an international legal scholar. Debate has become an essential component of the production of legal thoughts. Ideas are no longer mulled over for years in an – often dusty and messy – isolated study and kept secret until the day of their solemn revelation through publication in a top-tiered international law journal. While still being the product of a long individual cerebral effort, ideas are now shared, tested and further refined through peer-to-peer experimentation at an earlier stage of the scholarly thought-making process. This is not to say that international legal scholars are – and should be – pursuing debate for the sake of the debate and systematically rushing to the professional agora as soon as they come up with what they perceive as an original or refreshing idea. Ideas need not to be hastily disseminated among peers before they are ripe. And broadcasting them through conventional law journals or books remain the best means to secure formal ownership thereof.[2] Yet, legal scholars of the twenty-first century have grown more faithful in the Socratic virtues of the exchange of ideas which they now see as instrumental in the mutual development and sharpening of legal thinking as a whole. Eventually, thanks to the new means of transfer of knowledge, scholarly debates have simultaneously undergone a process of deformalization. Lack of seniority no longer bars access to the experts' debate and the implicit hierarchies of the profession have ceased to constitute compelling barriers to the expression of disagreement. Legal blogging has been both the cause and the consequence of these fundamental changes in the debating culture

---

[2] See chapter 9 above.

of the international legal scholarship of the twenty-first century. Bemoaning the existence of experts' legal blogging among international lawyers boils down to an atavistic negation of the cultural upheaval that has unfolded in the international legal scholarship over the last 15 years.

## II. LEGAL BLOGGING AND ITS HAZARDS

Not all the arguments of the detractors of legal blogging are erroneous. Legal blogging does not come without – serious – hazards: hasty treatment of information, ephemeral and cursory writing, dissemination of half-baked ideas, superficiality of analyses, overly emotional reactions, and all kind of impulsive expressions of thoughts which the author of a post may subsequently regret. Once written and thrown to the web, such ideas, emotions or statements ceased to be within their author's control. Because of the magnifying effect of the web, any indiscretion can then take on very harmful proportions for its author. It is true that this is no different from ideas advertised through books or peer-reviewed articles. Yet, the pace of blogging is faster, the barriers almost inexistent and the audience much wider. The risk of hastiness and impulsivity – and hence of self-inflicted harm – is far greater when scholars are simply one mouse-click away from the global agora of the profession. While the deliberative virtues of blogging lie precisely in such accessibility, legal blogging can also contribute to the broadcast of non-experts' opinions and convey self-reinforcing glaringly uninformed views. Eventually, legal blogging can also be seen as intensifying what has been called the "proliferation of international legal thinking"[3] that has long already affected conventional channels of legal scholarship. These dangers are well-known and have been discussed elsewhere.[4] It is not necessary to dwell upon them here.

## III. LEGAL BLOGGING AND ITS VIRTUES

Mindful of the abovementioned hazards of legal blogging, it is argued here that the cost of legal blogging is outweighed by two fundamental

---

[3] J. d'Aspremont, "Softness in international law: a rejoinder to Tony D'Amato" (August 13, 2009), 20 *European Journal of International Law*, (2009), 911–17.

[4] B. Leiter, "Why blogs are bad for legal scholarship", 116 *Yale L.J. Pocket Part*, (2006), 53 http://www.thepocketpart.org/2006/09/20/leiter.html.

virtues, namely the efficacious and rapid dissemination of information about current legal developments (1.1), and the platform for debate within the profession which legal blogging offers (1.2).

## 1. Informative Virtues

Legal blogging is construed, first and foremost, as nothing more than journalism within the epistemic community concerned. It is meant to inform peers of discoveries and new developments which they may have overlooked. As far as international law is concerned, it is undeniable that the world has turned so complex and – although in multiple ways – regulated that it has become an uphill battle for each of us to keep track of the factual and legal changes occurring on the international plane. In that sense, legal blogging is a medium which helps disseminate more massive and complex information. Moreover, it does so at an accelerated pace, for one no longer has to wait for the selective accounts of practice and case-law found in expensive and long overdue yearbooks. Dissemination of information is not only easier and faster. It is also made non-contingent on intermediaries, like editors of international law journals. If so construed, legal blogging is nothing more than journalism for experts by experts without intermediaries. At the same time, it inevitably shorts fall of the critical distance that makes legal scholarship so unique and irreplaceable. It should accordingly not be considered as anything like legal scholarship properly so-called. In that sense, the present author would support a distribution of roles between journals and legal blogging, analytical and evaluative legal scholarship being better suited for the former whilst informative materials fitting better with the latter.[5] Another remark must be made on the informative dimension of legal blogging. Even as regards its informative aspect, legal blogging should not be considered as neutral. It is uncontested that there cannot be a descriptive account of an event – be it factual or legal – devoid of biases and subjectivity. Likewise, it has never been claimed that the information shared by virtue of legal blogging is objectively chosen. Unearthing the "politics" of informative blogging should thus certainly not be neglected by the profession, especially as international lawyers turn more to blogs to glean information.

---

[5] For a famous attack on legal scholarship that is reduced to journalistic reports on cases, see P. Schlag, "Spam jurisprudence, air law, and the rank anxiety of nothing happening (a report on the state of the art)", 97 *Georgetown Law Journal*, (2009), 803.

## 2. Deliberative Virtues

Besides constituting an invaluable informative tool for the profession as a whole, blogging bolsters freedom of expression within the epistemic community concerned. Indeed, legal blogging allows scholarly debates to be no longer exclusively carried via distant and slow-reacting proxies (like international law journals). It simultaneously opens the scholarly debates to a greater number of experts, for it allows the entire profession to informally participate and exchange ideas in contrast with classical forums of debate which restrict – and carefully select – the happy few entitled to express their thoughts. Likewise, it often leaves room for a more informal tone and some humor – a welcome development in a rather stiff profession still beset by ancestry codes. This does not mean, however, that legal blogging should unravel the codes and hierarchies of the profession. It only does so as far as scholarly debates are concerned. Once we log out from such electronic platforms, international lawyers still have to make their way through the profession by abiding by its fundamental rules and codes.[6] And this should not be otherwise. Yet, if international lawyers can accept that some of these rules and codes are – temporarily – kept at bay to allow a global conversation within the profession, legal blogging could constitute the sign of an international legal scholarship growing more amenable, not only to the value of critique, but also to that of mutual enrichment.

There is one particular aspect of our debates which legal blogging can best accommodate. It is not contested that professional self-reflection constitutes one of the most important *acquis* of the various waves of criticisms endured by the mainstream international legal scholarship in the second half of the twentieth century.[7] The sociological enquiries which originate in that – welcome – change of mindset in the current legal scholarship have yielded a new kind of sociological thinking in international law more centered on the study of the dynamics of the profession than the examination of international law itself. While international law should remain the main focus of our cerebral activities, international lawyers should not bemoan this greater interest of international legal scholars in the sociology of the profession. Yet, legal blogging being the platform for the global conversation of the profession,

---

[6] See Introduction above.
[7] See chapter 6 above.

it is possible to see the blogosphere as a far better place than peer-reviewed journals to express our sociological findings about the profession.[8]

## IV. SAFEGUARDS FOR A USEFUL BLOGGERSHIP

Confronted with the above-mentioned hazards of legal blogging, it would be tempting to say that international lawyers should simply beware of them and resort to legal blogging with extreme care. Using a – coarse – metaphor popular among legal scholars – as is illustrated by the famous and oft-quoted car-analogy made by Ian Brownlie[9] – one could thus say that it is not because a car can travel as fast as the insane speed of 200 miles per hour that we should not drive it (there actually are more compelling environment-related motives to curb the use of cars). Well, this is as far as this unsophisticated metaphor can get. Indeed, the difference between cars and legal blogging is nonetheless that the latter can hardly be harmful to others, leaving aside distracting them from their work by deluging the web with half-baked thoughts. Most of the potential harms of blogging are born by the author of the post alone. In that sense, it is all about personal responsibility. It is only if bloggership were to be seen as a makeshift legal scholarship that it could be detrimental to the quality of our debates. If more modestly construed as legal journalism and a platform for a conversation among experts as is argued here, blogging is not to be feared by the professional community as a whole.

Yet, even modestly construed as journalism for the profession as well as a platform for experts' debate, a few elementary safeguards still need to be erected if international lawyers want to ensure that the benefits of legal blogging continue to outweigh the significant hazards described above. These are mentioned here.

First, it should be repeated that legal blogging should not be construed as an ersatz legal scholarship: as Ann Althouse rightly put it: "Let the law journal be the law journal and the blog be the blog".[10]. International

---

[8] On traditional platforms of academic writing see above chapter 9.

[9] I. Brownlie, "Comment", J. Weiler and A. Cassese (eds), *Change and Stability in International Law-Making*, (de Gruter, 1988), 110.

[10] A. Althouse, "Let the law journal be the law journal and the blog be the blog", 116 *Yale L.J. Pocket Part* 8, (2006), http://www.thepocketpart.org/2006/09/06/althouse.html.

lawyers should not strive to make legal blogging resemble legal scholarship. Moreover, international lawyers should remain mindful that, to a very large extent, securing formal ownership of ideas still hinges on publication in traditional international law journals or books.

Second, expertise must remain a passport to legal blogging. The determination of the membership – and thus the way in which international lawyers define expertise – surely is an extremely contentious issue. It carries the risk of reproducing the old hierarchies – and managerialism – which the blogosphere has helped overcome. It is undoubtedly a matter that should be actively and openly debated.[11] Experts' blogging must nonetheless still have some elementary scholarly restrictions in terms of *membership*.

Third, under any circumstances, legal blogging should be used with self-restraint by the members of that community. Self-restraint is the best guarantee against overwhelming our poor human minds. Too much blogging simply kills legal blogging – as well as the reputation of those who abuse it. Not every idea, opinion, or current development is worthy of a post.

Fourth, because it is not proper legal scholarship, legal blogging should not be rewarded or count for career-advancement – although it may inevitably bear indirect positive effects in this regard. Nor should it be cited as scholarly work. It should just remain what it is, that is, a global and informal conversation among professionals sharing their discoveries and their opinions.

Fifth, even if bloggership should never be conflated with legal scholarship, there still is one overarching guiding principle which bloggership and scholarship should have in common: mutual respect. Indeed, there can be no Socratic mutual enrichment through debate – in my view one of the main tenets of the culture of our profession nowadays – without mutual deference. It is only as long as we mutually respect each other's thoughts – however different these may be – that we can continue to reap the informative and deliberative benefits offered by legal blogging. Hence, it is not legal blogging that should be feared but rather the institutional constraints, the ever-growing competition within the profession and the ever-mounting pressure on its members, for they tend to make us oblivious of this elementary premise of any scholarly debate.

---

[11] See Introduction.

# Index

academic writing *see also* expert blogging; law publishing
  generally
    argumentative technique role of 225
    cult of citation, and 228–9
    pluralization 242
    technology role in 231–2
  tactics
    argumentative strawmen, and 231
    empiricism, and 229–30
    erudition, and 233–4
    generally 225–6
    new idioms/neologism, development of 234–5
    roughing-out 231–2
    scholarly intimidation 235–6
    self-gratification 233
    semantic instability, and 227–8
    textual aesthetics, and 228–9
    textual economy 227
accountability
  deformalization, and 90–91
  formalism, and 105
  for public authorities 90–91
  state role in law-making, and 117–20
Althouse, Ann 251
argumentative practice, law as
  access restrictions 13–15
  communitarian practice 3, 220
  confrontation, role of 23–6
  interdisciplinarity, and 56–8
  principles 1–3
  situationalism, and 6–8
  studies 4–9
argumentative techniques, generally 1–3 *see also* academic writing; dissemination; expert blogging; interpretation; methodology
  foundational doctrines, overlaps between 28–9
  situationalism, and 6–8
  social arrangements, and 5–6
  social validation of law, and 22–7
  socialization of lawyers, and 9–15
authority
  accountability, and 90–91
  international law, and erosion of 95–7
  law-making legitimacy, and 80–81, 94
  tradition concept 220

Bianchi, Andrea 215
Brölmann, Catherine 155–6
Brunée, J. 17

Charnovitz, Steve 116
cognition
  international law-making, and
    dynamic output-based approaches 133–5
    dynamic participation-based approaches 129–33
    dynamic pedigree-based approaches 135–7
    formal sources of international law, and 127–9
    input impacts focus 114
    instrumentalist turn 129–33
    legal personality, and 121–4, 126
    light subjecthood thesis 123–4
    natural law, and 126–7
    New Haven School 129–32, 135–6
    pluralism in 137–8
    qualification criteria 126
    relevance 107–8
    retroactive construction, and 134

rule or source-based 126–8, 131
social thesis 136–7
static pedigree-based approaches 126–9
static *vs.* dynamic approaches 115–16, 135–7
subject-based approaches 121–6
subjecthood paradigm 113–4, 121–6
theoretical divergence in 120–37
models
community of practice 17–18
epistemic community 16–17
interpretative community 18
multiplicity approach, benefits of 20–21
shared communication 19–20
communities of law, generally
background 4–5
communitarian practice 3, 220
community of practice 17–18
epistemic community 16–17
interpretative community 18, 219–21
meaning 10–11
models 16–21
pluralism 21
purpose 5–6
shared vocabulary 19–20
social validation 22–7
socialization 9–15
community of practice 17–18
constitutionalism
in international law scholarship, generally 63–4
rule of law, deformalization influences on 98–101
*vs.* contractualism
dialectical reconciliation 151–61
reconceptualization 159–61
tensions 141–51, 161–6
content-determination interpretation
constraints 214–17
disciplining rules 214–17
formalization, and 211–12
generally 207–9
law-ascertainment interpretation, and
constraints 217–22
differences 212–14, 222–4

similarities 209–12
power relations, and 210–11
purpose 212–14
research agenda 223
contractualism
*vs.* constitutionalism
dialectical reconciliation 151–61
reconceptualization 159–61
tensions 141–51, 161–6
Crawford, James 50–51
critical legal studies
deconstructivism, and 12, 195–7
disorder *vs.* order 198
influences of 197–8
post-modernism 196
situationalism, and 6
customary law
interpretation conflicts 208–9
sources of
deformalization, and 69–75
identification 71–5
law-ascertainment, and 69–71, 77–8
morality and public conscience, and 77
soft law, and 85–8
substantive validity, and 76–8

Dann, Philipp 80
Debray, Regis 237
deconstructivism
critical legal studies 12, 195–7
deformalization, of sources
agendas 88–9
creative argumentation, and 93
international law development, for 89
international law promotion, for 89–90
legal materials, search for 91–2
legal pluralism, and 94
legal scholarship, in 83–7, 91–2, 97
legitimacy, evaluation of 94
public authority accountability, and 90–91
contemporary applications 75–6

effect/impact-based conceptions of law 78–83
process-based conceptions of law 83–5
soft law role in international law, and 85–8
substantive validity, and 76–8
costs and challenges 95–101
  erosion of character and authority of law, and 95–7
  formal unity of international law, and 100–101
  international law critiques, and 97–8
  legal scholarship conflicts 97
  legal system viability, and 99–100
  rule of law sustainability, and 98–9
customary international law, and 69–75
formalism, resilience 101–8
  culture of 104–6
  generally 101–2
  Global Administrative Law 102–3
  Heidelberg project 103
  legal positivism, and 106–8
generally 63–4, 108–10
  benefits 89–94
  definition 65–8
  Global Administrative Law project 79–80, 81–2, 102–3, 114
  Heidelberg research project 79–80, 82, 103, 114
international law
  customary law 69–75
  relationship with 63–4, 69–75
law-ascertainment, and 65–75, 83–5
legal realism, and 67–8
liberal individualism, and 84
prospects for
  formalism trends 102
  generally 101–2
  Global Administrative Law project, and 102–3
  Heidelberg research project 103
dissemination, of law *see also* expert blogging
  academic publishing, and 239, 242
  argumentation, link between 27–8

communication *vs.* transmission 237
digitization, and 242
importance 237–8
law journals, and 240–41, 243–5
networks and hierarchies 238, 246, 247
order and sequence in 241–2
processes 243–5
quality control and certification 240–41

effectiveness *see also effectivité*
  definition 167–8
  scope 52, 167–9
  statehood, in law of 51–2
*effectivité*
  definition 167–8
  effectiveness, differences from 167–9
  scope 167–8
  statehood tensions, internal *vs.* external 38–9
effectivity *see also effectivité*
  benefits 171–2
  bridging function 169–71
  definition 167–8
  in international context 169–71
  negative aspects 172–4
empiricism
  as academic writing tactic 229–30
  methodological choices, and 187–9
  objectivism, and 188–9
epistemic community
  meaning 16–17
expert blogging
  advantages 247, 248–51
  criticisms of 246–8
  expertise, importance of 251–2
  law journals, influences on 242, 247
  legal scholarship, relationship with 252
  limitations and hazards 251, 248
  membership determination 252
  safeguards 251–2
  self-restraint, and 252
  sociological thinking, and 250–51

facticism *see also effectivité*

statehood, legalist tensions 36–7
Fish, Stanley *see* Fish *vs.* Fiss
    interpretation debate
Fish *vs.* Fiss interpretation debate
    constraints, standardization of
        216–17
    disciplining rules 213, 216–17
    interpretative community concept
        218–20
    rules, need for 216–17
Fiss, Owen *see* Fish *vs.* Fiss
    interpretation debate
formalism
    accountability 105
    culture of 104–6
    generally 101–2
    Global Administrative Law, and
        102–3
    Heidelberg project, and 103
    legal positivism, and 106–8
    vulgar *vs.* sophisticated forms 65
foundational doctrines, generally 1–3
    *see also* effectivity; institutions;
        law-making; sources; statehood
    argumentative techniques, overlaps
        between 28–9
    influences, continental *vs.*
        Anglo-American 29
    situationalism, and 6–8
    social arrangements, and 5–6
    social validation of law, and 22–7
    socialization of lawyers, and 9–15
Franck, Tom 84, 187
Fuller, Lon 77–8
functionalism
    contractualism *vs.* constitutionalism,
        and 141–4, 145–6, 158

Global Administrative Law project
    deformalization, and 102–3
    law-ascertainment interpretation
        81–2
    norm-generating processes 79–80,
        81–2
    on reconceptualization of
        international institutions 160–61
Goldmann, Mathias 80

Heidelberg research project
    deformalization, and 103
    law-ascertainment interpretation 102,
        103
    on norm-generating processes 133
hierarchy
    dissemination through 246, 247–8,
        250
    in international law, generally
        180–81, 184
    social validation of law, in 25
Higgins, Rosalyn 130

institutionalism
    liberal individualism, and 84
institutions
    international law tensions
        autonomy, role of 143–51, 156–8
        balancing, success in 161–6
        contractualism *vs.*
            constitutionalism 141–66
        *dédoublement fonctionnel* notion
            154–6, 159
        definitions 142, 147
        dialectical reconciliation, and
            151–61
        dichotomy avoidance mechanisms
            152–61
        diverging capacities 142–3
        functionalism, and 142–3, 145–6,
            158
        generally 139–40, 146
        institutional veil concept 155–6
        internal *vs.* external roles 142–3
        legalism and managerialism 157
        methodological choices, and
            183–5
        need for 161–2
        reconceptualization, and 159–61
        scholarship, criticisms of 164–6
    law of
        challenges 139–40
        characteristics 139
        development 163–4
        functionalism, and 145–6
        influences on 162–3
        self-reflection trends 141

international law, generally
  confrontational character 203–6
  effectivity in context 169–71
  institutional hierarchies 180–81, 184
  normative universe, commitment to 199–201
  purpose 129–30
international law-making
  approaches
    conflicts 113–14, 130–31
    dynamic output-based 133–5
    dynamic participation-based 129–33
    dynamic pedigree-based 135–7
    formal sources of international law, and 127–9
    instrumentalist turn 129–33
    legal personality, and 121–4, 126
    light subjecthood thesis 123–4
    natural law, and 126–7
    qualification criteria 126
    rule or source-based 126–8, 131
    static pedigree-based 126–9
    subject-based 121–6
  generally
    norm-identification 79–82
    public authority legitimacy 80–81
    purpose 129–30
    trends 111–12, 115–17
  legal cognition, and
    dynamic output-based approaches 133–5
    dynamic participation-based approaches 129–33
    dynamic pedigree-based approaches 135–7
    formal sources of international law, and 127–9
    input impacts focus 114
    instrumentalist turn 129–33
    legal personality, and 121–4, 126
    light subjecthood thesis 123–4
    natural law, and 126–7
    New Haven School 129–32, 135–6
    pluralism in 137–8
    qualification criteria 126
    relevance 113–14
    retroactive construction, and 134
    rule or source-based 126–8, 131
    social thesis 136–7
    static pedigree-based approaches 126–9
    static *vs.* dynamic approaches 115–16, 135–7
    subject-based approaches 121–6
    subjecthood paradigm 113–14, 121–6
    theoretical divergence in 120–37
  non-state actors, role in
    development 116, 117–18, 123–4
    regulation 118
    transnational regulatory networks 118–19
  pluralization
    instrument diversification, and 117
    international law character, influences on 115–17, 124
    non-state actor role in 116, 117–18, 123–4
    state dominance and resilience 117–20
    transnational regulatory networks 118–19
    trends 111–12, 115–17, 137–8
international legal scholarship *see also* academic writing; cognition; Critical Legal Studies; methodology
  anti-pluralism 76–7
  behaviourism 78–9, 82
  constitutionalism, generally 63–4
  contractualism *vs.* constitutionalism
    autonomy, role of 143–51, 156–8
    criticisms 164–6
    *dédoublement fonctionnel* notion 154–6, 159
    definitions 142, 147
    dialectical reconciliation, and 151–61
    dichotomy avoidance mechanisms 152–61
    diverging capacities 142–3
    functionalism, and 141–4, 145–6, 158
    generally 141–6, 150–51
    institutional veil concept 155–6

internal *vs.* external roles 142–3
  legalism and managerialism 157
  reconceptualization, and 159–61
  reconciliation mechanisms 159–61
  tensions 141–51, 161–6
 deformalization
  agendas 88–94
  creative argumentation, and 93
  culture of formalism 104–6
  generally 63–4
  Global Administrative Law project 79–80, 81–2, 102–3
  Heidelberg research project 79–80, 82, 103
  international law development, for 89
  international law promotion, for 89–90
  legal materials, search for 91–2
  legal pluralism, and 94
  legitimacy, evaluation of 94
  public authority accountability, and 90–91
  reductionist legal positivism 106–8
 generally
  effect/impact-based conceptions of law 78–83
  fluidity of 12
  Global Administrative Law project 79–80, 81–2, 102–3, 114, 160–61
  Heidelberg research project 79–80, 82, 103, 133
  interdisciplinarity and multidisciplinarity 189–91
  interpretation, research trends 222–4
  on law of international organizations 141
  morality and public conscience, and 77
  process-based conceptions of law 83–5
  public recognition of 193–4
  reform, need for 192–3
  socialization of lawyers, influences on 12–13
  soft law role in international law 85–8
  statehood, and 49, 51
  subjecthood paradigm 113–14, 121–6
 situationalism 6–8
 international organizations *see* institutions
 interpretation, generally *see also* content-determination interpretation; law-ascertainment interpretation
  authority, and
   absence of 204–5
   argumentative 206, 210, 213, 224
   power relations, and 210–11
   submission to 220
  conflicts in 202–3, 223–4
  confrontational character of international law, and 203–6
  constitutive and performative function 202, 207
  definition and scope 199–201, 222–4
  existing law and practice, focus on 200–201
  of facts 209
  formalization, and 211–12
  indeterminacy, influences on 211
  instabilities of 211, 220
  international scholarship
   limitations 214–17, 223
   research trends 223–4
  multi-dimensional nature 200–201, 207
  primary norms *vs.* rules of recognition 208–9
  tradition concept 220
  validation standards in 208
  veil of unicity, and 205–6
 interpretive community *see also* Fish *vs.* Fiss interpretation debate
  communitarian practice, and 217, 219, 220
  constraining role 220
  criticism of 220–21
  meaning 18, 219–20

Jellinek, Georg 38–40
Johns, Fleur 210

Kennedy, David 109, 195
Koskenniemi, M. 104–6, 195–7
Kuhn, T. 198

Lauterpacht, H. 44
law-ascertainment interpretation *see also* deformalization
  behaviourist approaches 78–9, 82
  challenges 74–5
  constraints on 213, 217–22
  content-determination interpretation, and
    differences 208, 212–14
    research agendas 222–4
    similarities 209–12
  customary law, and 71–5
  effect/impact-based conceptions of law 78–83
  Fish *vs.* Fiss debate 216–20
  formalization, and 211–12
  generally 208, 217–8
    Global Administrative Law project 79–80, 81–2, 102–3
  Heidelberg research project 79–80, 82, 103
  international law development, and 89
  international law promotion, and 89–90
  legal certainty, and 99, 220–21
  power relations, and 210–11
  principles
    generally 217–8
    natural law, and 77
  public authority accountability, and 90–91
  purpose 212–14
  research trends 223–4
  social approach to 218–21
  soft law role in international law 85–8
  substantive validity, and 76–8
  tradition concept 220
  treaties, and 71, 74–5

law journals
  blogging, influences on 242, 247
  digitization, and 242
  dissemination role 238, 239, 243–5
  law validation, and 238–45
  limitations 240, 242
  new/specialist journals 243–4
  quality control and certification 240–41
  selectiveness 240
law-making *see* international law-making
law publishing
  externalities of 239
  information dissemination role 237–9
  law validation, and 238–45
  limitations 240, 242
  new/specialist journals 243–4
  public good, and 239, 243
  quality control and certification 240–41
  selectiveness 240
lawyers, socialization *see* socialization, of international lawyers
legal positivism
  deformalization of sources, and 106–8
  methodological choices, and 185
legal realism
  compliance-based approaches to international law 82
  deformalization, and 66–7
legalism,
  statehood, and
    as agenda of 51–3
    facticist tensions 35–7
    interdisciplinarity, and 56–8
legitimacy
  deformalization, and 94
  evaluation of 94, 187–8
liberal individualism
  global institutionalism, and 84
  trends 187–8

McDougal, Myles S. 129–30
Manhattan Law School 84, 187

methodology
  methodological choices
    constraints on 180–82
    deconstruction, and 195–8
    empiricism, and 187–9
    EU *vs.* US traditions 185–6
    evaluation of 182–3
    freedom of 179–80
    inductive methods, and 185–7
    institutional background 183–5
    interdisciplinarity and
        multidisciplinarity 189–91
    legal positivism, and 185
    legal theory, and 177–9
    legitimacy 187–8
    liberal individualism 187
    perspectivism, and 194–5
    pluralism, and 194–5
    reform, need for 192–3
    self-awareness, and 198
    self-validation, and 84, 188
    systemic thinking, and 185–7
  theory, relationship with 177–9
Mitchell, Mark 220

natural law
  deformalization, and 99–100
  doctrine of sources, and 69–70, 126–7
  law-ascertainment, and 77–8
  minimum content 100
  morality and public conscience, and 77
  principles 77–8
New Haven School
  on deformalization 83–4
  on dynamic law-making 129–32, 135–6
  on subjecthood paradigm 113–14
non-state actors
  law-making role
    development 116, 117–18, 123–4
    legal personality, and 123
    pluralization of international law 111–12, 115–16, 123–5
    transnational regulatory networks 118–19

objectivism
  empiricism, and 188–9
  statehood, subjectivist tensions 35, 39–42, 51–2

Patterson, Dennis 221
peer review
  alternatives to 244–5
  quality control, and 241, 243, 244
  responsibility and civism 243–4
pluralism
  anti-pluralism 76–7
  deformalization, and 94
  methodological choices, and 194–5
positivism *see* legal positivism
post-modernism
  critical legal studies 196
proceduralization
  statehood, in law of 46–7, 54

quality control
  alternative forms 244–5
  in law publishing 240–42, 243, 244
  peer review, responsibility and civism 243–4

recognition
  of international legal scholarship 193–4
  rules of *vs.* primary norms 208–9
responsibility
  deformalization, and 65–6
  peer review quality control, and 241, 243–4
rule of law
  deformalization, influences of 98–9

Scelle, Georges 154–5
Schlag, P. 221
Schmitt, Carl 36
self-determination 46–7, 125–6
Singh, Sahib 195
situationalism
  challenges 7–8
  determinism, and 8
  generally 6–7
  research trends 7–8, 197

social validation 22–7
  challenges 23–4
  confrontational nature of law, and 23–6
  criticisms 25–6
  dissemination, and 234, 235, 237–8, 242, 243–5, 246
  foundational doctrine and argumentation techniques influences on 23–4
  hierarchies 25
  law journals role 239, 241, 242, 243–5
  of methodological choices 183, 191
  peer review, and 243–4
  persuasiveness, and 25–7
  principles 22–3
  quality control, and 240–45
socialization, of international lawyers
  access to legal argumentation, and 13–15
  argumentative techniques, and 5–6, 8–11
  background 4–9
  confrontational nature 23–6
  descriptive frameworks 11–13
  development 9–11
  fluidity of 12
  foundational doctrines, and 5–6, 8–11
  influences on
    education and training 12–13
    English language 15
    scholarship 13
  meaning 10–11
  shared consciousness, as 11–13
  situationalism, and 6–8
  sociology studies 4
  sources, role of 61–2
soft law
  internationalization role 86–8
  law vs. non-law continuum 85–6
  source of international law, as 85–8
sources
  customary law
    deformalization, and 69–75
    identification of 71–5
    law-ascertainment, and 69–71, 77–8
  morality and public conscience, and 77
  soft law, and 85–8
  substantive validity, and 76–8
deformalization
  agendas 88–94
  benefits 63–4
  costs and challenges 95–101
  creative argumentation, and 93
  customary international law, and 69–75
  definition 65–8
  effect/impact-based conceptions of law 78–83
  erosion of character of law, and 95–7
  examples of 69–75
  formal unity of international law, influences on 100–101
  formalism, influences on 65, 69–70, 98
  generally 62–4, 65–8, 108–10
  Global Administrative Law project 79–80, 81–82, 102–3
  Heidelberg research project 79–80, 82, 103
  international law critiques, influences on 97–8
  international law development, for 89
  international law promotion, for 89–90
  international law, relationship with 69–75
  law-ascertainment, and 65–75, 83–5
  legal materials, search for 91–2
  legal pluralism, and 94
  legal positivism, and 106–8
  legal realism, and 66–7
  legal scholarship agendas 88–94
  legal scholarship conflicts 97
  legal system viability, and 99–100
  legitimacy, evaluation of 94
  liberal individualism, and 84
  process-based conceptions of law 83–5
  prospects for 101–8

public authority accountability, and 90–91
rule of law sustainability, influences on 98–9
soft law role in international law 85–8
substantive validity, and 76–8
generally
 definitions 65–8
 importance of 63
 legal acts *vs.* legal facts approaches 85–6
 natural law, and 69–70, 126–7
 secondary rules on international law 217
 shared communication vocabulary 19–20
 socialization role 61–2
 studies, precedence in 61–2
 will of state, and 69–70
treaties
 law-ascertainment, and 71, 74–5
statehood, law of
 agendas in
  anthropomorphism 45–6
  disentanglement of law 43–4
  effectiveness, and 52–3
  elucidation 46–8
  epistemological self-rehabilitation 54–9
  explanation 43–6
  generally 33, 42–3
  interdisciplinarity, camouflaged nature of 56–7
  international law comprehensiveness 50–51
  international state membership and control 49–50
  legal scholarship 58–9
  legalism 51–3, 56–7
  objectivism, and 51–2
  proceduralization 46–7, 54
  regulation 49–54
  self-referential dynamics, and 43–4
  sophistication as redemption, and 55–6
  territorialization 48
 ubiquity of international law, and 59
 development 33, 59–60, 162–3
 epistemological tensions
  effectivité, internal *vs.* external 38–9
  facticists *vs.* legalists 35–7
  subjectivists *vs.* objectivists 35, 39–42, 51–2
  three elements doctrine 38–40
 interpretation 33
 methodological developments 59–60
 studies, criticism of 33–4
subjecthood paradigm 113–14
subjectivism
 statehood, and
  objectivist tensions 35, 39–42, 51–2
subjects, doctrine of *see* statehood

three elements doctrine 38–40
Toope, S.J. 77–8
tradition *see also* customary law
 concept of 220
treaties
 deformalization, and 75–6
 law-ascertainment interpretation 75–6
 Vienna Convention
  drafting conflicts 215–16
  formalization of interpretation, role in 212, 214
validity, of law
 dissemination, and 238–45
 interpretation rules, generally 202–6
 law journals role 239
 quality control and certification 240–41
 selectiveness 240
 self-validation 84, 188
 social validation 22–7
  challenges 23–4
  confrontational nature of law, and 23–6
  criticisms 25–6
  dissemination, and 237–8, 243–5

foundational doctrine and argumentation techniques influences on 23–4
hierarchies 25
law journals role 239–41
of methodological choices 183
peer review, and 241, 243, 244
persuasiveness, and 25–7
principles 22–3
quality control, and 241, 243, 244
substantive validity 76–8
symbolic validation 10
Verdross, Alfred 215
Virally, Michel 158
von Bogdandy, Armin 80

Waldock, Humphrey 215–16